1984

SPOT NEWS
P M OPERATED
UPON CONDITION
VERY GRAVE

1984

The Anti-Sikh Violence and After

SANJAY SURI

HarperCollins *Publishers* India

First published in hardback in India by HarperCollins *Publishers* 2015
4th Floor, Tower A, Building No. 10, DLF Cyber City,
DLF Phase II, Gurugram, Haryana – 122002
www.harpercollins.co.in

This edition published in India by HarperCollins *Publishers* 2025

2 4 6 8 10 9 7 5 3 1

P-ISBN: 978-93-6213-575-9
E-ISBN: 978-93-5177-071-8

Typeset in 11.5/15 Adobe Caslon Pro at
HarperCollins *Publishers* India

Printed and bound at
Thomson Press (India) Ltd.

MIX
Paper | Supporting responsible forestry
FSC® C010615

This book is produced from independently certified FSC® paper
to ensure responsible forest management.

Contents

Author's Note

Anniversaries do get a little more commanding when they hit round numbers, they demand a little more remembrance, at the least some less forgetting. So reminders are on offer that this year marks 40 years since the murder of more than 3,000 Sikhs in Delhi over just a day or two in 1984.

The calendar-fed reminders have been very much less commanding than the counter-urge to forget that whole lot, beyond the forgetting that the passage of time naturally wads us with. Those dead are now distant numbers, a forgettable aberration whose recall should not be forgotten. Numbers can be numbing. How many years? We have a number. How many dead? We have numbers if not the number. These numbers have a way of bouncing off.

Off most of us that is. For survivors, for surviving families, forgetting has not been easy. Anniversaries arrive like another twist of the knife. That is tens of thousands of people, still. They are still grieving, they are still angry.

The call to forget is not new, it began right then, before bodies could be cleared from the streets, before families could manage what last rites they could. Those rites weren't easy, how do you cremate someone who's been burnt alive, or his reassembled body parts? And who dared then step out to do any cremating other than the police who lit up piled bodies, to destroy evidence more than to cremate?

What's happened has happened, we were all told, the Sikhs as much as anyone else. Awful what's happened, but now forget and move on. If that was within the first few days, why bother now only because 40 is a multiple of ten?

For a start because Sikhs have not forgotten. They never really will. 'Those killings have now become a part of the recall of Sikh sacrifices within the daily ardaas,' Tarlochan Singh, Press Secretary to former President Zail Singh in 1984, and later MP, and head of the National Commission for Minorities tells me. 'Sikhs can forget their achievements, but their sacrifices, never.'

Forgotten they could have been, even to Sikhs, if they hadn't been so many killed so quickly.

If only in a peripherally political way, no one quite has forgotten 1984. The year 1983 came and went, as did 1985, and the years before and since. 1984 doesn't go away. The calendar magnifies it once in a while but never manages to erase it. It has cast a long shadow, if now a weakened one. 1984 set Punjab further from Delhi than it was ever before.

Less tragically but no less certainly, it isn't easy for some of us to forget, who witnessed those killings—and many of us did. People were murdered before our eyes, and we have been told ever since that the right thing to do is to look the other way. Forgetting was made easier by who those killed were and who they were not. They were nothing but now dead carpenters, charpai weavers, bicycle mechanics who had worked too many hours a day for too few rupees. People of no consequence.

These were no Jessica Lal murder cases where an outrage over an acquittal brought a fast-track retrial and then conviction. The media likely spent endlessly more time over this and the Arushi murder case than it has over those thousands of murders together.

Some of us not involved then do feel nudged by the calendar to remember those few thousand murdered people a little more than we do otherwise. The rest are annoyed that we won't forget all about them. In getting murdered so much, these people became an embarrassment. India has better stories to tell.

That makes recalling 1984 more of a reproach than an observance. The usual nuggets of received wisdom—remembering will not bring the dead back to life, move on and look to the future, never look back—could have been commonsensical enough had those families mourned natural bereavement. How many who proffer such advice have watched their father or husband ringed with burning tyres around their neck? And would they have forgotten as they now advise.

We don't forget an unanswered call, a WhatsApp message not acknowledged. How soon will we forget if someone slaps us in the workplace before our colleagues? And we want all these people to forget the murder of their own. To forget your father's killer as he walks down the street where you lived and he killed, forget that the killer never was arrested, that the police, the government supported the killing and then blocked justice. Consider what it is we expect, and over what.

What happened has not ended with its happening. Latent anger bursts through unsuspected pores—rebel music that becomes massively popular, mass protests over issues not on the face of it about 1984, election results that speak of separation, unrest among quite a significant numbers of Sikhs abroad that has the government shaken, a desperation among Sikhs to emigrate. Other Indians no doubt push to leave. Once out they usually turn towards India with a fondness they never found while in it. Among Sikh groups successful emigration often triggers quite the opposite.

1984 did not bring the level of open revolt feared then but it has left behind a residual sullenness that India wouldn't want, and certainly not in a border state. If not outright alienation, it has left behind a shaky oneness. We're all very lucky it was no worse. 1984 wasn't the turning point, not even necessarily a turning away point, but it has been an unsettling point, a point of unease. The passage of time has enfeebled anger but hasn't erased the unease. The reason we haven't altogether forgotten 1984 is that it won't let us.

~

Of late a 'progressive' argument has arisen against the recall of 1984. It broadly suggests that now is not the time to bash the Congress party, we need to back the Congress to fight the fascism of the BJP. The argument does not necessarily dispute the facts: that Congress party leaders led and backed killers, that the party-led government failed to protect Sikhs and later prosecute the killers in all but a small sprinkling of cases. For those failings, the argument goes, the party has been punished, we removed it from power, did we not? But today the Congress is the voice of secularism, we need it to strengthen it to fight the communalism of the BJP.

At the base of this argument runs the continuing ding-dong of the TV studio kind between the BJP and the Congress over 1984 and the Gujarat killings of 2002. You killed in 1984 ... but you killed in 2002 ... it goes on. The arguments and counter-arguments, more abuse and counter-abuse really, don't quite cancel out. They both only add up to the disrespect for the dead and disregard for justice.

In 1984 a Sikh family on the run hides in a disused well. They are discovered, they scream hopelessly for mercy. They are doused with kerosene and burnt alive. In Ahmedabad in 2002 hordes of killers break into a Muslim's home and slash everyone to death. Do murders have a political way of canceling one another out? Can we tell the survivors of either of those families that failure to protect then, or to hand justice now, is in some ways okay because think what happened to the other? Why would we raise Gujarat to dilute justice over 1984, or the other way? We are arguing our way out of justice both ways.

Again, those numbing numbers, this time for balancing. In Gujarat, as the official count goes, 790 Muslims were killed, as were 254 Hindus, with 223 reported missing. Without doubt the real numbers were higher. In 1984 as the official count goes, 2,733 were killed. And we know if only from the hundreds of deaths on the trains that the real number was higher.

The progressive argument of today would have us forget the screams in the Nangloi well in the cause of a greater morality. What would we be saying to the families of those people burnt in the well? That we don't want to know because we want the son of the Prime Minister then to be Prime Minister now? Political arguments can have their validity. But can we be called upon to deny murder in the name of morality? Such arguments would summon one act of brutality to look away from the other. Point to the supposedly right thing said today to cancel out a murderous past.

Odd how many of our brightest are not shy of such equations. This has been the stuff of those ding-dong TV debates over decades now. One genocide becomes the ding, the other the dong. Sound them in one program, and proclaim balanced journalism.

Surely the 1984 killings cannot be dropped in the name of Gujarat and in the cause of the politics of today. You killed here, I killed there, call it quits? In truth the law failed at both places. That does not cancel culpability, on the contrary, it calls for the law to be applied more rigorously over both mass killings. Because Rahul Gandhi has secular views, no one murdered in 1984 is any less murdered than he was. No one killed at either place was any less murdered than the other.

~

This third edition adds the short chapter 'BJP Shadows'. Not by way of blaming the BJP to 'balance' accusations out or reduce the imbalance. The chapter points to the support provided to the killers who were leaders of BJP's predecessor, the Jan Sangh. And it points to some decisions taken by the BJP government that have turned out to be protective of killers, notwithstanding the eventual conviction of Sajjan Kumar in a freak court decision. This revised edition also adds to the earlier chapters on Kamal Nath and on Rajiv Gandhi. It substantially revises the chapter 'Commissions and Omissions' to record a fair bit more by way of both.

~

Ten years back I had asked, why now? Why thirty years later? Ten years on, 1984 is still unfinished business.

This book got going, suddenly one afternoon in 2014, in the course of a chat with my friend and colleague Sagarika Ghose. 'Why haven't you written a book on 1984 yet?' she asked. I didn't have an answer as good as the question.

We spoke when 1984 was back in the air. Rahul Gandhi, had just given an interview in which he duly denied that his party, or the Congress-I as it was once called (after his grandmother and former Prime Minister, Indira Gandhi) had a hand in the killings of the Sikhs in Delhi following the assassination in 1984. Rahul also insisted that his father, Rajiv Gandhi, and his newly formed government then had done all they could to stop the violence. The usual volley of allegations and counter-allegations followed.

I thought I had something to contribute to this debate, away from the usual blame game. It would be in the form of a record of what I had seen and reported through 1984, a resurrected diary of sorts.

I had reported on the violence that had erupted in Delhi as a crime reporter with *The Indian Express* newspaper. Later, I submitted affidavits based on my eyewitness accounts before two inquiry commissions, headed by Justices Ranganath Mishra and G.T. Nanavati.

This book brings in all that but seeks to do more than staple earlier submissions together. It brings three offerings.

One, I include here detailed interviews with critically important police officers who were at the forefront of dealing with the violence in 1984. For this, a delay of thirty years might not have been bad at all. These officers are now retired, and could now speak far more freely than they ever could before. What they do say now is telling.

Second, I place my experiences and encounters within the context of the law and required legal procedures as they stood then, and still do. The debate over 1984 has continued far too long without a close enough reference to the law.

Finally, I bring into this account my own experience of reporting and witnessing the events of 1984, in Punjab as well as in Delhi. This I could never do before as a reporter tied only to newsy facts. This, now, is an account of the person, such as I am, running into those events, such as they were.

The following pages include much that is historical but make no claim to be the history of those days. They arise from what I directly saw and personally understood. I believe that the account is not historical also because it adds up to a case for steps that are still possible to take—just about.

Finally, this sharing was made possible by the guidance of Krishan Chopra at HarperCollins, and the astute reading by the editor Somak Ghosal. And now my warmest thanks to Udayan Mitra for his patience with the new edition, and for allowing me to share more than I could earlier. And to Aadrit Banerjee for his astute editing of this second edition.

I

The Politicians

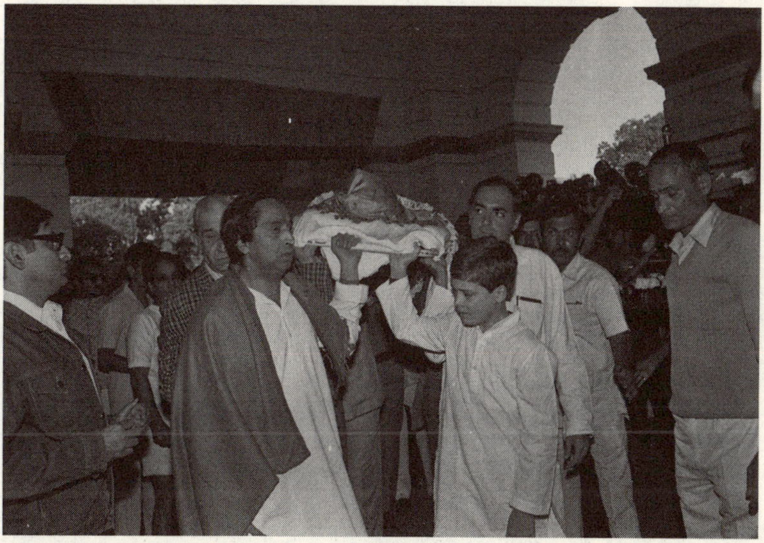

1

Upside Down in Karol Bagh

The call to the office of *The Indian Express* newspaper in New Delhi came in the afternoon. 'The police have arrested many men for looting Sikhs,' the voice said. 'A Congress MP has come to the police station. A big confrontation is taking place now because he wants the men from his party to be released.' Not the exact words, but this was more or less what the man had called up to say.

Could this be true? Would a Congress-I member of parliament (MP) show his hand, the party hand, so openly? Would he really come to claim men hauled up for attacking and looting Sikhs after the assassination of Prime Minister Indira Gandhi as the party's own? And then ask for them to be released?

It was an anonymous call, hard to believe. Politicians drop hints, they send word, they find ways of letting it be known what it is they want. It was hard to imagine an MP turning up in person at a police station to make such a demand.

But that wasn't the only bit hard to believe. Could it be that the police somewhere had actually taken steps against the hordes of men who had attacked, looted and killed Sikhs on the streets of Delhi? We had seen, I had seen myself, the police deliberately do nothing to protect Sikhs through the violence that arose after Mrs Gandhi's death. In those days, for the police to arrest such criminals would itself be news.

The man had spoken with great urgency; his tone rang true. My gut feeling was that this information needed to be checked out. In the business of reporting you learn to make room for what is neither likely nor logical. What sounded more unlikely was an indiscretion by a Congress leader in publicly claiming ownership of men arrested for criminal acts, and not the fact that ruling party men had engaged in violence, with the backing if not leadership of their seniors.

I had run into killers just a couple of days earlier on the streets of Sultanpuri in west Delhi. Their Congress connections seemed evident. Through the worst of the killing in days earlier we had all witnessed a collapse of the ruling Congress government and its agencies. The government had emphatically failed to protect Sikhs, at the political level through its decisions and indecisions, and at the administrative level through the inaction of the police. But no Congress leader had publicly gone so far as what the caller was now claiming.

No doubt the caller had his interests. That would not be unusual— newsrooms do get information as a matter of course only because it suits someone to pass it on. A beat crime reporter makes it his business to invite such information discreetly. The caller could have been from an opposition party, he could have been a concerned citizen, a dogooder from within the Congress, someone who wanted to nail the MP, someone within the police. I didn't know and it didn't matter. The question was whether this was worth checking out.

A couple of us in the newsroom, and there were just a couple of us around at that time, were dismissive of the tip-off. None of us thought it likely that a Congress MP would go to a police station with such a demand, even if it were his men who had been taken in. But a fellow reporter I spoke with agreed that the scenario would be quite extraordinary if true. Could this be the chink through which the hand of the Congress leadership might become visible?

I had no immediate word of any new violence in the city at that time. It was 5 November. By then, the killing was done. So I took my old Vespa scooter and headed out to Karol Bagh police station.

I could hardly have suspected then that this expedition would lead to just about the firmest evidence I ever would see of the involvement of Congress-I leaders—along with top police officers—in the looting and the killing that came with it. It led, in fact, to the most direct evidence so far of the party's involvement at such a senior level that I've seen anywhere yet. Nor could I have anticipated that the visit to the police station would lead further to an encounter over the incident with the Prime Minister, Rajiv Gandhi—and later bring me up against the defence of the Congress offered by his son Rahul ahead of the parliamentary elections in 2014.

~

I could hear shouting inside the police station as I parked my scooter. Some men just within the gate in the courtyard were raising slogans against the police. A couple of constables stood to a side watching them. Behind them lay the office of the station house officer (SHO), the inspector in charge of the police station. As I walked past the noisy bunch towards that office, I could hear what sounded like loud arguments within.

Approaching the door, I saw Hukum Chand Jatav, the additional commissioner of police for Delhi range, seated in the SHO's chair. He saw me at the door, and could hardly contain his anger. He ordered a junior policeman in the room to send me away. I had to leave.

In those moments at the door, I had seen something of the scene within. The officer heading the central district police, the deputy commissioner of police (DCP), Amod Kanth, was sitting to one side of Jatav. The SHO of the police station, Ranbir Singh, not a Sikh, was standing to a side in the room. I remember Ranbir Singh as much the Haryana man he was with the authority of a 'policeman' written all over him, even if he now stood sidelined.

Near him was the officer one rank above him, the assistant commissioner of police (ACP), Ram Murti Sharma. And on the other side of the table from Jatav, Congress MP Dharam Dass Shastri had taken centre position among a group of men, all protesting loudly against the local police.

Shastri was the MP for the Karol Bagh constituency (far larger than just the Karol Bagh police station area). I heard one of the men on Shastri's side particularly loud. He was Moti Lal Bakolia, a senior Congress leader.

On the police side, the room had packed in almost the entire chain of command of officers there. Delhi was then divided into two 'ranges': called Delhi range and New Delhi range. The officer in charge of a range was an additional commissioner of police, only one rung below the rank of the top man, the commissioner of police (CP). Within each 'range' lay three police districts. Delhi range comprised the central, north and east police districts, the New Delhi range included New Delhi district and the west and south police districts.

A district police force was commanded by a DCP. Within a district a set of two or three police stations would be led by an ACP. Each police station would be headed by an inspector, the SHO. Karol Bagh was one of the police station areas within the central district of Delhi range.

In the pecking order inside that room, Jatav was the top officer, heading the three districts of Delhi range, followed by Amod Kanth, DCP, central district. One rank below Kanth was ACP Ram Murti Sharma and one step below him, the SHO, Ranbir Singh. The SHO was the juniormost among the officers gathered but most critical; it is the SHO who stands invariably at the cutting edge of policing.

My eviction from the doorway to the SHO's office didn't send me far. The voices rose loud. I could hear everything from outside. And no officer was present outside to send me away from the space around the SHO's office. From the doorway, I'd seen a window on the far side of the office with an open compound beyond. I walked round to that side to stand close to the window.

Within, Bakolia and Shastri were both protesting to Jatav against some arrests made by the local Karol Bagh police. Some phrases arose again and again: '*Matlab kya hai* ...' (What does it mean ...), '*Bina baat* ...' (Without reason ...) One word I heard again and again was that the police had been '*badtameez*' (badly behaved). I heard Kanth defending his SHO's actions.

At one point, Amod Kanth turned right upon the Congress-I leaders. 'You are protecting criminals ...' Kanth said, or words very similar to that. This he spoke plainly and directly. That provoked the most frenzied shouting I'd heard until then, aimed at Kanth and the SHO. I glimpsed Bakolia get up from his chair and square up to the SHO, as if almost to assault him. Some of his companions grabbed him to calm him down. Shastri did nothing to stop him, he appeared to back all that Bakolia was saying.

Kanth confronted the shouting Congressmen again and again. I heard him say several times that those looted goods had been found in the homes of these men. This was the thrust of the confrontation: the local police had picked up men for looting Sikh homes, the Congress leaders were now claiming them as their own and demanding their release. The caller had been right.

I heard Jatav cut short his DCP time and again, demanding explanations from him in the presence of the Congressmen. I'd never seen anything like this before. The top police officer was sitting there backing the Congress leaders against his own SHO and the local police. The next senior officer in that room was defending the local police team—and was being opposed by his own senior for it.

The confrontation calmed down in a bit. ACP Ram Murti Sharma stepped out. I walked round to speak with him. He looked very upset. I remember almost exactly what he said: 'Whenever the police try to do any work, the politicians stop us.' He pointed to the SHO's office. He looked disgusted.

Soon, Jatav stepped out. I asked him why he had not supported his officers. His reply was unforgettable: 'No such thing happened,' he said. 'But I saw it,' I said.

'No, you have not seen it.'

I asked him what the shouting was about then. 'It is all the fault of Amod Kanth,' Jatav said. 'Mr Kanth does not know how to behave with politicians.' Barring inconsequential details of phraseology, that is what he told me.

That remark came as yet another indication of how policing had broken down during the three days following the assassination of Indira Gandhi. I cannot imagine that in normal circumstances an additional commissioner of police would tell a reporter that the deputy commissioner of police did not know how to behave with politicians. Jatav walked to his white Ambassador police car and left.

Jatav gone, I stepped towards Dharam Dass Shastri, who was now standing just outside the gate of the police station. I asked him why he was protesting against the arrests. 'The police could have taken away the property, but should not have arrested the people,' he said. 'Just because some property has been recovered, these people are not criminals.' I asked him how he could expect the police to recover looted property and not arrest the men from whom it had been seized. The two together, I said, were inseparable within the offence. By this time, a few people had gathered around us outside the police station. One man heard my question and demanded that Shastri answer it. This man, needless to say, was not a Sikh—a Sikh could still not be seen on the streets of Delhi.

'These men are all innocent,' Shastri replied. He said he was angry because the police had misbehaved while conducting raids. The police had used 'foul language' and had upset him. He didn't want that argument to build up, and left.

I now walked up to Amod Kanth, standing outside the SHO's office. He seemed trembling with emotion, I saw tears. I had seen him humiliated by a senior officer for doing his job and for protecting his men who had done theirs, and he knew I had. I asked him what he would now do. 'Just take leave and go away,' he said. He did not look like he wanted to say much more, and left. I too headed back to my office.

I did not hear then the concluding part of those exchanges within the SHO's office, how the quarrel was resolved. But the Congress leaders had left a satisfied lot; Jatav had walked away authoritatively. Kanth and the local police officers looked shaken. Perhaps the kindest possible viewing of the police here was that they had 'defused the situation'—Delhi Police have a stronger record defusing situations than dealing with them.

Laying tact over truth is an uneasy business though. It meant that an upholder of law had decided to abandon it. My memory of that encounter carries a heavily upside-down feel. Shastri was accusing the police of arresting men they had found to have broken the law.

Later that evening Jatav issued a statement, a copy of which I received at *The Indian Express*, declaring that the police would continue to take action against antisocial elements. The statement made no reference to the incident at the Karol Bagh police station. The official line he had handed me was after all that nothing had happened there. I had Jatav's word for it: I had not seen what I had or heard what I did. I could hardly have taken Jatav's word for it of course, and I reported the exchanges at Karol Bagh in *The Indian Express*, which carried the story in a bold box on the top of the front page the next morning.

~

Jatav's statement would no doubt be filed away to show how this police officer had issued very proper instructions that antisocial elements be dealt with. What was a reporter's word against an officer's record? I was a witness to what had transpired, but could I find witnesses to testify to what I had witnessed? The remarkably simple counter that Jatav had used—that no, I had not seen what I had seen—was used later by the Supreme Court judge, Justice Ranganath Mishra, who led an inquiry into the killings. The police, to the extent that they were represented by Jatav, were 'denying' the story, and we are all accustomed to reading the ringing stamp of authority in such official denials.

As it happened, the officers junior to Jatav inside that police station later filed affidavits before the Mishra Commission confirming what had happened—and in line with what I had reported. Their word, or mine, made little difference to Jatav. Just what was submitted to the commissions of inquiry, and what they did with those submissions, is another story that emerged later (Chapter 13).

The Kusum Lata Mittal inquiry ordered in 1987 into police conduct through the killings found that 'the role of Shri Jatav during the riots appears to be somewhat dubious and his conduct questionable'.[1] The report says Jatav removed the officers who were taking effective action and took a 'lenient view against miscreants.' The report found that 'it is more than obvious that he is accountable for the total breakdown of law and order in many areas under his charge'.

This inquiry found Jatav's role 'questionable, partisan and inexcusable'. He was 'in sympathy with some local leaders and disinclined to take action against the culprits'. Its recommendation was that 'such an officer is not fit to be retained in a disciplined force'.

Jatav was not sacked as recommended but in the wake of such findings and other complaints, the government instituted an inquiry against him. Justice Nanavati notes in his report in 2005 that 'the inquiry against Additional Commissioner of Police, Shri H.C.Jatav, was concluded with imposition of penalty of 30 per cent cut in his pension for a period of five years'.[2]

Jatav had been charge-sheeted for negligence and dereliction of duties in March 1992, two weeks before his due retirement. The cut in pension was ordered in 2000. Jatav challenged the government proceedings against him in court. But the government itself stepped back from its move earlier. Its counsel told the court in 2005 that the 30 per cent pension cut had been restored to Jatav and that the government was considering paying the interest over delayed dues that Jatav had claimed in his appeal. The court ordered payment of interest over the delayed 30 per cent payment as Jatav had claimed.[3] The government dropped all charges against him.

I did not see Shastri again, though he too, like Jatav, simply denied everything I had reported. This was denial with the additional stamp now of an MP on it. As Shastri said, he was upset by the use of 'foul language'. In the midst of all the killings and breakdown, here was an MP getting agitated, supposedly, over verbal indelicacies. Delhi Police's vocabulary has never been known to include an offering of words sweet and gentle. Foul language comes to the police as inevitably as breathing and is expected by everyone too. The issue here was not of failed niceties of expression—the fact that this was being suggested at all by

Shastri implied a return to the usual business of cover-up that no one believes in or is expected to. Shastri was being a politician again, and not a very good one.

One moment the MP was speaking about the police arresting innocent people, at another that it was okay to recover property from these people but not arrest them, and then he was saying it was the police's language that had not been right. No doubt he believed this whole exchange was between him and the police; it was not something he expected to see front-paged in *The Indian Express* the next morning.

Left unresolved at that meeting, left unresolved to this day, is the question of law. Later police reports I saw are silent on the question of prosecution or any convictions following the arrests. The compromise of the moment seemed to have been that the police hold on to the stolen property, but release the suspects rounded up. On the impossibility of separating the two, there had been no reply by the MP. The trouble with that simple question of law is that it never was asked by those who effectively could.

You don't have to pass a law exam to figure that the two cannot be separated—you cannot split the fact of stolen property being recovered from whom this property had been recovered from. Shastri wanted the police to look at a stolen television set and even to take it away, but not look at the one who stole it and whose house it had been recovered from. It was in so doing that he had incidentally announced that the men the police had hauled in for loot were all Congress party men.

What finally emerged from Karol Bagh police station was a Congress leader's ownership of men arrested for loot; what emerged also was the government's refusal to apply the law after a rare bunch of policemen those days had acted as required by law.

2

Loot and Law

The Indian Penal Code (IPC) unfolds its sections a great deal less pedantically than one might expect. It might even be 'recommended reading' not because we must all know the law, but as just an interesting read for use of precise language of the Victorian era—it had come into effect, after all, in 1860.

We all know Section 420 of the IPC that covers thievery through trickery; it's had films named after it, it's a daily metaphor in Indian life. The spell in jail it could hand out isn't as light as the metaphor though: 'whoever cheats and thereby dishonestly induces the person deceived to deliver any property to any person' could be jailed up to seven years, and fined.

Theft stands as obvious offence; you don't need to produce numbers from the IPC to establish that it is. But theft alone was not the issue at the Karol Bagh police station that afternoon, the declared reason for the arrests was not that these men had been caught while stealing. It was that stolen goods had been found on them, and seized from them.

That takes us to numbers within the IPC such as Sections 411 and 414 that are not quite as popularly known as Section 420. But Jatav, a police officer, would have known them all. He would have known that under Section 411 whoever dishonestly 'receives or retains' any stolen property that he knows or even 'has reason to believe' to be stolen can be punished with three years in jail. Jatav would have known further that under Section 414 someone suspected of doing no more than assisting in dealing in stolen goods, or goods that he could have reason to believe to be stolen, could be sent to jail for just as long.

Consider these two laws and Jatav's defence of the men who had been hauled in after stolen goods were found on them. For a start, did he think the police had cooked up the story entirely? Unlikely, not because Delhi Police are not known to cook up evidence, but because he could not instantly have had time to gather evidence to lead to such belief. Police officers are, as a matter of course, reluctant to consider such possibilities, and they usually never do.

The abuse from the Congress MP and his party colleagues inside that office did not add up in itself to evidence that the police had concocted evidence. If Jatav had evidence from some other source, he didn't say so. Given his aggressive sympathy for the party leaders, he'd hardly have kept any such evidence quiet.

In any case, if he did suspect the police had acted on false evidence, he would be bound by the law and police codes to order prosecution of the concerned police officers. This, he did not do. Under the law, Jatav had two choices. He must either prosecute his juniors for assembling false evidence or support the prosecution of the arrested men.

If Jatav did not think the local police themselves criminal, he would have good reason to believe, prima facie as they like to say in police jargon, that the local police had indeed found stolen goods on these men. In backing the Congress leaders' demand for release of these men, was Jatav assisting them in concealing or disposing of these stolen goods? Once let off, these men would of course do all they could to remove any trace of what they had done. Was Jatav effectively supporting men who had broken the law? Preposterous in thought, but not illogical in law, was there a case for Jatav's juniors inside that police station to have arrested their boss?

You can't look back on 1984 and forget the law as the police then did. It was the standard to judge police action against, it was the standard they had been trained in. Recalling the law today brings a measure of just how much had gone wrong in 1984, a measure more precisely of just how far the top cop was wandering from law at the Karol Bagh police station.

Jatav would have known that protestations of innocence would be for a court to consider, and in the correct course he could have told the

Congress leaders they could argue their innocence before a magistrate.

At that particular moment it was legally enough for the police to have arrested the suspects and made the seizures with no more than 'reason to believe it to be stolen property'.

Why talk of these stolen goods at all? When lives were being lost, who cared for the loss of a television set? Not even those it had been stolen from. The quarrel at the police station was over detentions over stolen goods, but the issue was about much more than that. And not just that the Congress hand had shown itself. A top officer's intervention on behalf of the detained men had axed the possibilities of uncovering far more than television sets. There never was some 'A' gang that killed and 'B' gang that looted. It was the same people. Could investigation of men caught for theft have opened up prosecution for murder?

The law offers that opening. If within a mob someone looted, and someone else killed, they would be a part of the same 'transaction'. The police would be required to investigate members of such a group for both offences. The Karol Bagh police were within reach of something more serious following the arrest of these men on the relatively minor matter of possessing stolen goods. Interrogation of the looters could have led the police on to the more serious—and associated—crimes of killing and injuring.

Jatav would have known Section 221 of the Criminal Procedure Code (CrPC): 'If a single act or series of acts is of such a nature that it is doubtful which of several offences the facts which can be proved will constitute, the accused may be charged with having committed all or any of such offences, and any number of such charges may be tried at once.'

The law builds a lot of muscle for the police to push much further arrests made at first on a relatively minor charge. If 'the accused is charged with one offence, and it appears in evidence that he committed a different offence for which he might have been charged … he may be convicted of the offence which he is shown to have committed, although he was not charged with it.' This meant the arrested persons could have been interrogated and potentially booked through this very case for murder, if investigations led that way and it were to turn out later that the charges relating to recovery of stolen property would not themselves stand. Sections 219 to 223 of the CrPC arm the police extensively to arrest on one charge and later book on another following investigation.

The stolen goods had opened a doorway; instead of leading his police through it, the top officer in the police station was closing the door shut. Jatav knew the law, but he knew more. He knew he could disregard it and get away with it, because he did.

~

Consider a moment all that would have to be true if, as Dharam Dass Shastri said, the arrested men were innocent. If these were innocent men, as claimed by the MP, then the SHO had led his force into manufacturing false evidence to arrest the right-hand men of the ruling party MP.

The police, of course, knew at the time of the arrests that these were Congress party workers. The men would hardly have failed to declare who they were—the Congress stamp was their best bet against arrest. The 'don't you know who I am' culture is pervasive in Delhi, always has been, alongside its cousinly 'don't you know whom I know'.

SHO Ranbir Singh and his men had not just made arrests; a good deal of looted property had been recovered. For Shastri to have been right, the police would have had to recover these stolen goods from other looters, carried them over to the homes of the Congressmen, 'recovered' those planted goods back, and then arrested the Congress members and leaders living in those homes. False charges would have to follow faked recoveries.

Anyone can judge the likelihood of the local police doing all this against ruling party leaders riding a post-assassination wave of political sympathy.

For local policemen to have found stolen goods in the homes of criminals to then carry to homes of Congress-I leaders would need an extensive conspiracy of active police criminality involving a very large number of junior officers and constables—if the SHO had at all set out to carry out some such agenda against the Congress, for some reason not easy to guess. No SHO would dare order his men into such a criminal conspiracy, nor would an extensive police force carry out such orders without some promise of lifelong silence. They would risk arrest and the end of their careers. What reward could they hope for against such risks?

The more you looked, the more facts arose to deny the Congress-I denials. The stolen goods were stolen from somewhere; in time descriptions from victims or witnesses would follow of what was stolen and from where, or of what had been found and recovered from where. The police acted on specific information to seize particular goods from a given place, from identifiable people, people identified as local Congress leaders and members. And there was no doubt at all that the men arrested for loot were Congress party men—we had Shastri's word for it.

The discovery of these goods would at some stage have to match complaints of what was stolen. For Shastri to have been right, a lot of Sikh families would have had to decide all of a sudden, and all together, to go to the police with an agreed and extensive lie about thefts and robberies in order to target some bunch of innocent Congress workers.

Who again would believe that such a scenario might remotely be possible? The looted Sikhs were a poor and shattered lot, hiding in fear of both the attackers and the police. Which Sikh in Delhi those days could have commandeered others to generate false evidence against the Congress and its leaders? For a start, some Sikhs would have had to step out of their houses at the risk of their lives. How could such a conspiracy have been hatched? Mobile phones weren't around those days, no social media on which to connect. Landline phones were few, and only for the privileged few.

Any multiplied fiction produced by the police in such conditions never could stand in court. And would the DCP have protected such a local police conspiracy against the Congress-I and, in effect, joined such a conspiracy to go after innocent Congress-I people? Dharam Dass Shastri could never have been right to suggest that these were innocent men unfairly picked up by the police.

Dharam Dass Shastri was angry really that the police had dared to police. An unwritten law had taken over from the written law, and the unwritten law then was that the police would not enforce the law against Congress party men, that they would not protect Sikhs. In stepping up to proper policing, the Karol Bagh police had acted in law but betrayed the norm. Shastri wanted enforcement of the norm, which was to disregard the law.

~

'We were told we were saved by an SHO by the name of Ranbir Singh,' a young Sikh inside Zohra Emporium told me when I went back to Karol Bagh in 2014, thirty years after I had witnessed that scene at the police station. The young Sikh must have been a kid in 1984, maybe he wasn't born then. Yet, he knew the name of Ranbir Singh. As do other Sikhs in Karol Bagh. It's not often you see a mere SHO turn into a legend.

Karol Bagh today is no more Delhi's sole magnet for wedding shopping that it once was. But given all the growth of money and people, the wedding-wear business still buzzes. But up until the 1980s, generations of middle-class Delhi couldn't marry without a visit to Karol Bagh. It's where you'd go to buy that red kind of glitter mandatory for brides, and the near-bridal. That would take you to places like Zohra Emporium in Gaffar market, down the road from Karol Bagh police station.

Zohra Emporium was a giveaway name then too; the shop board boasted its name in Punjabi script as it still does. Like so many Sikh businesses in Karol Bagh, this shop was fortunate it could go on with business as usual past 1984 that brought no more than a few days of shut shop.

In those first days of November 1984, shops weren't just shops, where you could change money for goods. They stood as targets for looters, not as magnets for buyers. Gold sat within to be looted, dresses to be burnt, if not stolen. Ranbir Singh and just a few of his men stood in the way. Policing that at other times might be routine was in those days heroic.

Ranbir Singh died some years back, an officer at the Karol Bagh police station told me. The police station has now expanded from what it was then: the SHO's office is now lodged in a newer block. But the old structure stands just as before; a board announced the old SHO's office as now the office of the inspector for investigations. I wandered around to revisit my vantage point of thirty years earlier, to the courtyard by the side of that old office, where I had witnessed the drama within.

From here I walked past the duty officer's room on the way to the new SHO office. Two policemen came by carrying a metal wardrobe to the backyard, next to the malkhana (storeroom) where recovered stolen goods are stacked. Presumably, this was some stolen wardrobe. It looked good. Theft now looked reassuringly secular, just a normal transaction between thieves and the owners they had relieved of their goods. A 'good thief' is neither religious nor political in the course of his job. Whether that wardrobe was stolen from a Sikh or not did not matter, and how I liked that.

In 1984 theft—and more—had been permitted selectively by the state; it was fine to steal so long as you stole from the Sikhs. Karol Bagh had stood as an exception to that sanction but admirable as that was, it was not for this that I remember, and recall, Karol Bagh. What made Karol Bagh exceptional was that this dump of a police station had thrown up evidence of an involvement of Congress party leadership that it could never deny itself out of.

Most of us 'knew' that Congress party men were behind the criminality and the killings. But who could produce evidence of such involvement? From those very first days, the Congress-I had been demanding evidence from all of us who were seeing that involvement. In our newsroom, as through the city, we could not instantly produce evidence of the kind that could stand incontrovertibly in court, that would prove the active involvement of a top Congress party leader.

After that incident at Karol Bagh we could, and did.

~

Arguments over some petty thefts had in one stroke set up two momentous pointers—both to police collusion and political involvement. I had seen the hand emerge out of the defensive glove. And that is the reason to talk about Karol Bagh at all.

I'm mindful that I do not overstate the significance of the Karol Bagh incident simply because I witnessed it. And I'm fearful of any boastful tone that might ride along in incidental, if unintended, ways.

Journalists are a breed stuffed with self-importance over what they might 'exclusively' have done; evidence of the importance of such exclusivity usually is known exclusively to themselves. What journalists routinely recount of the government-shaking power of their stories is sadly not matched by evidence of governments actually shaking.

My 'boast', if any, can only be that I happened to be at the police station that day. No great achievement this. Much of this reporting business is about being at a certain place at a certain time. I am trying to look at the content of what I witnessed, and not boast that I had been there to witness it. The content of what I saw I believe to be the most definitive pointer yet of top-level Congress party involvement in the aggression against the Sikhs.

This suggestion is of course open to review and disagreement. If more firm evidence were to arise of the hand behind the killings, we all would want to see it, whether the hand were that of the Congress or of any other group or party. The evidence from Karol Bagh counts not as a political handle to beat the Congress with, but because it brought a definite pointer—where it pointed to was another matter. The facts that emerged at the Karol Bagh police station just happened to point to the Congress.

The Congress party hand that showed here wasn't visibly bloody, but it was identifiable. Far more serious allegations arose over other Congress leaders, but these lie trapped in the contested space between accusation and denial. The Karol Bagh police station emerged as an unlikely slot for a peep show into the politics behind the attacks.

Hand-in-glove with the politics, Karol Bagh had shown up just how lethally the police leadership held hands with the Congress-I. I had seen deaths in the days earlier, too many. But this quarrel at Karol Bagh brought its own trauma, and it remains disturbing to this day. It was the trauma of witnessing a deliberately ordered abandonment of policing.

It was one thing to have witnessed lawlessness on the streets, but another to then see it followed up by orders from a top police officer to reverse a rare enforcement of law. And to do so not in the heat of the street, but through official instructions inside a police station. An officer in the second seniormost position in Delhi Police sat there ordering the abandonment of law.

The evidence I had seen was firm enough to be presented to court. That it wasn't was the consequence of a continuation of the abandonment of law that followed. But at the least it brought some political consequences for Dharam Dass Shastri. He was denied a party ticket in the December 1984 elections after that Karol Bagh story got into the press.

3

Rajiv Gandhi

That Dharam Dass Shastri was denied a Congress-I ticket in the parliamentary elections of 1984 as a result of the incident at Karol Bagh police station, I came to know directly, and most unexpectedly, from Rajiv Gandhi the following month, in December.

The media attention had shifted to Rajiv Gandhi. Delhi's Sikhs who had survived the attacks on them somehow, tens of thousands of them, had crowded, cold and fearful, into all sorts of shelter homes, in schools, gurdwaras, even police stations. I hardly had time to report this as fully as I'd have liked. I was assigned to cover the elections due end-December. That took me trailing Rajiv Gandhi in Amethi, the favoured constituency of the Gandhi family about 150 km east of Lucknow.

I was to cover Amethi and neighbouring Rae Bareli, the constituency then of Arun Nehru, Rajiv Gandhi's very influential cousin in the Congress party. Rae Bareli had been Indira Gandhi's constituency, it was handed to Arun Nehru in 1980, and he, of course, won it then, and again in 1984. Rajiv Gandhi had inherited the Amethi constituency from his brother Sanjay, who was killed in an air crash in June 1980. That air crash launched Rajiv Gandhi into politics.

Amethi was expensively, but dubiously, nurtured. Rajiv Gandhi was the MP when I first visited the constituency, but the remains, ruins rather, that Sanjay Gandhi had left behind were everywhere to be seen in the shape of abandoned windmills that had been intended to power irrigation. These projects had never been thought through, they barely outlasted the inauguration. Soon these abandoned fans were dotting the roadsides as pictures of failed development. Nobody removed them either. Who would dare remove an intended windmill set up in Sanjay Gandhi's name even if it had decayed into a rusting fan?

Rajiv Gandhi, who was an Indian Airlines pilot until his brother's crash in a club aircraft launched him into politics, began to develop the constituency his own way. He roped some flying buddies into a local flying academy, and declared it a prize landmark in the name of development. Constituents of Amethi found jobs in the academy as cooks and sweepers, not as pilots. Big companies set up factories in the constituency area; like the windmills, these too soon came to a standstill.

After the assassination of Rajiv Gandhi in 1991, Amethi elected Captain Satish Sharma, a flying pal of Rajiv Gandhi who had landed himself in the inner political circle of the Gandhis. Along the way, the Bharatiya Janata Party (BJP) has managed to break thc Gandhi family hold. But Amethi has remained an electoral anchor of the Gandhi family; it returned Sonia Gandhi, then Rahul Gandhi.

In 1984 there was little doubt that Rajiv Gandhi would be reelected. Amethi was a non-contest. His main Opposition-backed opponent was Maneka Gandhi, his brother Sanjay Gandhi's widow. She had no hope of winning and never came close to it. Rajiv Gandhi was nevertheless going through the rituals of campaigning in Amethi, and it was at an election rally that I ran into him.

Running into Rajiv Gandhi, who was then Prime Minister after succeeding his late mother, was surprising, and from a security angle, shocking. A stage of the kind usual at election rallies had been erected in a ground somewhere in Gauriganj, close to Amethi town within the constituency. Aspiring young leaders from the party were delivering speeches in loyal passion they must have hoped would get noticed. As is the practice, they were warming up the rally, and no doubt gaining time for the spaces at the back to fill up, or be filled up.

I had headed for that rally ground and then walked up towards this stage when I saw Rajiv Gandhi standing behind it to a side, looking very pink in his white kurta-pajama. He didn't appear to be listening to the obsequiousness thundering over the mike; the speeches weren't going to catapult those poor speakers into a spectacular political career.

To my surprise, Rajiv Gandhi stood there alone; some others were around, but at a respectful distance of several yards. Just that sight was shocking—he would have been easy target for a trained sniper. This was an open ground, with trees and houses and low buildings all around. I had strolled to the stage towards Rajiv Gandhi without passing through anything like a metal detector, without being stopped or questioned.

The assassination of Indira Gandhi was very much on everyone's minds, security and the failure of security was being debated all the time. And yet, here the new Prime Minister of India stood out there in open space alone. You don't often see a Prime Minister unguarded in public, certainly that wasn't how anyone could expect to find the Prime Minister of India in the month following the assassination of the previous Prime Minister. You'd have thought that security would be excessively unrelenting for her son now.

This was my second security shock in Amethi. A couple of days earlier I had stepped into one of those public works department rest houses in Uttar Pradesh, where I was informed Rahul Gandhi and Sonia Gandhi had both been staying. And I had been able to go up to Sonia Gandhi there unchecked. She chose not to say anything, but nobody stopped me getting close enough to ask her a question.

From the security angle this time it got worse, though for me better. Unbelievably—and unbelievably to myself at that time—I just continued to walk up all the way to Rajiv Gandhi, expecting someone to come up, to call out, to stop me. Nobody did, I was surprised at every step I took.

I was up to handshaking closeness with Rajiv Gandhi. I introduced myself as a reporter from *The Indian Express*. The election was a noncontest, so I asked him about the involvement of Congress party leaders in the Delhi killings. 'In one case there was evidence, and we took action,' he told me. That would be Dharam Dass Shastri. The front-paged report from the Karol Bagh police station had created a stir if not a storm. It was confirmed to me later by a top officer of the Delhi Police that the Prime Minister's office had demanded a report on the incident, which had backed what I'd reported despite Jatav's denials to me. Speaking to an *Indian Express* reporter, it would be Shastri that Rajiv Gandhi was talking about.

The single question and answer did not develop into a conversation. Quite suddenly, a couple of armed policemen stepped up, to send me quite firmly in the direction of the crowds where I rightfully belonged. But through that momentary security lapse, I discovered that Rajiv Gandhi, then Prime Minister, of course, had accepted that Dharam Dass Shastri had intervened wrongfully to protect looters, and to unwisely claim them as his own.

So here was Rajiv Gandhi seen talking of some sort of action against a senior MP from his own party once he got evidence of involvement. On the face of it, that would make the case for a clean chit for Rajiv Gandhi, it would suggest he had acted fairly and honourably against his own when he saw reason to. Could a leader who had shown such intentions have ordered some pogrom against Sikhs? It would seem not. But facts on the ground raise questions over Rajiv Gandhi. They point to the other side of the chit that did not appear quite as clean. This was after all only some limited steps over a single case that Rajiv Gandhi had talked about.

~

For a start, denial of an election ticket to Shastri was some form of punishment handed out by Rajiv Gandhi in his capacity as the Congress party boss. Rajiv Gandhi and his fellow party leaders decided they didn't want an MP who launches himself publicly into illegalities—or indiscretions over illegalities. But Rajiv Gandhi was not just a party leader, he was Prime Minister. He had snubbed Shastri as head of the party, he did not order legal action as head of government. What had happened inside that police station was abortion of law induced by political muscle. Shastri had been punished for political misdemeanour, he was not prosecuted for violation of the law that such misdemeanour amounted to.

Attempting to interfere in the course of justice is a clear offence. As is any attempt to prevent a public servant from doing his duty—though such a charge would in this case be complicated by Jatav's opposition to his own officer. The Prime Minister did not respond with orders for police investigation, which should have arisen as logical and legal consequence to Dharam Dass Shastri's actions of which he had knowledge, and that he had acknowledged as unacceptable.

It was self-evidently outside of law for the Prime Minister to have 'punished' Shastri by cutting short his political career rather than by facilitating a process of law to take its course. Prime Ministers don't pursue cases at police stations, but this one Rajiv Gandhi knew of. He knew also that his MP had been wrong to take the stand he did which is why he was punished at the party level. Rajiv Gandhi chose the ways of a durbar above rules of government.

Rajiv Gandhi would have done himself a world of political good had he correctly ordered legal steps instead of nudging Shastri politically aside. For Rajiv Gandhi to have publicly ordered investigation of his party MP would have changed the entire debate about the Congress party's role in the violence if that is what he had wanted. An order to the local police to pursue action against Shastri and his own party workers, coming even after the killings were over, could also have sent a strong signal out to the police to take action where they had found evidence of an offence. This was a moment where Rajiv Gandhi could have taken steps both principled and politic. He lost that moment. Whether through inability or will, we may never know.

The kind of 'punishment' Shastri was given, or not given, only sent out a signal further discouraging police investigation of criminals. The message went out that if any action was to be taken at all, it would be at the party level, that if the Congress bosses did not touch Congress leaders, the police wouldn't either. Only on the face of it was the Shastri case an instance of Rajiv Gandhi taking some action against the guilty. In effect it was only evidence of a refusal to take legal action in the face of admitted facts that demanded it.

~

That question has always hovered over the 1984 killings—what Rajiv Gandhi did and didn't do.

Congress party leaders have always asked an apparently fair question in defence of Rajiv Gandhi. Where is the evidence that Rajiv Gandhi may have ordered the killings? It's unlikely there will ever be such an evidence. It's almost impossible that someone will one day produce some secret note from Rajiv Gandhi ordering a massacre of Sikhs in Delhi. Surely, no such note exists. But there the Congress case for denial does not rest.

It's the impossibly simplistic nature of the demand for such smoking gun evidence that is the problem, not the lack of any evidence that would meet such expectation. For a start, no one would ever 'write', or visibly order, some such action. Such a communication—if ever there was one—would go out in whispered suggestions, not as written orders. And this here is no whispered suggestion that there might have been any such.

The closest person to the inner circle of the government I spoke to on this was Tarlochan Singh, who was in 1984 the press secretary to President Zail Singh, and later MP, and Chair of the National Commission for Minorities. We met at the India International Centre in Delhi in May 2024.

'Arun Nehru had called a meeting of senior local Congress-I leaders in the afternoon on October 31,' he said. 'By then everyone knew Indira Gandhi had been shot dead, though the official announcement came in the evening. He asked why there has been no protest, no demonstration.' Tarlochan Singh said that Mahinder Singh Saathi, then mayor of Delhi, had attended the meeting. And then reported the outcome of that meeting to Zail Singh. Zail Singh told me this is what Saathi had said.'

The attacks, Tarlochan Singh said, began only after that. 'The first attacks came at INA Market. Nothing happened before the directive came. The violence was directed. It was not spontaneous violence on such a large scale.'

The next day, he said, the President tried several times to call Rajiv Gandhi by way of an SOS for Delhi Sikhs, but could not get through on the phone.

Later that day, he saw the attack at Gurdwara Rakab Ganj. 'The back side of Rashtrapati Bhavan overlooks Rakab Ganj gurdwara. Two Sikhs were burnt alive; we heard their screams but we could not do anything. I could see the attack taking place, I could see the police just standing there doing nothing.'

Tarlochan Singh here reports what Zail Singh had told him of the Mayor's report to him. Admittedly this is indirect, under the circumstances, there would never have arisen any communication that could have been direct and incontrovertible, we would have heard had there been any such. This is indirect word, but word from very responsible people in government then. So did this happen as Tarlochan Singh reports, is his a credible account? This would have to be a judgment call for anyone who considers this.

Irrespective of a view on this, I believe Rajiv Gandhi carried prime responsibility for most of those deaths. He simply did not do what it would have taken to prevent them.

Must we accept that Rajiv Gandhi wasted no time in accepting the position of Prime Minister but that having accepted it, he could not be expected to do what a Prime Minister then must have done about no less than mass killings before his eyes. If we have no evidence that Rajiv Gandhi directly ordered killings, we have no evidence either that he directly ordered the police chief of Delhi to stop the killings when they were happening. He was in close communication with the team overseeing funeral arrangements for Indira Gandhi that necessarily and prominently included then Police Commissioner Subhash Tandon.

What inhibits us from reading backwards into that killing inaction of Rajiv Gandhi then? What kind of correctness should blind us into seeing that this inaction was consistent with all that Rajiv Gandhi said and did—and failed to do—later? Could we pretend that it was not the same man, the same mind? The lazy dismissal of such an exercise would be that it is speculative. And speculative it would be to summon guesswork or hearsay to assert that Rajiv Gandhi 'must have' ordered the killings. But it is not speculative to note that following on from a wide broadcast of an appeal for calm, Rajiv Gandhi took no executive or administrative steps to stop the killing. And it is not speculative to see that in that image of the earth shaking upon a mighty tree falling, he saw the killings as inevitable, and not possible therefore for a government under him to have stopped them.

The difference lies between ordering killings and failing to prevent them. How much less is the second kind of guilt than the first? Less, certainly, but how much less? On that we will all have our own views. But views cannot be held in disregard of facts that point the way they do. These facts point to a clear responsibility for failing to protect Sikhs, even if they stopped short of any active command to kill coming from Rajiv Gandhi. So much of what he said, and did, spoke at the least of a passive aggression that encouraged the killings. And this he followed up with decisions that were guaranteed to deny justice later.

Rajiv Gandhi's metaphor for the killings shook Delhi, it certainly shook the Sikhs of Delhi: when a big tree falls, the earth shakes. The metaphor sought to turn the killings on the streets and in homes into an inevitable, even automatic consequence of the assassination of Indira Gandhi, with no possibility of intervention between cause and consequence. The tree metaphor in effect said this: two assassins who happened to have been Sikhs had assassinated Indira Gandhi; the murder of a few thousand innocent Sikhs was therefore the logical result; the murders were the shaking of the ground, the tree having been felled.

The inevitability suggested by the image of the falling tree would absolve Congress leaders of any hand in the killings, the police of responsibility in preventing them, and finally Rajiv Gandhi himself for failing as head of government to protect his people. The metaphor had of itself announced a view that prevention of the killings was not possible, and that prosecution for them would not be possible either.

Tragically, the metaphor did not remain a matter of choice of language. Government conduct had fallen in line with that metaphor, lethally.

The metaphor might have found some limited acceptability if it did not cover as many as three thousand murders and more. Indira Gandhi was no doubt a towering figure suddenly felled. That set off tremors that shook everyone at the ground level. Everyone I knew was shaken, but none of them turned killers. Rajiv Gandhi had summoned that metaphor not to describe the emotional state over our shock at the assassination; he had summoned it to explain away mass murders in a few districts of Delhi. In those early days after the assassination of Indira Gandhi, India had a Prime Minister who had demonstrated that he could not tell the difference between feeling shaken and going out to kill.

Rajiv Gandhi had deployed that metaphor at an election rally at the Boat Club in Delhi on 19 November, well after the assassination of Indira Gandhi. He said in that election speech: 'Some riots took place in the country following the murder of Indiraji. We know the people were very angry and for a few days it seemed that India had been shaken. But, when a mighty tree falls, it is only natural that the earth around it does shake a little.'

As *little* as to cause almost 3,000 murders in three days in Delhi? Because, by then, the death toll was known, certainly known to him. Were those just 'some riots'? And justifiable, because we knew, didn't we, that 'the people' were very angry? Of course, people were angry. But it wasn't 'the people' who killed.

'The people' were people everywhere, Indira Gandhi was the Prime Minister of the country. And Sikhs live everywhere in India. Nowhere did 'the people' go after 'the Sikhs', not even in Delhi. It was, as Ved Marwah, later police commissioner, found in his inquiry, small groups on the move that looted and killed, and in some areas very much more than in others. It is this lot, and they were not a lot, that had to be stopped. And it was these groups that the Prime Minister failed to stop.

Rajiv Gandhi was sworn in as Prime Minister on the evening of 31 October. At the time he was being sworn in, civil order was beginning to break down in Delhi. Rajiv Gandhi had had to take over undoubtedly in deeply tragic circumstances for him personally. But leaders are set different standards, in accepting leadership they accept they would be judged by a capacity to act exceptionally in exceptional times.

The police had their written codes, the codes for leaders are unwritten but known. Some pardonable neglect that might be indulged in by the ordinary cannot similarly be allowed a leader. Rajiv Gandhi had to act as a Prime Minister with responsibilities, not as a son bearing a loss. He was tested immediately, and he failed.

The tree metaphor that followed suggested that he didn't think he had. It suggested that the Indian Prime Minister thought that 3,000 murders in Delhi following the failure of his government to prevent them were okay. It suggested, and we saw, that he didn't believe there was any reason to later prosecute those guilty of the murders. The metaphor came with perpetual injustice written into it. Rajiv Gandhi's government governed in line with the injustice of that metaphor.

True, the police were never openly ordered to not protect Sikhs. Some correctly worded orders were also circulated routinely and blandly. Later, inquiry reports dug some of these out of records to make the case that Rajiv Gandhi therefore carried no responsibility for the killings, and that he had supported the proper course. What appeared lacking, and appeared dangerously so to Congress workers and the police, was the energy and will of a leadership resolute against the breakout of violence.

Missing was any tough message circulated early to the police on behalf of the Prime Minister ordering the police to go all out to take protective measures for the Sikhs and punitive steps against the rioters. In the face of such a command, Delhi could not have seen the patchiness it did, where just a few officers could go the way of enforcing law, and the rest the way of sabotaging it. That variation was itself evidence of a lack of effective government command to keep the law.

As it turned out, the gangs on the streets and the police interpreted this limpness in government signals as a non-verbal message that people were free to attack Sikhs and the police should let the attacks take place.

The need to provide protection to Sikhs was never remote, it was right before Rajiv Gandhi. Within walking distance of the Prime Minister's house, Sikhs were being 'necklaced' with burning tyres. Of course, the Prime Minister wasn't taking a walk on the streets, but even without the benefit of all the intelligence and government reports he undoubtedly had, he would have seen columns of smoke rising in the skies all over Delhi, and around him. He would have seen and heard the crowds baying for blood as they filed by Indira Gandhi's body at Teen Murti Bhavan. Rajiv Gandhi could hardly have been unaware that the city was in breakdown all around him. In the end, whether Rajiv Gandhi ordered the killing or just failed to take steps to prevent, or at least reduce, the killing made no difference to those killed and their families.

Those three days Rajiv Gandhi did not lead. Criminal or not, it turned out to be tragic. He perhaps did not see a need to lead if all he was observing was a cause-and-effect phenomenon of shaking of the earth on which a mighty tree had fallen. The leader reduced himself to an observer, or an incomplete actor. He made appeals for calm, he did little to enforce them. The Sikhs of Delhi did not need to hear speeches on the right thing to do, they needed the right thing done. And that needed government force that did not come, that Rajiv Gandhi did not effectively order.

For a mere citizen to have looked away would be condemnable but perhaps pardonable; for a government and its police to look away was culpable. And it still is. And it is still punishable. It's punishable particularly for the police, on many counts in law. The offence stands, evidence of it stands, many of the guilty are still left standing. The government failed then. So have successive governments since: the United Progressive Alliance, National Democratic Alliance, and whatnot have all failed to launch effective prosecution over those crimes.

The arm of the government that could have stopped the killer was the police. The police looked the other way, and could be seen looking the other way by the government, as much if not more than by anyone else. Just that deliberate police decision to look the other way makes an arguable case for conspiracy or at least abetment to murder—the fact that Delhi Police enabled murders through deliberated decisions they took is a fact that is inescapable, overwhelming and chilling. And if the police was culpable, so was the Congress government that controlled the police.

The police cover of correct communication proved to be a thin one that everyone saw through. Some top officers made some symbolic spot visits, though they were quicker to visit places where some scattered Sikhs had hit back in self-defence. The evidence gathered through the course of the police inquiry led by Ved Marwah established beyond doubt that the police were failing, and failing deliberately.

Marwah has spelt out at length what he found (see Chapter 7). Locally too, the police created some records to suggest that the right moves were being made. But the tone of the communications was rarely a firm command to effective steps. The adopted police strategy was to appear to make moves and to then make sure these moves would not be effective. A 'tone' is not the sort of thing that is tangible. But killings are. The mismatch between minimally correct communication, and the blood and fire on the streets, was unmistakable. Marwah's inquiry nailed this mismatch.

Clearly, the police were nowhere overwhelmed by mobs of such size they could not have controlled had they wanted to. The typical group on the rampage was no more than a few hundred men, Marwah's inquiry found. Delhi Police is used to handling crowds hundreds of thousands strong at frequent rallies in Delhi; they have managed to control enough riots down the years. Controlling these scattered and relatively small groups was hardly beyond them. They didn't because they didn't want to, and because they were not ordered firmly enough to. That signal—that did not come—had to have come from the leadership of the police and ultimately the government.

Rajiv Gandhi betrayed more than governmental and even moral failure of leadership—his failure became dangerously political at a time when India was closer to a precipice than it ever had been before, or has since. Comparing 1984 with riots that have taken place since in Mumbai or Gujarat is as macabre as it is pointless. But in 1984, after Operation Blue Star and then the Delhi killings, India seemed more dangerously close to a breakdown than I have ever thought or felt.

India was in real danger of losing its internal oneness with Sikhs. In Operation Blue Star in June 1984 the Congress government, led by Indira Gandhi, was seen by Sikhs to have brought down the Akal Takht, the fountainhead of their faith. It was seen to have killed hundreds of Sikhs within the Golden Temple. And now the inactions of the Congress government, with Indira Gandhi's son as Prime Minister, were seen killing yet more Sikhs.

Those days, the very survival of India was touch-and-go, the danger appeared immediate that the government couldn't have killed so many in Amritsar, and now in Delhi, and hope to get away with it. Rajiv Gandhi was failing at the moment when the country needed him most to govern.

Indira Gandhi launched Operation Blue Star in June 1984 to target Sikh militants who had fortified themselves within the Golden Temple in Amritsar under the leadership of Jarnail Singh Bhindranwale. How Blue Star was strategized and executed is another matter. But outside of all those arguments, one way or another, Blue Star had been a traumatizing blow to Sikhs. Just a few months after Blue Star, Sikhs, and all of Punjab, needed a calming hand—not the murder of another 3,000 Sikhs because two Sikh policemen had assassinated Indira Gandhi.

Governance demanded from Rajiv Gandhi just about everything needed to prevent another Sikh massacre—and in Delhi many times more Sikhs were killed than in Blue Star. But government policy as seen handed down to street level appeared more provocative than protective.

The immediate fear then accompanying the killings of Delhi was that Sikhs would turn upon Hindus in Punjab, because people who appeared outwardly as Hindu had slaughtered Sikhs in Delhi. Miraculously it seemed, in reaction to the massacre in Delhi, no more than some small and sporadic incidents of unrest erupted in Punjab— almost no Hindu was targeted by any Sikh in Punjab in any form of revenge attack. What limited the Sikh anger in Punjab?

Two reasons came to the fore then—and one hardly for Sikhs themselves to be proud of. From all that I gathered through connections with family and friends in Punjab, and through conversations with police officers with access to intelligence reports, word had spread fast from Delhi just 'which' Sikhs had been killed. People in Punjab were saying that those killed were not all Sikhs in the 'proper' sense of the term.

Very large numbers among those killed in west Delhi were Sikhs seen as only turbaned men from Rajasthan who did not speak Punjabi— and so, not 'proper' Sikhs. Worse, most victims were from the lower castes, and almost all were very poor. They were seen as poor and distant cousins, not true brothers of the 'proper' Jat Sikhs of Punjab. This distance in caste, wealth and location diluted Sikh anger in Punjab. Had 3,000 Jat Sikhs been killed in Delhi, we would have faced another story, possibly another India.

I ran into another, perhaps more parochial, reason through conversations with the same sources. Word had spread fast in Punjab, quite accurately, that it was never Punjabis who had attacked their Sikh neighbours, and that, on the contrary, thousands of Hindu Punjabis right across Delhi had done all they could to save Sikhs. This was perhaps the prime reason why there was almost no Sikh backlash against their Hindu neighbours in Punjab. In any case, there is much intermarriage between Hindus and Sikhs; whether in Delhi or Punjab, rare is a Sikh family without Hindu members or the other way round. Punjabi Hindus and Sikhs are not inaccessibly 'other' to each other.

People, just people, saved India from its own government. It appeared impossible then that they might, and it appears incredible now that they did. Rajiv Gandhi was just lucky that the ground stopped shaking without a helping hand from him.

4

Rahul Gandhi

'I remember, I was a child then. I remember that the government was doing everything it could to stop the riots …' Rahul Gandhi said in an interview to Arnab Goswami from Times Now channel in January 2014. Challenged with counter-allegations, Rahul Gandhi defended his position by repeating himself: 'The government in 1984 was trying to stop the riots, trying to stop the killings …'

It was the standard party position, and Rahul Gandhi no doubt would have resisted any allegations against his late father. The party has been one with the family for so very long now that defending the party was much the same as speaking up for dad. And it is the same party, even if it has now dropped the 'I' of the Congress-I then—'I' was for Indira Gandhi, to describe a split section of the party loyal to Indira Gandhi. The other side of the split had rapidly faded away, and it was the Congress-I that was the Congress then, and continued to be.

Rahul Gandhi was in 1984 all of twelve years old. How exactly a boy of his age knew what the government was doing then to stop the riots, as he believed, he did not say. He had little to say in response to questions put to him suggesting Congress involvement in those killings; his essential response was repetitions of denial. It was an interview he no doubt regretted giving; the repeated assertions that the party had done all it could to contain the killings—without spelling out what it was the party had done—seemed to do him no good at all.

Rahul Gandhi did admit in the interview that 'some Congressmen probably were involved'. He added: 'There is a legal process through which they have gone. Some Congressmen have been punished for it.' What, or who, was he talking about? He did not name those Congressmen who he said had gone through this legal process, he did not say who had been punished, and how.

Were Congressmen put through a 'legal process' and punished? The public seems to have missed this. What the public have not missed is the opposite—the fact that Congressmen, several of them, were in fact protected over their role in the riots. Where there was punishment, it was routed outside of the legal process.

Very little had happened within the legal process through those days of killing or later. On 31 July of the following year, high-flying Congress MP Lalit Maken was gunned down outside his house in Kirti Nagar in west Delhi along with his wife, Geetanjali. The killing followed widespread allegations of his involvement in the killing of Sikhs. Maken was elected to Parliament in 1984. But he was no ordinary Congress leader before then; he was the son-in-law of the former Indian President, Shankar Dayal Sharma, and he had been close to the Gandhi family, particularly to Sanjay Gandhi. Three Sikh extremists were later arrested for the murder.

On 5 September 1985 Arjan Dass, a Congress party councillor who was a close friend of Rajiv Gandhi, was shot dead along with a policeman guarding him. The killing was led by the same assassin, Harjinder Singh Jinda, who had shot Lalit Maken, and who later killed General Arun Shridhar Vaidya, who was the army chief during Blue Star. Rajiv Gandhi publicly castigated the police for security lapses that led to the killings.

No doubt such killings could not be allowed to continue. Extraordinary protection became evident around Congress party leaders after the killing of those two Congress leaders in Delhi. What we hadn't seen from Rajiv Gandhi was correspondingly strong steps to protect Sikhs through those three days of killings in Delhi.

Rahul Gandhi spelt out the correct position—that it was wrong to have taken out anger over two assassins on an entire community they happened to come from: 'What those two people did to my grandmother was two individuals,' Rahul Gandhi said in the course of that interview. 'I don't turn around and take my anger, which existed then and frankly doesn't exist now, and brush it on to an entire community ... I don't take my anger against two people and overlay it on millions. I think that's criminal ...'

So very correct. But what Rahul Gandhi chose not to say was that what had happened in Delhi was the precise opposite of what he now spoke of as the right thing to have been done. If everyone had thought in Delhi as Rahul Gandhi did, not a single Sikh would have been attacked in the city. Who carried the responsibility then of ensuring that this correct principle was upheld? It was the Congress party and its government—the very two entities led by his father—that had failed.

What Delhi had seen then, that the boy Rahul Gandhi had not, was that many Congressmen were actively in the lead in taking out anger over two assassins on an entire community. Rahul Gandhi was speaking in that interview of what might have been, what should have been, but so very obviously wasn't. 'Innocent people died in 1984, and innocent people dying is a horrible thing and should not happen ...' he declared. Of course, such a thing should not happen. Rahul Gandhi was distancing his party from the killings through declarations of ideal morality that stood far from the facts on the ground. The tragedy of November 1984 was that Congress party leaders had failed to live by the values Rahul Gandhi was upholding in the interview. The lesser tragedy of

2014 was Rahul Gandhi's insistence that they had. He failed to underline that verbal insistence with facts, he couldn't possibly have.

~

Rahul Gandhi's advisers made sure he gave no more interviews. That one did him no good then, and it seemed to have done the party no good when the election results came in. He did also appear in need of better advice in speeches that he delivered in Rajasthan in October 2013—that his nemesis Narendra Modi later picked up on.

A speech in Kherli in Rajasthan offers an extraordinary view of the events in 1984 as Rahul Gandhi saw them, and an even more extraordinary view of the man now recalling those events. Today we have the very ordinary option of listening to that speech on YouTube.

This now ordinary option would have appeared to us reporters of those days a possibility beyond imagination. We reported in the pre-Internet age, when the very thought of anything such as the Internet would have been out of some Hollywood film of the futuristic kind. But now we can look, and listen.

Here in this election speech in Kherli was a man approaching middle age (branded young only by the standards of Indian politicians) recalling what he experienced as a twelve-year-old at the time of the assassination. The eyewitness account Rahul Gandhi shared in that speech about the assassination and after is revealing of what the twelve-year-old saw, but it reveals a great deal more of the man now standing there on that election stage and doing the recalling. It's a spe-ech that deserves to be heard again. Here is a translation:

> It was a time of terrorism, there was a fight on, there was anger in Punjab, there was anger elsewhere. It was not anger in the

hearts of people, it was planted there. People were provoked to fight ... In 1977 everyone had deserted us. But Sikhs, those I could see, they were around in the most difficult days of my grandmother. They were standing by her. In five or six years, there was anger.

I spoke to you about my grandmother, I can tell you about Satwant Singh and Beant Singh [the two policemen who assassinated Indira Gandhi]. I knew Satwant Singh and Beant Singh. In a way, they were my friends. Just like these bodyguards (pointing to security men behind on stage), they were there, they were my friends, teaching me badminton, teaching me to exercise.

One day, in anger, my friends killed my grandmother. Just like in him (now pointing to a lone Sikh in the crowd), there was anger in me too, anger why they did this. There was anger in me that was like a burden. That anger was throttling me. And one day I understood. This is what happened ...

Let me tell you in detail. I was in school, there was a geography lesson on, and I was looking out of the window, there used to be a petrol station there, I was looking out of the window, and one person came and said I have to go to the principal's office. I was a badmash, I used to end up there every day, so they took me there. When I got there, a woman who used to work in the house was on the phone. She was screaming, I'd never heard anything like this.

I asked, how is Papa. Because I was scared, because such was the environment then. He was in Bengal, and she said Papa is fine. Then I asked, how is Mama, and she said Mama is fine. I was nervous, I asked, how is grandmother. She said just come back. And put the phone down.

My heart stopped beating for two or three seconds, as if someone has hit me hard in the stomach. I went home. On

> one hand, my grandmother had been murdered. On the other, the one who taught me badminton, the one who taught me exercises, had been killed [Beant Singh]. The question is, why did this happen? And I want to give you the answer. As I said before, anger is planted. It doesn't happen, it is planted … I too am a victim of terrorism. And it's not just me. In this country lakhs have been hit by terrorism. Anger is planted.
>
> Yesterday a policeman came to my room. We were talking, I asked what are you doing, he was from the intelligence … he said he was tracking victims [of the Hindu–Muslim riots in Muzaffarnagar in Uttar Pradesh in 2013] who are angry and want to go to Pakistan. First you plant anger, then you ask, why are you becoming a terrorist? A terrorist is born because anger is planted in him. And if there is one thing the opposition does, it is to plant hatred in the hearts of Indians. Getting Hindus to fight with Muslims is their full-time job. And when people die, they are nowhere to be seen …
>
> I have been hit by this blow twice. Anger will not take this nation forward. Love will take it forward … we will live as one, we will die as one.

Narendra Modi, then only a BJP leader, retorted at an election rally in Jhansi in Uttar Pradesh, a couple of days later: 'Is it true that all Congress people were angry? Is it not true that in that anger your party people burnt thousands of Sikhs alive? And not one has been punished as yet? That you were angry over the killing of your grandmother I can understand. But were you ever angry over the killing of those thousands of Sikhs? Did you feel any pain? And now, when there are elections in Delhi, you have sprinkled salt on those wounds, those families whose young were burnt alive, those thousands of Sikhs were killed, and today you talk about your anger. Nobody who believes in humanity will forgive this language of the Shehzada (as Modi described Rahul Gandhi).'

~

Just what was Rahul Gandhi saying? There are 'two' Rahul Gandhis here, the boy of then, and the man of now recalling the experiences of that boy. And what Rahul Gandhi the man now recalled, what he remembered and now chose to say—say it the way he did—brought some remarkable glimpses into those days from within the Gandhi family, brought home to us now what the boy of then suffered. It also offered us incidental insight into the mind of Rahul Gandhi here and now.

Who could possibly be unsympathetic to what the boy had to go through after being hauled to that phone call during the geography lesson? But the adult Rahul Gandhi did recall that moment oddly: 'On one hand, my grandmother had been murdered. On the other, the one who taught me badminton, the one who taught me exercises, had been killed.' He recalled them as twin shocks. For the boy of then they well might have been so; conceivably he had chummier relations with Beant Singh who taught him badminton and exercises than he might have had with a grandmother who had much to do besides spending time with a grandson. A boyhood pal is so much more real than a remote grandmother.

But it was the now adult Rahul Gandhi recalling those times—on a public stage. An adult might be aware that it could be less than respectful to speak of the killing of his grandmother's assassin as some hyphenated twin shock to the assassination itself. The clubbing together in language and tone was odd given his place in the family. To me his simplicity sounded worrying: 'One day, in anger, my friends killed my grandmother.'

In one who was aspiring then to lead the country, some might have expected a keener sense of what to say where, and how. And have at least the politic good sense of saying a word about the thousands massacred in Delhi, to add to his expressed sentiments over the double loss of his grandmother and his 'friend' Beant Singh. Modi pounced on this thoughtlessness in his own election rally counter, that in speaking of his own anger and hurt, Rahul Gandhi had spoken not a word about the thousands killed in Delhi. Except to say that killing is in itself such a 'horrible thing'.

That it is. Failing to stop killing when one had the means to, and when it was one's responsibility to, is also a horrible thing. In covering up for 1984, Rahul Gandhi tied himself into a web of Congress narrative woven from thirty years ago. He could have stepped away from it; he chose to step right into it. Rahul Gandhi had no hand in the decisions of 1984; but in publicly adding his own little patch to that old cover-up, he announced ownership of an action he had not then been a part of, and that he need not now have owned.

In the course of the Times Now interview, Rahul Gandhi seemed to make a distinction between the Congress and Congressmen. 'Some' Congress-I leaders were involved, he had admitted, but the Congress was not. It doesn't take a lawyer to argue that a party is not other than its members and its leaders—the party is not its posters, not its office space, and not even just the top leader. 'Some' of the party's top leaders cannot be parenthetically dismissed.

'Some' is really a lot. The terrorists who had shaken Punjab were also only 'some'. The Sultanpuri and Trilokpuri killers too were only 'some'. The allegations over leading the carnage at street level in Delhi are only against 'some' Congress leaders. Rahul Gandhi's defence of the Congress would be the equivalent of a defence that Pakistani agencies were not behind the 26/11 killers because only 'some' people had landed up in Mumbai to kill, Pakistan itself had not turned up.

It had taken only 'some' to do all the killing in Delhi. The police have documented that looters and killers went out in crowds each numbering no more than a few hundred. These were not massive mobs on the streets, they were relatively small groups. Delhi then had a population of around seven million, going by the 1981 census; to that add a couple of million or so of the undocumented and what is called the 'floating' population. Among those millions, gatherings of hundreds that in all added up to no more than a few thousand were only 'some', and they would need far fewer to lead them. Rahul Gandhi was offering 'some' defence of the Congress in 1984.

~

Moreover, in offering that rapid overview of 1984 in his election speech, Rahul Gandhi had inadvertently raised serious questions about the Congress and specifically about his grandmother's governance in the years leading up to 1984. The simple gloss Rahul Gandhi was offering could not possibly hope to cover the shattering developments through those years leading up to 1984.

In 1977, Rahul Gandhi said, Sikhs were standing by Indira Gandhi. Within years, they were gunning at her. The merely outward appearance either side of those seven years might be more or less as Rahul Gandhi described: in 1977 few signs appeared publicly of any militant Sikh opposition to Indira Gandhi even though festering issues had by then acquired a long history; 1984 brought what it did. What changed through those seven years, and why? Any extensive analysis of this change is outside the scope of this diary. But 1984 makes no sense without at least a glance at the perilous signposts through that period.

To me that change had a face. General Jagjit Singh Aurora was the Indian hero of the 1971 war; he led the Indian military in its operations that broke Pakistan. What was East Pakistan became the independent country Bangladesh. The Indian Army had cracked

Pakistan's hold in the east: at first surreptitiously through a force that came to be called the Mukti Bahini, and then frontally in a military assault led by General Aurora. Through that assault some 90,000 Pakistani soldiers were taken prisoner. Past 1984 I met General Aurora several times; he was now a bitter man struggling for justice and dignity for Sikhs.

'In five or six years there was anger …' That was Rahul Gandhi's simple summary at the election speech. It wasn't five or six years. The seeds of unrest were laid over much longer.

To glance briefly back at some of those deathly milestones, the first seeds of the conflict were the Punjabi Suba movement that began in the 1950s to demand a Punjabi-speaking state. Punjab was not then what it is today: it included what is now Haryana and Himachal Pradesh. Many in that extensive state, too many as some Sikh leaders saw it, had declared Hindi as their primary language, and not Punjabi as written in the Gurmukhi script.

I myself grew up in that political dispute, though I didn't recognize it then to be so. My parents were Punjabi, who had migrated over from what is now Pakistan. At home we spoke both Hindi and Punjabi, but the script I learnt was Hindi, and not Gurmukhi. Moving to Delhi early from Punjab took me to the periphery of the dispute, rather than leaving me at the heart of it. Millions within Punjab, mostly Hindus, spoke the Punjabi language but did not choose Gurmukhi as the script to write in. Leaders from the politico-religious Akali Dal party wanted Punjabi in Gurmukhi script as the first language to be taught in schools.

They had their way—in a way. And this they did thanks to Indira Gandhi, who became Prime Minister of India first in 1966. She accepted the primary demands of the Akali leaders that very year, but in a territorially reduced Punjab. The Akalis had their way, but within a smaller Sikh-majority Punjab.

This didn't end the Akali agitation. Party leaders wanted more Punjabi-speaking areas to be included in the new, reduced Punjab and they wanted Chandigarh, a Union territory controlled by the Central government, as its capital. Chandigarh was the shared capital of Punjab and Haryana, administered by the Central government. To this end, Akali leader Fateh Singh launched a fast unto death in 1966, but was persuaded by Indira Gandhi to give it up. In August 1969, Akali leader and Rajya Sabha MP Darshan Singh Pheruman actually starved himself to death over the party's demands. The Akali agitation led to a resolution passed at the Anandpur Sahib gurdwara in Rupnagar in the Ropar district of Punjab in 1973. The location was significant. Anandpur Sahib is a historic gurdwara founded by Guru Tegh Bahadur, the ninth guru, and where the tenth and last guru, Guru Gobind Singh, set a martial stamp upon Sikh beliefs.

The resolution was to become the basis of militant agitation leading up to Operation Blue Star in 1984. The Anandpur Sahib resolution asked for more power for state governments in relation to the Central government 'to obviate the possibility of any danger to the unity and integrity of the country'. That language was seen by many as a veiled threat. The resolution made specific demands such as Chandigarh as the capital solely of Punjab state, a greater share of the waters of the Ravi and Beas rivers flowing through Punjab that also fed states downstream, and 'second language' status for Punjabi in the states surrounding Punjab.

Akali Dal leader Harcharan Singh Longowal emphasized that the Sikhs had 'no designs to get away from India in any manner'. But Indira Gandhi saw the resolution as secessionist. Politically, the Akalis were a low force through the early 1970s. The Congress had emerged as a strong party at the Centre and in Punjab itself the Congress ruled with a substantial majority. The Akalis later came into government in partnership with the Janata Party, following the Emergency imposed by Indira Gandhi between 1975 and 1977. But through those years in government the Akalis themselves made no energetic push within the government for implementation of the Anandpur Sahib resolution— power has a way of easing agitation. After 1980, when Indira Gandhi was voted back to head the government as Prime Minister again, the Akalis took to the streets to demand constitutional changes in line with the Anandpur Sahib resolution.

Through the early 1980s serial—and serious—conflicts arose between the government and Sikh leaders. The Congress government found itself confronting the Akali Dal, and lethally, Jarnail Singh Bhindranwale, whose name came to strike terror, and whose men actually did. Bhindranwale's militant opposition alongside the political opposition from the Akalis shook up the government. His opponents and innocent people—both Sikh and Hindu—were killed in terrorist attacks carried out by men associated with Bhindranwale and inspired by him.

The gaunt and hardy Bhindranwale had come to head the Damdami Taksal, an institution of Sikh learning based in Chowk Mehta, a village about 40 km from Amritsar, actually by accident after its leader was killed in a car mishap in 1977. Many of the Damdami Taksal's leaders before Jarnail Singh Bhindranwale, and since, have carried the name 'Bhindranwale'.

The Congress party courted Jarnail Singh Bhindranwale to set him up against the more established Akali Dal leaders. Bhindranwale had become a popular religious leader at first for his strong opposition to the Nirankaris, a sect that traditional Sikhs consider heretical. Then followed a race to the extreme, with some Akali leaders competing with Bhindranwale to establish their own rebelliousness to counter Bhindranwale's popularity—and expanding militancy.

This very Bhindranwale had in one election actually campaigned for the Congress party. It was widely believed that Indira Gandhi had set up Bhindranwale as a foil to the Akali Dal, in a policy that went disastrously wrong for her party, for Punjab, and eventually for herself. Bhindranwale was widely spoken of then as Indira Gandhi's Frankenstein.

From about 1980 a spiral of killings and assassinations brought an eruption of violence. Lala Jagat Narain, editor of the influential *Hind Samachar* group that opposed Sikh militancy, was killed in September 1981. Bhindrawnwale was suspected of conspiring in the murder, arrested and later released. Later that month, Sikh separatists hijacked an Indian Airlines plane to Pakistan.

The relations between Bhindranwale and the Akalis shifted constantly, and I doubt these were ever quite clear to the leaders themselves. The Akalis saw Bhindranwale as a sort of cousinly rival variously to be feared and competed against, or joined in some alliance of convenience. Following his arrest, the Akalis began to court Bhindranwale and to campaign for his release from jail. Akali leaders began to push their demands for Chandigarh and river waters with renewed vigour, but round after round of talks with the government collapsed. All the while, the killings rose, in tandem with a strengthening agitation by the Akali Dal.

In April 1982 Bhindranwale joined the Akalis in launching a Dharam Yudh Morcha, declared as a peaceful march, to demand implementation of the Anandpur Sahib resolution. Indira Gandhi's government decided to prevent the march forcefully, and did so disastrously. More than a hundred people were killed in firing upon agitators, more than 30,000 Sikhs were arrested. These killings provoked Bhindranwale into open militancy against the Central government that he considered synonymous with the Congress party

In October 1982 Akali leader Harcharan Singh Longowal threatened to disrupt the Asian Games, due from 19 November and which had been carefully choreographed to showcase the party heir apparent Rajiv Gandhi on the world stage. The government threw a tight security ring around Delhi—Sikhs travelling to Delhi were stopped and searched, often humiliatingly. This in turn fed both experiences and perceptions that the Central government was targeting Sikhs.

By 1983 people were being attacked and killed in Punjab every other day. In October 1983 six Hindu passengers were separated from Sikhs in a bus in Punjab and shot dead. The same day two government officials were shot in a train. These attacks followed targeted and random killings in Punjab and Delhi throughout the year. After the bus attack, Indira Gandhi dismissed the Punjab state government and imposed Central rule. The violence only got worse: on an average five or six persons were being killed in attacks across Punjab every day. That is when Indira Gandhi ordered Operation Blue Star that came in June 1984. The army stormed the Golden Temple complex. Bhindranwale was killed in that attack, among hundreds of others inside the temple, and hundreds more from the army.

~

'In five or six years there was anger …' Really, over more than five or six years, there was more than anger. Of course, Rahul Gandhi could not be expected to deliver a history lesson at an election rally, not even a brief one. He was to be expected at an election rally to speak for the Congress, and not to examine its performance down the years analytically. But were his election rally offerings betrayed by a shortfall in awareness of essentials that the adult he became might have gathered?

Rahul Gandhi had made a sensible remark over the Muzaffarnagar victims that could hardly be lost on Punjab: 'First you plant anger, then you ask, why are you becoming a terrorist?' That was exactly the question that arose in the 1980s in Punjab, and it was a question for the Congress to answer. The creation of Bhindranwale against the Akalis, the many slights to Sikhs up to and during the Asian Games of 1982, were provoking anger that 'some' carried over into terrorism (it only took some). The question Rahul Gandhi asked over Muzaffarnagar was the very question that hung over the Congress government's policies in Punjab leading up to 1984. This was the question that led on to the assassination of Indira Gandhi and then to the killings of Sikhs in Delhi that followed.

Delhi saw also a Congress hand in those killings that Rahul Gandhi didn't—and perhaps understandably wouldn't. A little more history lay behind the assassination and the massacres in Delhi than Rahul Gandhi's single sketchy line had allowed.

5

Kamal Nath

I wasn't expecting to find Kamal Nath by the screaming crowd outside Rakab Ganj Sahib gurdwara, where two Sikhs had only just been burnt alive. But there he was, a little to a side, in bright white kurta-pajama, not far from the usual white Ambassador car with its mounted red light and mini flag post by the front bumper announcing its officially important credentials.

The white of Kamal Nath's kurta and pajama was standard for a Congress-I leader. Not exclusive to the Congress, of course, leaders do wear it as near-uniform on occasions where they wish to appear leaderlike in public. That day the white no doubt doubled appropriately as mourning dress. It was the afternoon of 1 November, Indira Gandhi had been assassinated the previous day. Her body lay for darshan in Teen Murti Bhavan close to Rakab Ganj gurdwara. Mourners had been filing past all morning crying 'khoon ka badla khoon (blood for blood)'.

Rakab Ganj gurdwara was the nearest target from Teen Murti Bhavan where the cry for blood could be turned into action. There were certain to be Sikhs there, and there was the gurdwara itself to attack. At the gurdwara groups heading out from Teen Murti found the blood they had been crying for. Police indicate a wave of attacks on the gurdwara, and that someone within had fired to try to scare the attackers away. The firing in the air caused no reported injury. This was before I reached; when I arrived on my scooter, the crowd was advancing menacingly again towards the gurdwara.

But that wasn't the only shocking sight. What stunned me was that alongside the screaming men advancing upon the gurdwara stood a neat formation of policemen watching the crowd. And in this neat formation they continued to stand. Screaming men were advancing again and again towards the gurdwara—and the policemen just stood there, in a disciplined and very static column.

The policemen were from the Central Reserve Police Force (CRPF). The additional commissioner of police for New Delhi range, Gautam Kaul, stood by the side of the policemen standing in two or three rows, one behind the other. Kaul stood as static as the policemen, carrying a bamboo riot shield to protect himself. He was the second in command of policing in the area after the commissioner of police, the New Delhi range equivalent of Hukum Chand Jatav from Delhi range; the charge of these 'ranges' Delhi was divided into devolved to Kaul and Jatav from the police commissioner.

The sight of the still policemen assaulted my sense of what should be. The gurdwara was being targeted in the presence of a large force of disciplined spectators from the police and I didn't think it should be so. The designer platoon made no move to stop these men advancing on the gurdwara, Kaul made no move to order them to do so.

Within minutes of my arrival, some from the crowd rushed down the road again towards the gurdwara. Gautam Kaul saw them come and scampered to a side. By 'scamper' I mean a sort of sprint that lasted just a few steps. Those steps he took remarkably rapidly for a fairly senior person; I'd never seen Kaul run before. I felt embarrassed for him, and I can recall that feeling of embarrassment distinctly, for some reason it has remained for me an enduring experience of 1984. Here was an officer who had the command of a police force by his side. In the face of an advancing move by a murderous crowd, he issued no orders to the police, he ducked and ran.

Kaul later denied this; of course he would. Put to it, he could no doubt line up a neat formation of witnesses from the CRPF to 'confirm' the 'denial'. And who among that crowd would come up ever to say they saw the police officer in charge duck to a side the moment they took some steps forward? None of this silence alters the fact that I saw what I saw.

I had turned up at Rakab Ganj as the beat crime reporter of *The Indian Express*, I was out in the city to cover events as far as information, time, and my scooter could take me. I had no idea before I turned up that I would run into Kamal Nath, or Gautam Kaul, or anyone else. I have neither friendship nor friction with Kamal Nath, or with Gautam Kaul. My responsibility was to report fairly what I saw, and not tailor that to fit one set of interests or another. I didn't go there to 'nail' Kamal Nath, I wasn't out there to defend him.

What I did see then was that when the crowd surged forward at one point, Kamal Nath had only to gesture lightly, and they held back. Does that fact exonerate Kamal Nath? Because, on the face of it, he had restrained the crowd, hadn't he? Only of course if you were to see that moment as representative of the whole day. It necessarily wasn't, it has never been my claim—or my report—that it was. I could have made no such claim, and did not. All I could and did report was that by way of some intervention he did at that one point prevent the crowd advancing further towards the gurdwara.

Why did the crowd listen to him? Why, in a situation where a murderous bunch was advancing yet again, would the police continue to stand to a side (and the officer leading them duck to a side), and now watch the MP control that crowd? Why did a word from the Congress MP become more effective than any move from the police? What was the relation between Kamal Nath and that crowd that at that one moment he had only to raise his hand towards it and it held back?

Were these just people with no party connections who had seen an MP shoo them back, and promptly retreated because they held such innate respect for an MP, just any MP? They did not appear such a respectful lot. They did not appear like a lot who had killed, who were now out to kill more, but would suddenly hold back because some MP had signalled to them to hold back, a signal they must obey because an MP is necessarily a leader, if not their particular leader.

Kamal Nath and that crowd had a connection; he signalled, they listened. And they were only likely to respond to him if they were from the Congress party and accepted him as their leader, not just any leader. I doubt they would have responded with that alacrity to an MP from, say, one of the communist parties. Given the circumstances, that wasn't surprising. Kamal Nath had come down from Teen Murti Bhavan, the crowd too had come from there, as the Kusum Lata Mittal report into policing failures duly notes.[1] That does not of itself add up to a conspiracy or to any inference that Kamal Nath had brought the crowd there from Teen Murti in order to attack the gurdwara. But it does say that these were men from the Congress party, and that Kamal Nath, as I said in my affidavit then, had control over them.

Kamal Nath said later he was not leading the mob in any attack, that he had, on the contrary, only tried to control the situation. That defence itself betrays a connection. Kamal Nath's signal to the crowd, and their response to it, implied a right to instruct and a duty to respond. This understanding arose from a crowd owning a leader, and the leader the crowd.

Why was the controlling left to Kamal Nath? Was that not for the police to do? And if he was at the scene as only some responsible political leader, would it not be proper for him to do all he could to make sure that the police dealt with the situation? Surely, dealing with that situation must mean quick and effective intervention to disperse the crowd? For the police to be doing what they must, and for the law to mean what it did, it was for Kamal Nath to do his bit to push the police to disperse that crowd. Instead, he was there in direct communication with the crowd—with the police idle to a side. This was not just some ordinary crowd control situation. Murders had taken place there—committed by members of this very crowd.

If Kamal Nath was playing a role as responsible citizen and leader, he would have wanted later to follow up with the local police to ensure investigation and prosecution for the murders committed. We have seen no evidence he did that. No one was ever caught and punished for those murders. To all appearances, Kamal Nath was controlling the situation in his own way. That was not the legal way.

In failing to push for police intervention to disperse those crowds, and to push for arrests (if pushing were needed where murders had been committed in the presence of the police), Kamal Nath together with the police may well have done something towards making more killings possible. Because these very men were left free to attack Sikhs and kill wherever they went from Rakab Ganj. They left with the message that the police would not stop them. The crowd did finally go their way, and who could say where they headed. This was the afternoon of 1 November, the worst of the killings was to come that night.

I could not raise such questions about the implications of Kamal Nath's signals in my affidavit. The stuff of the affidavit had necessarily to be the bare facts that I had witnessed, and I stayed within those limits. A commission would want to know what I saw, not what I thought about what I saw. It would be well out of the scope of an affidavit to talk of implications; these would be for an inquiry officer or judge to take up. The bare facts had cast their shadows, and in those shadows lay disturbing and unanswered questions.

What did the police know about the crowd that they could stand back and decide to leave it in the hands of Kamal Nath? Indisputably, before their eyes, this was a Congress crowd. Just as indisputably, men from this crowd had killed two people, and were ready to advance to kill again. For a police force to stand by watching all this was itself illegal. The stillness of the police was actionable. They cannot delegate policing over murder that takes place in their presence. It is outside of law for a police force to stand and watch a political leader make moves to exercise control that was for them to enforce.

A senior police officer later defended that inaction to me. He said the police had been tactful in letting Kamal Nath lead the crowd away; they had taken this course to defuse violent confrontation. But violent confrontation there had been already. I had never before known the police to ignore murders because it might be 'tactful' to. Tact has its limits: it cannot include suspension of law and disregard of murders in police presence. For how long and how far could they rely on Kamal Nath? Soon after waving the crowds back, Kamal Nath got into his car and left. Soon after, the crowd too began to fade away from the scene—and not because the police had pushed them away. That crowd killed no more that day—not at least at the Rakab Ganj gurdwara. But killings followed all around the city.

~

Who were these men that the police had stood watching and Kamal Nath controlled? For a start, those men at Rakab Ganj, killers among them, had come from Teen Murti Bhavan, the

Kusum Lata Mittal report declared, based on police records. That was where Mrs Gandhi's body lay in state for darshan. Every senior party leader in town had turned up at Teen Murti Bhavan that morning. Kamal Nath too was there, as he later mentioned. Mourners had filed through Teen Murti Bhavan all morning. More anger than grief was in evidence. Columns of frenzied mourners screamed 'khoon ka badla khoon' ['blood for blood']. They were live on the state-owned Doordarshan, the only television channel around at the time.

It wasn't long after that they were acting on their intentions. The Rakab Ganj gurdwara lay just a couple of kilometres from Teen Murti Bhavan and it was this lot that made their way to the gurdwara. No neighbourhood existed around Rakab Ganj that could have generated these angry mourners. No Sikh shops or homes existed on the way from Teen Murti to Rakab Ganj to distract the mourner-murderers from their mission.

I knew that road outside Rakab Ganj gurdwara well. It was a part of the bus junction outside Central Secretariat that housed important government offices. The stop for buses to the Delhi University campus was located on that precise road, and I had used it for years. The road buzzed with bus commuters and devotees visiting the gurdwara. On festive days in the Sikh calendar the roadside became home to a row of stalls.

The road was never crowded the way I saw it that afternoon of 1 November. These were people going nowhere; no buses were running by that afternoon to get in or out of.

These men had come from Teen Murti, but how did they get to Teen Murti in the first place? Delhi had come to a shocked halt that day. The city had woken up to reports in the local newspapers of attacks on Sikhs around the All India Institute of Medical Sciences (AIIMS) the previous evening, and to images on state television that morning of a call for blood. And it had woken up after groups had driven around the city through the night shouting out warnings over loudspeakers that Sikhs had poisoned Delhi's water supply. It was a lie, but it got people scared for a while. And rumours were circulating of Sikhs preparing to launch attacks from fortified gurdwaras.

It was a morning when few were stepping out of their homes. Who would take them anywhere? Most of the buses plying in the city were privately owned, and hardly a bus was to be seen. The DTC (Delhi Transport Corporation) buses should officially all have been running as scheduled. A small number of buses went out in the morning but by afternoon these too disappeared.

Taxis were off the roads. The mourners hadn't hailed cabs to get to Teen Murti—in any case the vast majority of cab drivers at the time were Sikhs, and no Sikh was driving a cab about on daily business that morning. The Sikh cab drivers had fled for their lives—those who could. Just the night before, taxis at stands on Janpath, a few minutes' drive from Rakab Ganj, and at Mohan Singh Place by the side of Connaught Place had been burnt. Those drivers fortunately had left their taxi stands the evening before.

The city was at a near-curfew-like standstill that day except for the looters on the street. This wasn't the morning when the man next door dressed up in white looked for public transport that was not to be found, or risked his life in his own private transport to set out for Teen Murti Bhavan, driven by grief and some compulsion for a last glimpse of a beloved leader.

The columns of men filing through Teen Murti simply could not have been individuals who may have travelled individually from home through a burning city. It was extremely unlikely that a spontaneous mourner determined to catch a last glimpse of Indira Gandhi's body would get as far as Teen Murti Bhavan and back on his own that day. Those men at Teen Murti and then at

Rakab Ganj were brought there—nothing else explains that level of presence there, at that time, and of that kind.

Who could possibly have fed that level of mobilization, at such speed? The mobilization, the uniformity, had to have had an organizational push behind it. The organization behind such mobilization could not but have been the Congress; it is after all no surprise that those most eager and available to have been brought there would have been workers from the party whose leader had been assassinated. Ordinary citizens did not risk that journey to Teen Murti Bhavan in order to mourn a little and to then call for blood. And after raising that cry, to go for it.

These at Rakab Ganj were among the first killings to take place in Delhi. No one had pursued those crowds leaving Teen Murti, nobody tracked where some of them went after leaving Rakab Ganj. I did not stay much longer after Kamal Nath left, or long enough to see the crowd fully disperse, or to wait for normal access to the gurdwara myself. Deadlines had to be met, reports filed back in the newspaper office.

6

Close Encounter

It was the afternoon of the second day after the assassination, 2 November, and killings had been taking place on the night of 31 October, all day on 1 November, that night, and again on 2 November. We were getting to hear of more killings from people here and there—we still had no word from the police on just what was happening and where. We asked, of course, because through the wireless the police were closest to getting the full picture of the violence. But the police were switched off from any communication with media—they were switched off policing itself. The police knew of most of the attacks on Sikhs through their wireless network but by way of action they produced almost nothing; by way of communication absolutely nothing.

The worst massacre at Trilokpuri came to light because Mohan Singh escaped to come to our office at *The Indian Express* to tell us about it. The next day we began to hear about mass killings in Sultanpuri, another of those resettlement colonies that had been launched during the years of the Emergency (1975–77) by Indira Gandhi's son, Sanjay. I could again find no photographer to accompany me to Sultanpuri.

But our chief editor, B.G. Verghese, made an exceptional provision: he made an office car available. That was a relief, but it came with a catch: the office could not find a driver willing to go out into the city. The office never would give us cars without a driver, but that one day it did. I was given a noisy old Ambassador that I would have to drive myself.

A full team of us set out. I was joined by fellow reporter Ashwini Sarin, another reporter I knew as Joshi from the Hindi newspaper *Jansatta* of the Express group, and Sevanti Ninan, then special writer at the *Express*. Ashwini Sarin sat on the front seat with me, Sevanti and Joshi were at the back, a seating arrangement that was to have consequences. My little reporter's pad and pen were in my shirt pocket—unfortunately prominent as it later was to turn out.

It was a fairly quick drive across to Sultanpuri, we noted along the way how little traffic there still was. The fear that had gripped the city was not letting go so soon; almost everyone stayed home. But empty streets still looked better than roads with looters running wild—along that route the looters seemed to have retreated. A few people were about, but among them no Sikh was to be seen.

Once we got to Sultanpuri, discovering where the killings had taken place turned out to be simple enough. A couple of people on the roadside told us of the streets we should head to. Another pointed to a particular street that he said had seen the worst. I drove in that direction.

A chill gripped me as I turned off the road in the direction of that street. I saw a little park on the side of the road I was turning away from that looked extraordinarily tidy. It looked like it had just been swept clean. The sight struck me as unnatural. It wasn't a grassy park, just sort of fenced ground with perhaps a cement bench or two in it. A broom had left fresh lines over the soil.

It didn't look like it had been swept so strenuously by some enthusiastic municipal sweepers going about their daily job. The city had shut down, why would some exceptionally dedicated municipal man go about doing a routine job so carefully? I didn't reason this out at that moment, it wasn't such logic that brought unease; it was just an awful feeling. The freshly swept ground looked scary, the lines on the soil from the broom ominous. There was nobody in the park.

I turned into a narrow street as directed by the resident who had pointed to the scene of the killings. The street was for practical purposes one-way because it wasn't wide enough for more. It didn't look like a street used much to a car coming along at all. Who among those families crowding those poor little two-room tenements could think of owning a car those days? There was no movement on the street at all, it looked ghostly but for a bunch of men mostly in white kurtas and pajamas standing in the middle of it further down. The men, perhaps about a dozen of them, maybe up to twenty or so, stood still watching our approaching car.

I had to stop the car as I approached them, they were in the way. They knew we were journalists, the car had 'Press' written on the windscreen. I lowered the window and asked if the Sikh residents there were all right. All was well, they said, all was peaceful. They spoke in emphatic unison, many of them rushed to say there had been no trouble at all. Again, like the sight of that park across the road, it wasn't anything definite I could point to, but the collective reassurance sounded more disturbing than reassuring.

This group looked different from just people you might find on a street in Delhi. They certainly were different from the people we had spoken to along the way who had given us directions and pointed to killings down this street. This was a well-knit group, they spoke as one, standing amidst the silence all around us. They told us firmly we should leave.

In a moment, I thought I saw why. Down the street behind them a door had opened a crack, a hand was calling out to us. I thought it might be a Sikh, though I could not see this immediately. I told the men we would drive up, find a place to reverse and then head back. They stepped aside. I drove on towards that door down that street where the hand had appeared. I stopped outside. Hiding behind that door that had been opened a crack, stood a frail Sikh man, almost quaking on his feet. He had cut his hair and his beard, quite obviously only recently.

He begged for help. He said hundreds of Sikhs had been killed on that street and around the night before. If we couldn't find someone to rescue them, he said 'those people' would finish the rest of them that night. By 'those people' he meant the men on the street we had encountered on our way. He had gestured towards them, he knew they were there, he knew who they were. The years since those days have erased all sorts of details from memory. They haven't erased that look in his eyes. The eyes looked like he was some prey being hunted.

It had been 'those people' down the street who had been telling us all was well, that we should turn around and leave. The significance of some of what happened that day sank in only later. It became clear that the man behind the door was speaking of that single, definite group we had encountered—he was not speaking of angry people generally, nor of neighbours. It was that bunch that he described as the killers. That could no doubt mean the men standing on that street at that moment, and others like them who may have joined them.

I said we would find help and stepped back into the car. I could see that bunch of men still standing in the middle of the street, they had turned around to stare at us now the opposite way. I drove a little further, found a place to turn the car around on a side street, and headed back the way we had come. The men were waiting for us. They didn't look like they were about to move.

They blocked the way, and I had to stop the car. The minute I did, they rushed us from both sides. One pulled open the door to my side, threw a punch my way, and made a grab for my shirt pocket which had my reporter pad. He snatched the pad away, tearing my shirt. The men crowded around the car, they shouted that we were liars, that we were making trouble. Ashwini Sarin by my side was trying to calm them down, but failed.

Bizarrely, in the middle of all this, I saw the *Jansatta* reporter on the back seat pushing desperately against the back of the front seat, as if to push the car out of that spot. Fear does strange things. Even at that moment I could summon a fleeting sense of physics over the *Jansatta* reporter's efforts.

All this happened in a flash. Sevanti Ninan was to the left on the rear street. One man pulled open her door, and made a grab as if to pull her from the car. She struggled to close the door, away from the man's grabbing hand. He snatched away the reporter pad she had with her. At that moment I decided to make a break for it.

The car engine was running. I pushed up the gear lever and hit the accelerator. A man ahead tried to block us, I wasn't going to stop for him. He pulled away just in time, I think the right-side fender brushed past him. I remember thinking I could not stop, even if I had to run him over. Some of the men ran after us as we drove off, the rest stood shouting abuse on that still street. Soon we were out of that side street and into the safety of the bigger road by that park.

Did these men later attack the man who had spoken to us? Sickeningly, I never came to know for sure one way or another. But I know that if they had, nobody was around to stop them. The Sikh in that home told us that killings had been going on down those streets night and day. But not a policeman was to be seen there. The first SOS we could send out was only on return to the office, where I called all the senior officers I could. I appealed desperately for the army to be deployed immediately in Sultanpuri, and in any case before nightfall. I did so with a sense of inadequacy; who could be sure anyone would listen? But there was nothing else to do. We could think of doing no more in the face of a massacre that had taken place, and in the face of another massacre that seemed imminent.

I was told by a police officer that the army had been deployed in Sultanpuri later that evening. I doubt my calls had anything to do with that though. The army was being deployed in several areas that evening, and the police would have known centrally through wireless about the killings in that area—the death toll on just those streets we had visited was later confirmed, even in police reports, to have run into hundreds.

Word of army deployment in Sultanpuri had given me some uneasy hope but not absolute reassurance. The following day I was told that the army had imposed some sort of curfew and had begun patrolling the area. An officer told me no more killings took place there that night. But I could not be sure; I could not say even whether this officer would know for sure.

~

Who were those men in white kurta-pajamas down that street? From what appeared then, and from what emerged later, three things stand out: one, they were among the killers; two, they got away with the killings; and three, they were Congress party men.

On what evidence do I say this? I couldn't produce photocopies of some Congress party membership cards that they may have been carrying—and of course they wouldn't be carrying any such. I couldn't match their photographs with some register at a Congress office had such a record existed that I could access; I couldn't pick them out in an identification parade. I never came to know their names, their addresses. What I did come to know was what everyone I spoke to told me on a follow-up visit—that it was members of the Congress party who had killed on those streets; that it was members of the Congress party who had set upon our car. Word of that car incident too seems to have spread in the area. Neighbours remained unseen, but it seems enough were seeing. No one I spoke to had any doubt who these men were. The Sikhs in the refugee camps who had fled Sultanpuri told me this, as did just about every non-Sikh I spoke to in that area who was prepared to say anything at all.

This was the constituency of Sajjan Kumar. I have read a barrage of reports of Sajjan Kumar's involvement in those killings, of his leadership of the local killers. In limiting myself to my own encounters and experiences, I say nothing about Sajjan Kumar; he wasn't among those men on the street that day. I am not suggesting by any means that Sajjan Kumar is innocent so far as I knew—only that the scope of this account is limited to my own experiences.

By way of evidence of the kind that could be admissible in a court, I accept that this statement of mine that these were Congressmen can be challenged. To back this I would have to go back to local witnesses who, even then, were prepared only to whisper out such information. Many did speak up before the commissions of inquiry.

But far more thorough investigations than mine confirmed that it was Congressmen that killed in Sultanpuri. The Kusum Lata Mittal report has the following to say: 'It seems the pattern that was followed was that first the SHO Shri Bhatti (of Sultanpuri police station) and Head Constable Jai Chand ordered and threatened the Sikhs to go inside their houses otherwise they would shoot them. After the Sikhs went inside the houses, they were attacked by the mobs with the full connivance of the police.'[1] The report adds: 'The affidavits which were investigated by the Mishra Commission through the investigating agency also indicate that the allegations made by the deponents were by and large correct.'

The report found the killings were politically instigated. It noted that there had been no violence in the area on 31 October. 'However, in the morning of 1st November 1984, a local Member of Parliament addressed a meeting which was also attended by SHO Inspector Bhatti and other police officers of Sultanpuri. In this meeting, the gathering was instigated to take revenge on the Sikhs. Immediately thereafter, violence started with full fury.'[2] That local member of parliament was Sajjan Kumar of the Congress party.

The Mittal inquiry found the violence Congress-led, everyone in the area knew this. And at gut level I knew at the very moment of that encounter that these were Congress party men. Of course it isn't evidence to 'say' that I 'knew'. I am not here offering evidence in court. I'm aware too that I do not for that reason have the licence to speak irresponsibly, or to make airy accusations against innocent people. But my instinctive thoughts at the moment were confirmed by local witness accounts, both Sikh and non-Sikh. The Mittal report came much later.

Forget gut thoughts a moment, or even the inquiry report; look at the circumstances. Remarkable at the moment of that encounter was the collective lie the men on that Sultanpuri street were offering, and which stood exposed within minutes as a lie: hundreds had been killed in those streets by the time the men were insisting to us that nothing had happened there. Could it be that they did not know? They didn't say they didn't know whether killings had taken place, they had been emphatic in speaking in one voice that no one around had been killed. The only men out on the streets just after a massacre could hardly have been ignorant of the killing that had taken place all around where they stood, most of it the night before.

Theirs was not a gathering, they were a team. What had they teamed up for? To the extent we directly encountered them, to put out a lie over the killings, and to snatch our notes that might have recorded facts there, and then to do what they could to stop us getting out of that street. Only the Congress party was saying the killers in Sultanpuri were not from their party; everyone else said they were. If innocent the Congress party was, it might have produced to the police its list of local party men and offered evidence of their innocence. Innocent Congress members would naturally want to produce firm alibis to establish they were in the clear. Nobody in the party ever offered to do any such thing.

Missing from the streets of the killings, what did the local police know? It is inconceivable that the local police would not know that hundreds had been massacred a few minutes' drive from their police station. The police would almost certainly know who the killers were, given particularly the findings of the Mittal report. But at the least, they would have suspected that the killers could perhaps be from the Congress. Did that likelihood become a reason for the police to stay away?

The men who came to kill would have known, and seen, that the police were not going after them. Who were the kind of men the police would want to spare to carry out hundreds of murders? Take away the politics and would even the Sultanpuri police decide to let a few hundred murders take place around them because they couldn't be bothered about stopping them? Call this deductive, call it even speculative, but to me then, and later, the circumstances stood as unmistakable signposts. These men were from a single organization with a common purpose, and there was only one organization that the police would have indulged to carry out mass murders.

When do a bunch of men step out on a street in Delhi to speak a collective lie? People who gather spontaneously do not come with a shared script to narrate. When do a bunch of men decide in unison to mislead the visiting strangers that we were unless they had a strong and common reason to do so? What was that reason that they did not want us to know? What was it that would threaten them if we did, and subsequently did come to know? Our drive down that street was a threat to these men—as journalists we carried the means to uncover their lie, and they had seen that we had uncovered it.

That was why they attacked us. On the face of it, all we had done was to drive down the street past them, speak to a man, and head back. Why had just this become such provocation that they assaulted us? Those men were not innocent, not by any means. They were doing what they could to stop us getting the word out from those streets. They knew we had spoken to one who would have known of the killings, who himself stood in fear of being killed.

I have not a moment's doubt that our survival then was touch and go. Hundreds had been killed all around us. Four more burnt alive in a car would be just that many more killings. It would have been easy to kill us and then blame Sikhs for it. These men had killed those who were no threat to them; and we had become a threat to them for what they could see we had probably discovered. They knew they had good reason to stop us; we were just lucky to get away.

Overwhelming allegations arose in that neighbourhood and all around Sultanpuri that Congress-I 'workers' engaged in the killing were ordered and led by the Congress-I MP for that area Sajjan Kumar. Two judges from the Delhi High Court finally sentenced Sajjan Kumar to life imprisonment in December 2018 after a long and convoluted legal course, whose trajectory did not necessarily follow the political colours of the government.

The Congress-I had kept Sajjan Kumar in its fold for long after 1984 despite his record. The BJP was in government when Sajjan Kumar was finally convicted by the High Court. But that was only after the case was initiated and prosecuted by the CBI under the Congress-I that returned to government in 2005. The former MP was finally seen as giving the party a bad name. In the end this proved a rare judgment—the only judgment really—where we saw some justice finally done in line with all that we saw on the streets of Delhi.

II

The Police

7

Aborted

It wasn't announced with any fanfare, but crime reporters knew that Ved Marwah had begun to conduct an inquiry into police failures through the 1984 killings in Delhi. Marwah had been brought back to Delhi Police as additional commissioner of police heading the Crime Investigation Department (CID) following the violence. The new police commissioner, S.S. Jog, who had replaced Subhash Tandon, had asked Marwah early in 1985 to carry out that inquiry.

It was 'reliably whispered' that this report would nail police failures in those three days after the assassination of Indira Gandhi. We kept hearing through 1985 that the inquiry was almost complete. Over the years that 'almost' turned into 'never'. Questions about its fate brought no reply, not from Marwah, not from anyone else. It became Delhi's most secret report never written; none of us knew at the time that Marwah's inquiry had been stopped in its tracks, that it had been aborted just before completion.

Marwah himself could not speak immediately as a serving officer on why the inquiry was cut short, and he was kept a serving officer of the government a long time after he wrote the report that the government aborted. He was appointed police commissioner later in 1985. At the end of a career in the police he was appointed adviser to the governor of Jammu and Kashmir and then to the governor of Bihar. He was governor himself later, of Manipur, Mizoram and then Jharkhand right until 2004. His government connections ended twenty years after those 1984 events he had inquired into.

It was ten years after he left government, so thirty years after the killings, that I got to speak to him about his inquiry. There was an opening to my request for a conversation. We had both joined a discussion on CNN-IBN just after Rahul Gandhi had repeated the Congress party's declarations in a television interview that the Congress government had done all it could to contain the violence. Marwah had something to say about this—though he did not name any party. In a fragmentary way, I had seen something of the Congress hand through the riots, and shared a few remarks on that basis. Following that television discussion, I requested a chat with Mr Marwah, and he very kindly agreed.

We met over a cup of tea at his house on Amrita Shergill Marg in Delhi, just across from Lodhi Gardens. Remarkably, Marwah, now eighty-two, looked much the same as before—tall, slim and distinguished—a little inevitable greying apart. It was the first time I'd visited his house, the first time we had ever sat down to chat. He'd hardly have considered that sort of a chat in his days as police commissioner, when I was a junior crime reporter.

It was not without some embarrassment that I put that question to him about thirty years late: what had he found in his inquiry? His report was never completed, but he knew what he had found. I wasn't surprised that he recalled his 1984 inquiry as though he had only just completed it. Maybe he remembered other experiences in his long years in government just as clearly, but that inquiry seemed to stand as sharp in his memory as though he'd conducted it a week before we were sitting down to talk about it.

What was it about 1984 that those memories never seem to fade? They haven't for me: I can hardly remember most of my reports over two years as crime reporter before 1984, or over the four years after 1984 that I continued as crime reporter with *The*

Indian Express. I can say accurately that I remember very much more of that day of the assassination and the few days following than I can of the rest of my six years as the crime reporter of *The Indian Express*. Those memories keep returning sickeningly in grainy detail. I do believe that none of us who witnessed those events, however fractionally, was ever quite the same again. An equivalent perhaps might be witnessing scenes from the Partition, or the collapse of those towers in the 9/11 attacks.

Through those few days I had gone about in the city to the extent I could. Ved Marwah's inquiry was another story; he had inquired into the entire scene in Delhi through access to police records and communications, and presumably intelligence reports—he was after all heading the intelligence units of the Delhi Police when he conducted his inquiry.

I spent just about an hour with Marwah. Through that hour he said a good deal. I play back below what he said, but pause in between to share my thoughts on the implications of what he said, to not read between the lines but to think what the lines meant, what they meant to me as one who was a crime reporter out in the city those days. But it's only right that we should hear from him directly without my thoughts in the way, and so I separate the conversation clearly from my thoughts about it.

~

SS: So, what happened with that inquiry?

VM: I was given three months to inquire, and only into the role of the police. I took my job seriously and I worked round the clock. I completed the inquiry in the stipulated time. (That would have been towards the middle of 1985, within a few months of the killings).

SS: What did the inquiry involve?

VM: I collected all the relevant documents from the police stations, control room, and spoke to a large number of police officers, spoke to a large number of people who were witnesses, people from the NGOs, various other categories. But I still had left [to speak to] some senior police officers, the commissioner of police (in those days of 1984, Subhash Tandon). I left it to examine them at the end, so that then I would get a clear picture.

SS: And then?

VM: Then I got an order. The commissioner told me (then S.S. Jog), first informally, and then followed it up in writing, to stop my inquiry. So there was no report, I had not finished examining all the officers. The inquiry was into the role of the police, and how could the inquiry have been completed without examining the seniormost police officers?

SS: And whom did he [Mr Jog] get his orders from?

VM: I didn't ask him. It was quite obvious. You don't embarrass a commissioner by asking him why you are stopping my inquiry. It was quite obvious who was interested.

SS: How close were you to completing your report when it was aborted?

VM: Very close. I was very close to completing my report, just a few days from it. Because only a few top people had to be examined, and that was more a formality. Otherwise I would have written the report, maximum within a couple of weeks.

SS: How much of the report had been written by then?

VM: I had made notes, I noted the documentary evidence. S.B. Deol was assisting me with the inquiry. His exclusive charge was to help me out. So all the documents and everything was with him. The documents were in the police headquarters. They were then all handed over to the Mishra Commission. All the daily diaries and the rest, everything was given to them.

SS: And the notes?

VM: The notes I made were for my report. In the end they were of no use since I never wrote that report. I didn't keep anything in personal custody for obvious reasons. Maybe I kept some jottings, but I don't remember.

SS: And what did you note?

VM: It was quite obvious that the police was remiss in doing their job. The police control room records showed that every few minutes there was a distress call. And this was being recorded in the central control room. But the most affected police stations didn't show any movement of the police at all. They just stayed put in the police stations, they didn't go anywhere. Nor was there any record of [police] people who were already out in the field come back to say that anything had happened. The police just decided to keep their eyes shut. Now that was an explanation that had to be taken from the senior police officers. And that is where my inquiry was heading. And these people knew where the inquiry was heading.

SS: The concerned police officers?

VM: Yes. First, some of the police officers went to the high court to stop my inquiry. One was Chander Prakash, who was DCP South. Another was Sewa Dass, DCP East. The high court didn't stop my inquiry. So then they moved their own people, I don't know. And then my inquiry was stopped by an executive order. Jog (the police commissioner) had given me the order to start the inquiry, and Jog ended it.

SS: What did you do after the inquiry was aborted? Just put this aside and carry on with other work?

VM: This was additional work given to me. I was posted as additional commissioner, special branch, CID, as it was called. I had the crime branch and the CID under me, so that was my job.

SS: Later you became commissioner of police. Did this issue over the aborted inquiry come up again?

VM: It was mentioned, how could it not be mentioned? For one thing, I was facing and fighting cases then onwards. There were many cases. Some action was being taken, whatever was possible without getting into the area of the commissions and the committees which were there [conducting inquiries]. Because you can't have two parallel government procedures going on at the same time.

~

Marwah had very rapidly made two things clear: that he had found the police remiss, and that his inquiry was stopped at the last minute by the government. And government it was, the Central government; then police commissioner Jog who had ordered the inquiry did not on his own stop it. And Marwah did not think in any case that Jog had stopped it at his own level.

That Marwah found the police had decided to keep their eyes shut was what many of us had seen those days—in place after place I went, I had seen the police actually looking the other way. Marwah's inquiry documented that as a citywide pattern. The police had been in shutdown mode right across the city, he had found; what I had seen for myself was pretty much the picture at other places too that I could not visit.

But more, Marwah said his inquiry had been terminated by an executive order—after the high court turned down a petition demanding an end to it. Twice he had said it was 'quite obvious' who could have terminated the inquiry, that it was 'quite obvious' who would be interested in ending that inquiry.

Certainly, the police officers who had petitioned the court in vain would be interested in having that inquiry terminated—but they had no executive means to end it, they were far junior to Marwah. Once their moves failed in court, it wasn't then these junior officers who could have ordered or even influenced then police commissioner Jog to stop the inquiry. The decision would have had to be taken by the government of the day, and the government would have taken such a decision at a political level—at the very top political level. It wouldn't, it couldn't, have been some official in the home ministry taking the call on such a very sensitive order.

Marwah said it was obvious who could have ended it. What was obvious? The obvious does sometimes need to be said: who else had the means to abort that inquiry, and in who else's interest was it to do so? It is obvious that this inquiry—this of all inquiries—could not have been ended without the knowledge and approval of Prime Minister Rajiv Gandhi. It's inconceivable that the Prime Minister might open the newspaper one morning to find that some junior official had taken such a decision unknown to him. This was, after all, an inquiry into police failures behind thousands of murders in the city following the assassination of the earlier Prime Minister, the present Prime Minister's mother.

Rajiv Gandhi could not have been merely incidentally informed of such a decision either; he would be advised, and consulted, and would have to approve it even if he had not initiated it. Rajiv Gandhi necessarily had a hand personally in aborting the inquiry; and ultimately he was responsible for that decision, as head of government.

Rajiv Gandhi was both leader of the Congress party and the Prime Minister. The inquiry had been limited to police failures, but it was always likely to throw up political pointers. It appeared certain that it incidentally would, and necessarily must, given the mesh of policing and political facts. Most killings took place in the south, east and west police districts. It is in these districts that thousands had spoken up about the involvement of the Congress leaders from the area. The indication was dangerously clear that if police officers in these areas were booked and potentially prosecuted, the Congress hand, still publicly hidden through much of the killings, might begin to show so very openly that it could then not be withdrawn.

The ultimate oneness of the political and the governmental was that it was a Congress party government in charge. Speaking of the obvious, it is obvious from the Congress government's decision to terminate the inquiry abruptly that there was something potentially serious here that the Congress government did not want revealed. Could that have been the failure of a police officer here or there? No government has ever shown that kind of loyalty to just some DCP or other, why would it? It would in fact have suited the government admirably to fix the blame credibly on a few erring police officers, and have them punished for it. That would have turned fingers of accusation away from the party and earned Rajiv Gandhi credentials for impartial and just administration.

In making a sudden last-minute move to block the truth as dug out by the Marwah inquiry, the Congress government of the day could not have been covering up for some police officers—it was covering itself. Such separation as lay between the police and the politicians was an obviously porous one. The government had to have taken such an action only because it feared that the police inquiry would bring a political spillover that it was not prepared to face.

Strictly speaking, Ved Marwah's inquiry could only ever have been an unnatural half-inquiry. It was departmentally ordered, but the consequences of its findings could never have been departmentally confined. The failures of the police and of the Congress government were inevitably interlinked, if not one. The final and foolproof evidence of such link was not at hand then, we had imagined it might surface through this inquiry. The suspicion was overwhelming, even if immediate evidence was not forthcoming, of police links with the ruling party, of a link between the undeniable facts that the police had looked the other way, that this looking away suited Congress leaders, and that only the Congress government could have let them get away with this looking the other way.

The Congress hand, including that of a senior MP, had surfaced in evident view in the Karol Bagh police station incident. Rajiv Gandhi had himself acknowledged this and taken some form of action. But Karol Bagh could hardly have been the only place in Delhi where the Congress had had a hand; it had only showed up openly there.

That incident stands as an example of the difficulty with the artificially narrow circle drawn around the ambit of the inquiry: Mr Marwah was to inquire into the police and only into the police. But where the Congress leaders had been involved—as evidenced by their own conduct—in putting illegal pressure on the police, how then would such an inquiry deal with the limiting line around it? The inquiry must then focus on the police end of the pressure game, without considering the party leaders who were putting pressure on them. The terms of reference of the inquiry would be the equivalent of the police finding two suspects in a single incident holding hands, and being ordered to look only at one. Mr Marwah himself declined steadfastly to make any comment on the Congress party.

So far we have not seen evidence of communication from top people in the government that could incriminate them directly in the violence, and within that impossibly narrow test, we do not consequently see any guilt arising at the top. But we do see the guilt of the overseeing inaction that led on directly to killings. With the Marwah report, the guilt of inaction was threatening to surface in relation to the police certainly, and threatening also to drag in political links. The inquiry might not of itself have gone into those, but its findings could raise inevitable questions about them.

Ironically, the Congress showed its hand in that decision to throttle the inquiry. The Congress government order to stifle the Marwah report is of itself sufficiently an indicator of guilt, an announcement that it had something to hide. It is sufficiently a trigger to begin investigation to explore more.

Enough suspicion hangs heavy to warrant investigation—still. It would seem likely that the police officers who moved court, and also presumably government, to block the inquiry knew something that could have implicated senior Congress leaders—that seems the prime plausible reason for the Congress government to have taken a decision whose first immediate consequence would be protection of these police officers. Dharam Dass Shastri was brazen enough to have got caught in public view—or he was just unlucky that some reporter came wandering along. Evidence of involvement of more top Congress leaders would have been devastating to the party.

A great deal is obvious and not just by oblique inference. Four facts are indisputable, given the known events and circumstances then: (a) most of the killings took place in the areas of the police officers who had sought to stop the inquiry, (b) the political leaders of all of these areas were Congress-I MPs, (c) allegations from victims and witnesses pointed overwhelmingly to these leaders and to the police in these areas and (d) it was a political decision of the Congress government to stop the inquiry.

The government knew that police records had been gathered through the course of the inquiry, and that serious failure had been noted and documented. On the basis of these findings the time was at hand, as the Marwah inquiry neared completion, for a showdown with the police officers responsible. Police failings noted by such an inquiry would have had to lead to something more than the usual expressions of regret. The officers would have had to face some sort of action, if the government was not to invite further accusations of inaction and cover-up. In the end, the government prevented completion of the report, and covered up the fact that it had done so.

The government did in effect more than silence that particular report for then. True, the report was never finally written, but the facts it dug up had been assembled and recorded, they would be available for the government to call up at any time. The government made no move to summon those records at any stage later with a view to resuming the process begun in the course of that inquiry. The government was not shelving these facts; it was killing and burying them.

These facts were frozen into inaction after they were transferred to the Justice Ranganath Mishra Commission of inquiry. Justice Mishra could at most only make recommendations, and only eventually. Whatever the Mishra Commission found, it would still be the government that would have to take steps on the basis of its findings. The transfer of the records to the Mishra Commission through the long spell of its inquiry, from May 1985 to August 1986, meant that the government had surrendered records that could have triggered executive mechanisms.

With the police inquiry aborted, and the records transferred out of police reach, nobody within the police could find a handle to trigger any action—there had been a few, if very few, bold officers around. What Mishra finally noted in his report was only minor and tokenistic; in any case nothing noted led to prosecutions over police failures and of the police officers who failed. Nor did Mishra find any blame among the leadership of the Congress party. Justice Mishra was later, and not much later, made a member of parliament in the Rajya Sabha—by the Congress government. In the end the Mishra findings only legitimized a pardon of the guilty. For years later, the government could legitimately not do what the Mishra Commission had not specifically asked it to do.

From the point when the Ved Marwah inquiry was aborted, one paralysing process came to settle over another: transfer of potentially actionable records to the Mishra Commission, its findings, the government inaction over those, the final reward to Mishra himself … one step after another layered one procedure over another to bury the facts. In 2000 the BJP government appointed another inquiry led by Justice G.T. Nanavati—that commission produced its report only in 2005 by which time the Congress was back in power at the Centre. Unsurprisingly, no executive action followed the submission of this report either. The first step, the Ved Marwah inquiry, had come nearest to prosecuting a failing police.

Kill that inquiry the government did, but records have a way of surviving. They sit lodged in government files, and the files haven't gone away. The officer who conducted the inquiry would have the knowledge through his inquiry to share and to bring up if called to do so—if the government chooses to raise the issue, that is.

Rahul Gandhi's insistence in his 2014 interview on the innocence of the Congress in 1984 is a reminder that the conflict between records and claims is still real—his claims are at variance with records. The unfinished business of justice has faded from the media and from the public mind, but it does not stand eroded in record or in a legal compulsion for action based on that record.

And it has not faded from the minds of the families of the killed, or of survivors still living with the injustice.

In plain legal language, one who makes an active move to cover up a crime becomes a conspirator. And a conspirator is a criminal as much as one who carried out the actual crime. By law, prosecution of offenders, given the facts, is still possible; in fairness the need for action is compelling before it becomes impossibly late.

~

Mr Marwah had found the police remiss, but exactly what had he seen? To go back to a playback of the rest of our conversation before we think a little about some extraordinary observations he shared:

> SS: Did you find a pattern to the killings?
>
> VM: I found, and this was corroborated by every person in the police and outside that I spoke to, that there were relatively a small number of people who went on the rampage. And how a large number of Sikhs were ringed with tyres and burnt alive. The wife of one of the victims, when I went to her home to ask her, told me the terrible scene she went through for one hour. She said she saw her husband burning and nobody wanted to help. And she cried and she cried and she cried. And nobody helped her. So obviously this was not the job of an agitated mob. In my experience, an agitated mob doesn't indulge in this sort of cold-blooded cruelty. This is the handiwork of criminals.
>
> SS: Who mobilized those criminals?
>
> VM: Somebody obviously mobilized those criminals. And secondly, these criminals obviously had a tacit assurance that they will not be taken to task. Otherwise they could not indulge

in such activity so openly, so brazenly, in broad daylight in front of so many witnesses.

Crimes are not committed that way.

SS: And they were in groups of no more than hundreds?

VM: Not even a few hundred, in some places thirty or forty. In Khan Market, for example, 30–40 people came and ransacked the Sikh shops. There were no mobs at all—you can call them groups of rowdies. They were groups of rowdies being mobilized. There may have been some local people. Looting may have been done by some local antisocial people, but 3,000 Sikhs being killed was done by criminals ... 3,000 Sikhs being killed is no ordinary thing.

SS: So, on one hand, groups were mobilized by some organization, and on the other, the police failed.

VM: There was a policing lapse. And it was some organization I suspect that was behind it, behind the groups of rowdies, and those who organized all this.

SS: Where did you find the worst of the killings?

VM: Only three [police] districts were affected—east, west and south. North district and central were almost unaffected. In New Delhi [police district] there were some cases of arson but even that was not very much.

SS: Did you find that the police took firm action anywhere?

VM: Maxwell Pereira [then additional DCP, north district] took strong action. Pereira did a good job because his was the most vulnerable area. There's a big gurdwara [Sis Ganj] there, there was a big Sikh population there. So if it was just anti-Sikh riots, they were the ones who should have been attacked. There was no such thing. And elsewhere too there were no large mobs; only small groups that did all the damage, the people as such did not come out. You've seen this. In Delhi thousands of people collect in no time. There was no such thing [as a big mob].

SS: And so the two things that stood out in your findings were that these were small and organized groups of people, and second, that the police looked the other way as these groups went about looting and killing.

VM: These were the two things.

SS: You found that the police were remiss. But how can the police be just remiss? I, let's say, as a citizen can be remiss, but for the police to be remiss is criminal.

VM: Yes, there was some assurance to criminal elements that no action will be taken against them. And that is criminality. It's a very serious suspicion.

SS: And some police officers whose conduct you had inquired into have turned against you.

VM: Chander Prakash [then DCP, south district] has filed a defamation case against me after the high court threw it away [the appeal to stop the inquiry]. He has been launching one litigation after another. Even today a case is pending against me by Chander Prakash for defamation. And you know what is the basis of that? That a news item had appeared at that time in 1985 in a newspaper called *Sandhya Times*, that my inquiry was going to nail these three or four people, which included his name.

SS: What was his case?

VM: That no inquiry had really been made. I said *Sandhya Times* had published the news. I have not written that report (in the newspaper), I have not given the names. If *Sandhya*

Times has published something, ask them, who has given them these names. And you know, they have been hounding me for the last thirty years.

SS: But clearly any defamation case has to be against the paper. On what basis is the court proceeding?

VM: The petition has not been accepted, but it goes on and on and on. Thirty years, can you believe this? The last summons I got was some time in 2013. The people who brought the summons, they came and pasted it on my door. Can you beat it? A former commissioner of police? And being summoned like this? You see how brazen they can be.

SS: How are you dealing with these cases?

VM: The government is supposed to legally defend me in this case.

SS: Are they not doing that?

VM: If they were doing it, the summons would not be pasted like this. They have hired a lawyer. First the home ministry was doing it. Then the home ministry said they have no records, let the Delhi Police do it. Now the Delhi Police is doing it. It's unbelievable that in our system the culprits get away, and it is the inquiry officer who has to face this. The case is also against Kusum Lata Mittal, the IAS officer who carried out one of the later inquiries.

SS: This sounds incredible.

VM: As the inquiry officer, I am being harassed. But the court should end this one way or another. And there is no substance in the allegation of defamation. I am not the reporter, the question of me giving it to them does not arise. The newspaper editor should be hauled up and asked where did you get this?

SS: By law that has to be the first action in such a case.

VM: Yes, but they haven't done it. And the court is not asking that question.

SS: This is odd, how can a court not raise this?

VM: Thirty years. It was thrown from one court to the other. First, it was in a fast-track court, who knows what they have been doing?

SS: Some of the worst of the killings came in east Delhi. What did you find happened in east Delhi?

VM: In east Delhi, so many of the poor people were burnt alive. They were from Rajasthan. They were carpenters, not Sikhs in the traditional sense of the word, the way Sikhs in Punjab are. But those people were just burnt alive. Their whole place was set on fire, and this was not very far from the Trilokpuri police station. It was tragic.

SS: And in Palam area [close to the now Indira Gandhi International

Airport]?

VM: Many of the cases of burning by tyres was in the south district, in Palam. Normally there are no riots in Palam area, because you can't collect crowds there. But there were many, many killings of Sikhs there, they were burnt alive. That was in the south district. And in Sultanpuri [in west Delhi]. These are the three places that were the worst—Sultanpuri, Trilokpuri, Palam.

SS: In all three districts police action was missing?

VM: It was minimal, if at all.

SS: Did you get any indication that the Congress was responsible?

VM: I did not go into that. I won't go into that.

SS: But circumstantially ...

VM: I won't go into that. Even today I won't like to say [anything]. Because that would change the whole tenor of what I am saying. I am an apolitical person, and I would like to remain that way.

~

Asked to sum up as a newspaper man, I'd bullet-point this part of the conversation as below:

- One, it was actually only very small groups that carried out thekillings, that the people as such had never come out against the Sikhs.
- Two, that these groups were organized, these were not somespontaneously launched attacks.
- Three, there was an assurance to these groups that they could killand get away with it.
- Four, that far from nailing the officers he had found remiss, it washe, Marwah, who was being hounded over that inquiry, and that he has been hounded since he launched it.

All this, to add to what Marwah had said earlier, that the police had shut their eyes to the violence, and that his inquiry into the police failures was terminated by an executive order from the government just as he was completing it.

Marwah was very careful with his words, and he shies dutifully away from political remarks, but the implications of these points he made are enormous. They took the ground away from beneath Rajiv Gandhi's metaphor.

The inquiry brought up documented facts, that the earth was not shaking because some mighty tree had fallen. These facts would have come to the surface right then, had the government permitted Marwah to complete and submit his report. It became official, then, that just very small 'groups of rowdies' were out killing. It never was simply the non-Sikhs of Delhi who came out as a people against Sikhs. People were shaken by the assassination no doubt, but they were not shaking the earth to the extent that killing amounted to a shaking of the earth. And so far as it did, the earth wasn't shaking; not all of the earth in India, not all of it in Delhi even—it was three out of the six police districts in Delhi where the killings took place. And not just everywhere within these three districts either. The falling tree shook a few areas in three police districts in Delhi. Not what Rajiv Gandhi and his government could have wanted to hear by way of an official report based on facts they could never challenge had it come out in the open.

And was everyone within those districts shaken enough to go out to kill? The sense of magnitude of the earth shaking arose only from the very large number of killings. The Marwah inquiry found that in these places, only a very few people did all the killings. It's usual to think of a mob as something larger than a coming together of 30–40 people, a couple of hundred even. Not just larger, one thinks of a mob as a gathering that is more spontaneous, whose actions are uncontrolled, and whose violent ways are less planned. A mob may find a common enemy to target, but the targeting is usually not pre-planned, and the expression of its fury is usually more wild than deliberate. A small number of people out to murder in a few areas is no mob. The killing was the work, Marwah found, of organized groups.

This truth that Marwah's extensive inquiry brought to surface is not quite the broad headline truth that has stayed with so many of us, that large numbers of people were driven to uncontrollable rage by the assassination to turn against Sikhs. Amongst people at large, there appeared almost no outward reaction at all, almost no visible sign at all of any anger, or pain. Very few attended Mrs Gandhi's funeral— unlike the masses who had turned out for the funerals of Mahatma Gandhi, or Jawaharlal Nehru, when people poured out spontaneously to pay their last respects.

In scale, the violence caused was comparable to that caused by gangs of dacoits, not mobs of fury. Not only was this pattern not an instance of spontaneous public anger—it was evidence of the very opposite of what Rajiv Gandhi's tree image had suggested. In a city like Delhi, that kind of anger, or grief, could have brought hundreds of thousands out on the streets. As it turned out, not a single crowd amounted even to thousands.

This is not to say that the rest felt no anger. It's possible to be angry and stay civilized, to feel furious and stay within the limits of law, even to unfairly and by association blame a people—but without setting out to kill them. In its homes Delhi must have known spontaneous anger; but that anger stayed home, and within the limits of law.

Visions of those men who had attacked our car in Sultanpuri keep coming back. How many were they? Just a handful. And it was this little lot that the frightened man in Sultanpuri had pointed to. He had not pointed to 'the people' of Sultanpuri, not to any neighbours who had turned upon them. The scene in Sultanpuri was consistent with Marwah's findings: the killings were the handiwork of a lethal few.

It is only in the face of the scale of the violence that people assumed, or were told, that a proportionately large number of men were behind it.

The most potently revealing—and politically revealing, though Marwah couldn't say so—finding was that these men had been mobilized by some organization. This pattern of what Marwah found to be organized killing by a few, who had organizational backing, is not necessarily separate from the fact that the killers got away with it, and acted and killed as though they knew they would get away with it. They had organized support where it mattered.

Which could be the organization that would want to unleash violence on the Sikhs? Which organization would have the resources to do it? And which organization could make sure that they could do it and get away with it, who could then prevail on the government itself and the police themselves to look the other way? Surely it should be possible to ask one further question: who else? The answer, Marwah had said, was obvious.

Marwah saw the pattern of killing across Delhi as deliberate and cold-blooded, not killing by some furious mob that may set upon an identifiable target that came its way. He found that the killings came through controlled action rather than in uncontrolled anger. The woman who cried and cried out in desperation as she watched her husband burn to death within a flaming tyre was not appealing for mercy from some frenzied mob. Those killers, like the other killers those days, were going about their job in a methodical programme to kill. And using tyres to do so.

~

Tyres? As a murder weapon? Let's talk tyres.

This method of killing was gut-wrenchingly unusual. Everywhere, large numbers of Sikhs were ringed with burning tyres. In years of reporting crime I had never seen such a method of killing in Delhi, never before, never since. Over those three days, this became the chosen way to kill all over the city. How did this suddenly happen?

This variance from any 'popular' method of killing is as revealing to note as it is macabre to comprehend. Because if you were the organization that wanted to kill as it did, tyres made a lot of sense. Tyres, in fact, might have been the only method to kill that then made sense in Delhi.

The usual methods of killing were not appropriate for what these men had set out to do. The most commonly available weapon usually is some sort of knife. Picking up a knife to stab someone in street fury is not uncommon. It is also a favoured weapon of attack in premeditated assault, if only because knives are often at hand. Such a knife attack is usually launched on an unsuspecting victim.

Those days knifing would have presented difficulties. The target was not some unsuspecting victim who could be surprised. That victim would be facing up to the attacker, and the attacker would have to get very close to him. The other, prepared, would fight back. You could have a fight on your hands that could take too long, with yourself at risk. It would get messy and bloody. Knifing would bring other risks. It's very likely the attacker would get blood on his clothes, and that could be a deadly giveaway in case of any investigation.

Knifing is almost never used as a mode of attack upon large numbers of people. You never hear of knives used in genocide or in a pogrom. That is the weapon for an individual attack on a single target. Knives can be handy to pick up, but not necessarily easy to use. Any average bunch of men cannot all be trusted to use a knife skilfully enough for a quick kill.

Given the large numbers being targeted in the 1984 killings, it would have been difficult to hand out a set of sufficiently lethal knives for the job—the usual kitchen knife would not be suitable. And certainly no organization in Delhi would have a stockpile of long knives to hand out to kill someone with.

Or guns to hand out. A proper gun is always hard to get hold of anywhere in India; what is easy to find is the country pistol, the katta as it is called. But again, no organization is likely to have had some sort of armoury to produce these from, or buy them wholesale overnight. The katta is in any case notoriously unreliable, it fails and misfires often. If at all enough kattas could be produced, the average bunch of men one could find are unlikely to have had much skill in using the katta; using that kind of weapon does take time and training. Firing steadily from a proper revolver or pistol is hard enough—who could be trusted with kattas, and where would a relatively reliable lot of these be found? This option would be very much more difficult than wielding a knife. And it would take away any show of spontaneity.

If nothing as obvious as knives and guns, who would think tyres? They would have done a lot of thinking. Tyres could be found easily enough on streets and stacked in the open. They would only need the company of kerosene.

Kerosene would be even easier to find. Most homes in those resettlement colonies the murders happened in had no gas connection. Just about every home had a kerosense stove. And those neighbourhoods always had a kerosene depot where more could be bought.

Getting a kerosene agency wasn't just anybody's business; it was not an easy licence to acquire. These agencies were given to the carefully selected and well-connected. In any case, everyone knew where these were located in the neighbourhood. With connections or not, the owner would hardly be in a position to refuse an aggressive group that came with a demand for kerosene at that time.

Kerosene certainly was a familiar weapon. Delhi had by then developed a murderous tradition of burning young wives to death with kerosene around a stove. A great deal of my time as crime reporter was then taken up reporting cases of what came to be called 'bride burning', and 'dowry deaths', where a young and usually newly married woman would be burnt to death by in-laws, often for failing to bring enough dowry. Those killings took place mostly in just the kind of neighbourhood in which most of the killings of Sikhs took place.

Together with my colleague Sevanti Ninan, I had investigated the circumstances of many of these dowry deaths. We had together taken a hundred cases within a given and recent period, to look at each case through police records, home visits and collect the testimonies of relatives. In most cases of a woman burnt to death, the killings took place in the kitchen, often around a kerosene stove. Invariably, these were disguised as accidents. The murder weapon, kerosene, was 'naturally' at hand, many of these killings seemed to be copycat actions of known methods.

In 1984 someone decided to combine the commonly available kerosene with the commonly found tyres. Used tyres found a big market for resale after 'retreading'. These could be seen piled high in the open; rarely stacked indoors within some locked warehouse. In these piles of tyres someone had seen deadly promise. Tyres burn, and they burn over a long time. Topped with kerosene they burn more, they burn faster. A burning tyre contracts into itself, tightening itself around the space within. Ring a victim with a tyre, pour kerosene and set it aflame, and the tyre will turn into a killer garland. It will throw a restraint around the victim, and burn longer than kerosene splashed on clothes might. It was not a restraint the victim could run away from. The victim could at most carry the burning tyre around him the few steps he could move, if at all; he couldn't grab it with his bare hands to pull it away, or to pull himself out of it. Someone had thought this through methodically.

Tyres would be particularly suited to killing scenarios where a number of people, say anything from four to ten, could overpower a victim, force a tyre around the neck, set it on fire and run away. The victim could never run away from the tyre.

Through our reporting of those cases of bride burning, forensic experts told us that killing by burning offers peculiar advantages—the very method of killing destroys the evidence with it. Burning usually destroys fingerprints, it leaves no bullets or shells to identify the gun they were fired from, from which to trace a weapon and its ownership. Burning leaves no telltale bloodstains. A forensic team would be much limited in gathering evidence around a death by burning, even if investigation was ever to get that far; it rarely did in those dowry death cases. In 1984 it never did.

Why tyres, we may ask? Really, what else could be better under those circumstances, and for that kind of killing? A new weapon had been created—the kerosene-tyre. It seemed just right for killing in a pattern where small groups would target one or two victims at a time before turning upon the next. That kind of ratio would enable easy overpowering of a victim to ring him with a tyre and set it on fire, and the tyre would do the rest. An easy murder with almost no evidence left.

In other, more normal, circumstances the kerosene-tyre would never work. It couldn't be the weapon for an individual murder driven by some personal motivation. You couldn't hope to surprise a victim with a kerosene-tyre. The killing itself would be problematic. It would set off too much smoke, the screaming would get too loud, it would all attract too much attention. Not what anyone might want for the quiet murder they could get away with. Walking up to a victim lugging a tyre would hardly be discreet.

Tyres could never be used for bride burning. Such killing would be obvious murder, few could argue that a young wife had landed herself accidentally within a burning tyre. The kerosene-tyre was also unknown as a suicide method. But in 1984 killers felt no need to disguise their murders as anything else, to pretend these might have been accidents. They were confident they didn't need to.

It mattered nothing who saw the killers and how loudly and how long the man ringed with fire screamed. Or how high the smoke rose or how far the stench went. It was nobody's intention then to sneak upon some unsuspecting victim, the idea was to surround, drag out, burn and kill. From the organizers' point of view, it worked perfectly well. They had thought fast and acted fast. Until then it was thought tyres could kill if the tyre of a vehicle ran over someone. Now a detached tyre had turned killer.

In rare police action at the time, the central district police had to seal off the wholesale tyre market near Swami Shraddhanand Marg, the old 'red-light district' of Delhi. It was a well-known street, but not for tyres. Now and then the police would raid this area and make arrests among sex workers and their clients. This time the police descended on the area to protect tyres because these could be used to kill Sikhs. This is what Delhi had become.

These tyres had not just become the means to kill but a licence to kill. Groups that carried these tyres about were identifiable as groups with a particular mission with known targets. They would be seen to be so by the police. And nowhere in the worst affected areas did the police look out for groups carrying tyres to stop them.

Where precisely would these groups go looking for tyres? Yes, they were out in the open to pick up, but not out in the open on every street. People do not commonly know those shops that stock used tyres, these are on nobody's daily shopping lists. The groups would have had to be told by their local leaders where those stores were.

They found their ways to those shops in rapid and simultaneous forays across many parts of the city. The killers appear to have been centrally directed though not centrally supplied. But they were directed rapidly to the right places. It did not appear that these groups stripped their own vehicles of their tyres, or even took the laborious and risky route of loosening and then yanking them away from parked vehicles. The groups would need, and were given, precise instructions what to get from where. The tyres would have to be a certain size; scooter tyres might be too small, bicycle tyres too large.

The kerosene-tyre weapon would have needed, and got, other support. Tyres and kerosene are not easy to carry over long distances; no one was seen carrying tyres around their shoulders with cans of kerosene in hand; they wouldn't have got far if they did. Taking tyres and kerosene to targeted Sikh areas would have needed transportation. This, too, had to be an organized effort.

Someone had been smart to figure out the kerosene-tyre as a murder weapon, and then organized enough to spread the word to a select but sufficient number around the city who themselves were bound by an organizational glue to do as told. The logistics of communication could not have been easy, and if that message did not go further than it did, it was perhaps because communications were not then what they now are. There were no mobile phones those days, no Internet, no email and of course no social media. Communication could come only through landlines—and only between people who had a landline telephone.

The population of Delhi with such phones was then very small. It was far from uncommon that two people with landlines would not get through to one another because the phones were not working. The ones you could reach on such a phone would then have to reach others similarly, the risks of communication down the chain would only rise. The chain of such communication itself would get limited. More than phones, communication would have taken people actually travelling, and physically meeting, to take such plans further.

As a last step in that chain of command, communication would be needed to send these groups to targeted addresses. These groups were given addresses to get to, a Sikh home is otherwise hard to tell from outside. Who gave the killers the names and addresses? Who could have had such lists handy, and accessible, at such short notice?

At the Lawrence Road DDA flats in west Delhi, the tenant in a family flat there told me, an aggressive group had turned up to ask for Sikhs to be handed over to them: 'They showed us papers and lists, they knew which were the flats with the Sikh names. The rest of us just came out and made a wall, we did not let them enter the flats. After some time they went away.' This too was a pattern, where neighbours formed protective walls around Sikhs; I never stopped hearing of such instances.

But who were these people who suddenly seemed to have these lists of residents' names? Such lists are in the possession of the electricity office, the water board, the municipality, the house tax department— or political parties that maintain lists of voters. Assuming it wasn't the staff at the water or one of the other municipal kind of departments that had decided all at once to go for the Sikhs, the most likely source of the names was electoral lists, of which political parties have a copy.

The commonness of this newly acquired way to kill and the organized path that led from plan to execution was necessarily an expression of conspiracy, not of coincidence. Marwah did not name the conspirator, or the organization behind this conspiracy. He only implied it was obvious, and asked: 'Who else?' The question brings up an odd obligation to political correctness in discourse: it was OK for some to kill and get away with it, but some others cannot say the obvious about the killers and their godfathers and protectors.

The facts on the street then were clear, the confirmation through the Marwah inquiry is unmistakable: the multiplication of lethal little groups across the city was—it had to be—organized. The violence was focused on identifiable targets, the killers relied in common on an unusual weapon. The police no doubt would have spotted the stamp of the modus operandi had they decided not to look away. Or, as the facts suggest, they knew of a common modus operandi that they were instructed, whether by silence or by whispered suggestions, to look away from.

Again, that question, arising now over this particular murder weapon: which organization could have planned out the means to carry out such killing? And also, simultaneously, make sure the police would look the other way, because kerosene and tyres would need to be acquired and transported visibly and publicly? Once again, that question: who else? The means of determining truth does not have to be what some inquiring judge pronounces; it can be what we see. No judge can rule that we must not see what we do.

Could just unconnected individuals have been coincidentally smart in figuring out precisely this way to kill in different areas of the city? That by coincidence Sikhs were being killed with burning tyres in east Delhi, and in Delhi Cantonment in the south-west, while some policemen were trying to seal off a wholesale tyre market in central Delhi? That without any calls, without meetings, without emissaries, many people around the city thought of exactly this at the same time? Someone can assert no doubt, if they so choose, that it may indeed have been coincidence, and of that assertion someone else can think what they will.

~

And finally, the last of those bullet points. I found it disturbing to see the consequences that the officer had continued to face for approaching the truth over police failings at the time, for having come so close to revealing them formally and fully. That he should have notices and summons pasted on his door, and tossed about from department to department, none of them doing a very good job evidently of taking up his case effectively enough against allegations that seemed to add up to harassment by way of legal proceedings.

Why would a government allow such a situation? Anyone may file a case, but was the government answering that case in the best way it could? Why would an officer like this be led to say: 'It's unbelievable that in our system the culprits get away, it is the inquiry officer who has to face this'?

The inquiry officer, we began to discover from the days he took over as police commissioner in April 1985, was a quite extraordinary officer. My first encounter with him was memorable. A press conference had been called at the police headquarters for a meeting with the new police chief. A reporter congratulated the police commissioner on his new position of power. 'There is no power,' Marwah replied. 'It's responsibility. When you abuse responsibility, it becomes power.'

What was this? A Delhi Police officer thinking more of responsibility than of power? I remember what a journalist said in the corridor outside at the end of the press conference: 'What's wrong with him?' He added, in less than polite language, and with more than a few colourful adjectives, that Marwah was naïve to talk like this, that he would soon learn. But such noble remarks anyone might make; it was the rest of the press conference that proved unforgettable.

That press conference did not go according to plan at all. We crime reporters had just settled into our seats to face Marwah and his team of senior officers, when a junior officer by the name of J.P. Singh circulated a sheet around the room with comparative crime statistics down the years. The statistics were meant to make impressive reading: they showed, on the face of it, that crime had been declining down the years, that it was significantly lower in 1985 than it had been many years earlier. The suggestion was that

1984 should be a forgettable aberration, we should see just how effective Delhi Police had been in bringing crime down.

I was shocked by that sheet exhibiting those progressively and supposedly declining numbers. Those numbers were to me only official confirmation that the police were refusing to register large numbers of cases in order to bring down the number of cases on paper and records. The police were in truth announcing that they were cheating crime victims increasingly, and on a large scale. These victims were being denied justice at the very first stage; the police were refusing to register FIRs only to make a show of numbers to prove that crime was under control in their districts. Was the new police commissioner making a start with such a massive lie? Could such a man be trusted then with an honest inquiry into police failures through the 1984 killings?

I spoke up after a quick glance at the circulated sheet. I said the projection and the claims the police were making were false and unfair, and that the current numbers were being compared with older statistics when the Delhi Police were freely, or relatively freely, registering cases and complaints.

'You have taken the older figures, when there was free registration of cases, and compared them to newer ones to show there is a fall,' I said. That cannot be right, I had said. I was preparing for a pow-wow with him. To my surprise, Marwah offered no counter. 'There is something in what you say,' he replied. Marwah had agreed quite openly with me; he as good as admitted that the police had right there and then, in his presence, made a false projection. A battery of other top officers in the room sat through this exchange in uncomfortable silence.

The police commissioner's officer had circulated a sheet on his behalf suggesting one thing—and here was the police commissioner admitting that what his officer had circulated in his presence and on his behalf wasn't right. The precise comparative numbers offered suggested that crime had dropped by one-third over a recent number of years. 'Do you really believe crime has come down by one-third in the city?' I asked. Marwah's reply simply was: 'No'. My colleagues did not say anything to back up what I was saying; they didn't need to. I was being supported in criticizing those police claims by the police chief.

Marwah had been candid enough to admit openly in one stroke both that the police had been seeking to project a lie, and that massive failures were taking place routinely across the city that the lie had sought to cover up. He had to choose between truth or a cover-up for his officers who had prepared a falsifying report and were sitting with him right there. He chose the truth. I gathered from senior officers that Marwah was later furious with his juniors over the false projection. That was quite a dramatic start for an officer going public for the first time as police commissioner.

Over his 1984 inquiry Marwah maintained his silence during the months following. He had done his bit, he told me on one occasion when I asked. He said the rest was for the government to do. I did not then grasp the meaning of his measured words. Down the chain of command other police officers couldn't tell me much about this inquiry either; very likely they didn't know themselves.

At that first press conference, Marwah had made a bold if unexpected start. We reporters were to see very soon how he could lead on the ground.

In May 1985 Delhi was hit by a series of transistor bombs planted around the city. This was soon after Marwah had taken over as police chief. About seventy people were killed by thirty bombs that went off in Delhi and around. It was suspected, and indeed it turned out, that they had been planted by an extremist Sikh group in revenge for the killing of Sikhs in November 1984.

The men behind the transistor attacks were later caught. But 1985 continued to shake from the events of 1984.

Soon after those bombings came an incident where a confrontation between Sikhs and the police developed outside the Bangla Sahib gurdwara in the heart of New Delhi. Word spread that a vehicle had run over some policemen from a large paramilitary force that had been on duty near the gurdwara. They suspected a group of Sikhs within the gurdwara. Bangla Sahib had become the launchpad of Sikh political protest, it was here that Akali Dal leader Parkash Singh Badal had in earlier years burnt a sheet from a copy of the Constitution of India in front of a police force and invited media.

The air in 1985 was edgy with one fallout after another of the 1984 violence. The transistor bombs went off, Congress leaders Lalit Maken and Arjan Dass were assassinated, and now came this confrontation with the paramilitary policemen. When I arrived at the gurdwara, the paramilitary policemen appeared out of control. They were out in the middle of the road, trying to stop traffic, perhaps looking for Sikhs in vehicles. There seemed to be no containing their fury. And they were armed.

Within the gurdwara, a very large group of Sikhs had come out and formed a line of defence. Sikhs were, in those days, always preparing to defend their gurdwaras—so many had been attacked in 1984. That day they were preparing to face a possible attack from armed policemen who had abandoned all discipline. I could hardly overstate how very tense the situation had become, we were on the trigger of a new battle.

The parking area in between the road and the gurdwara had become practically a no-man's-land, with both sides preparing to confront one another. Nobody was parking there now, and nobody who was parked was stepping into that space to leave. Into this noman's-land, an official white Ambassador drove up. Ved Marwah stepped out, by his side was Maxwell Pereira, the police officer who had been such a hero during the 1984 killings. I saw Marwah speak to some officers from the paramilitary; they were still not being very effective in controlling their own policemen, and they did not appear to be trying very hard.

Everyone had their eyes on Marwah out there in the middle between the two sides. To everyone's astonishment, he turned away from the paramilitary officers and strode up—alone—towards the gurdwara. Seeing him, Pereira quickly stepped up to his side. The policemen on the road, the Sikhs inside the gurdwara, waited and watched. All eyes were on this tall and rather frail-looking figure of an unarmed police commissioner walking right up to and into the gurdwara crowd, just when someone from there was thought to have killed policemen, and just when this crowd at the gurdwara was preparing to face a police assault. Marwah reached the gurdwara and soon we could see him talking to a group of Sikhs there.

Others joined from within, presumably some gurdwara functionaries. I have no idea what words were exchanged. In a while, Marwah headed back, and waited at the scene for a while. The Sikhs stepped back into the gurdwara, the paramilitary police retreated into their trucks. The confrontation evaporated. Take that press conference, and this, and here was an officer whose findings about the 1984 killings, I believed, we'd all want to hear. I was perhaps right to believe that, but wrong to imagine there would be a report from him that I would report on. That there wasn't one spoke its own truth. But that truth dawned too, too late.

8

Sis Ganj

If those deathly few days of November 1984 produced a hero it was Maxwell Pereira. He has justly been feted for it, not always by some of his colleagues, naturally. He was as popular as he was competent. We crime reporters all knew Maxwell Pereira, or 'Maxi' as some of us would call him. I myself wasn't on 'Maxi' terms with him. But I knew, as did we all, that you could talk straight to him, and you'd get a straight response. We thought of him as something of a schoolboy cop, refreshingly different from the stuffy sahibs some officers came to play.

If ever Delhi needed a straight schoolboy cop, it was Maxwell Pereira then.

He even looked boyish, almost the good cop making his brief appearance in a Bollywood film. More, he spoke in synch with that image. We found it amusing to hear him speak of his constables as 'the boys'—it was hard to think of a Delhi Police constable from Haryana as one in a species of 'boys'. His juniors, the constables—'boys,' to put it his way—worshipped him. Here was an officer, and there weren't many, who would do, and do only, the professional and proper thing. When there was policing to be done, he would do it straight and smart.

That's just how he led the most effective policing by far in 1984. He was then additional DCP for the north district of Delhi Police. That he was only 'additional' DCP became significant sadly. The DCP for north district was a man by the name of S.K. Singh. The officer above S.K. Singh was additional commissioner of police, Hukum Chand Jatav, heading also the central and east districts.

We didn't know of Pereira's heroism on 1 November, the day he saved the historic Sis Ganj gurdwara in Chandni Chowk in the north district. That we didn't was in part a consequence of the usual paradox of the news business—we don't hear much when something goes right, or relatively right. Had something gone wrong that day at Sis Ganj— which means really that had Maxwell Pereira not been there, we might have heard of the consequences of an assault on Sis Ganj gurdwara that Pereira prevented. So would Punjab and the rest of India, and for a long time, if Sis Ganj had been desecrated and Sikhs there burnt alive, as they were being at so many gurdwaras across the city.

Given the innate perversity of the news business, just the fact that the police did anything at all then should have been news. This thought was to arise much later. At that time, very few of us reporters, no more than three or four in all of Delhi, were trying to get to places where the killings were taking place—that we could come to know of. Who could think of going to a place where killings had been prevented?

So we had to live with Maxwell Pereira's account that we heard only later. I heard that account in the course of meetings with him well after the day all that drama took place outside Sis Ganj. Between reporting of the aftermath of the killings, and following up on the assassination of Indira Gandhi, and then covering the elections, that story was lost in news space. Let's hear him again now. We didn't manage to be in Delhi at the same time in early 2014, so on this occasion it was a long conversation with him on the phone that reminded me of details I'd forgotten, and that he hadn't.

This time I heard the silences better. Like Ved Marwah earlier, there were some things he wouldn't say when asked. These were potent silences, and I do believe I must share my understanding of the possible meaning of those silences, based on my many years as crime reporter—the most work-packed years I ever have known. My familiarity with policing ways could, I believe, bring some pointers to understanding what he was saying but wouldn't in so many words. In his silences lay unspoken truths about the many failures through those days. Interpretations are always a tricky space to step into, and so I separate below any expression of my own understanding sharply from Pereira's own narration.

It's tempting to reproduce just the narrative of the Sis Ganj events as Maxwell Pereira himself experienced them and told me—as pure narrative, it's extraordinary. But dotting his story lie potent gaps, and apparently bland facts that carry unstated but sinister implications. Hence my intrusions. Those unstated implications add up to an extensive and disturbing picture of failures that the police can still be made to answer for.

The story of Punjab and of India, I seriously believe, might have been frighteningly different without this 'boy' cop's intervention at Sis Ganj. That much killing on the streets of Delhi had been traumatic enough for Punjab to hear of. An invasion of Sis Ganj, and killing of Sikhs within that gurdwara, would have been catastrophic. Punjab had witnessed the attack on the Golden Temple in Amritsar only a few months earlier. It had absorbed all it could and much more. It could hardly have taken an attack on Sis Ganj and killing of Sikhs within, and then kept as calm as it did.

Sis Ganj gurdwara stands tall and majestic in the heart of Chandni Chowk, itself a thriving bazaar centuries old. It marks the site where Sri Guru Tegh Bahadur, the ninth guru, was beheaded on the orders of the Mughal emperor, Aurangzeb, in November 1675. Just about every Sikh has visited that gurdwara at some time to offer prayers. The place finds a sacred spot in every Sikh's heart.

~

Maxwell Pereira so nearly wasn't at Sis Ganj that day. Below follows his account of how that morning began:

> They wanted me to take over the PM's security, there was no SPG (Special Protection Group, guarding top leaders) those days. The existing security set-up had been disarmed and totally confined to the barracks. The police commissioner then asked me to report to him at the Teen Murti Bhavan [where the body of Indira Gandhi lay].
>
> That was in the early hours of the morning of the 1st [November]. I'd spent most of the 31st night guarding my area. There were Sikhs being attacked, we were helping them reach home, and getting people to go back inside their houses. That went on for most of the night.
>
> It was the early hours of the morning, and I had to go home for a bath. When I just finished and was going back into the area again, that's the time I got the summons from the commissioner to report to him at the Teen Murti Bhavan.
>
> When I went [to the Teen Murti Bhavan], it was all still continuing, reports were coming [of attacks on Sikhs and Sikh establishments]. I asked the commissioner, 'What am I doing here, sir?' He just told me to wait. I was there beside Mrs Gandhi's body, and waiting. There were people coming [to file past the body]. But in the meantime my wireless operator was informing me of disturbances, of incidents going on in the north district. And then he told me of the Bhagirath Place fire (Bhagirath Place is a wholesale electrical goods bazaar at the edge of Chandni Chowk, across from the Red Fort, a few minutes' walk to the east of Sis Ganj gurdwara).
>
> That's when I told the commissioner I can't just go on listening to all this, there's no one there handling the situation, I need to go. That's when he told me, 'Yes, you go, but remain

available at a minute's notice to report back to me.' So I rushed to Bhagirath Place. I left sometime between 9 a.m. and 9.30 a.m. I reached Red Fort in my jeep. We were a total of six or seven people in the jeep. They had their hand weapons only—short batons.

I reached Red Fort, I found the Red Fort police post in-charge, he had about two or three people with him. I could see that Bhagirath Place was burning. I asked him to accompany me with his force. And we started a march towards Bhagirath Place—that would be ten or twelve of us. We kept walking up, beating our batons on the road, trying to disperse the crowds that were assembling. Many were just curious watchers. We went up, we kept marching, and meanwhile messages were given about the situation. I don't think there was anybody to dowse the fire. Those affected were trying to douse the fire.

~

Pause Pereira's narration here for a moment, there is reason to. It would have been known to the commissioner of police, and certainly to the north district DCP S.K. Singh, that Pereira was among no more than a handful of officers in Delhi who had been actively trying to control the unrest that began to develop on the evening of 31 October.

This would be obvious, and audibly obvious, from wireless transmissions of steps Pereira was taking on the evening of 31 October and into the night.

It would seem inevitable that the following morning there would be more trouble, and most certainly, in the north district too.

North district chief S.K. Singh would have heard or been given all the messages directly, and the picture arising would have been conveyed further to S.K. Singh's immediate senior, additional commissioner of police Hukum Chand Jatav, and further up to the police commissioner as a matter of course. It is inconceivable that the police commissioner did not know of the breakdown in different areas of the city, and what his officers were doing, including Pereira.

It is true also that the police commissioner would have had at his command a range of officers to pick from, who were not that morning on active police duty in the districts, to post in a static presence at Teen Murti Bhavan. Pereira had, after all, not taken over the PM's security as told. He was not ordered to take over the security force now around Rajiv Gandhi, but just to stay put at Teen Murti—not the best way to protect the new Prime Minister.

Heavy police deployment was in place at Teen Murti already to manage the mourners filing past the body of Mrs Gandhi, and more, for management of visiting VIPs. An officer who had rapidly established himself to be exceptionally energetic in protecting Sikhs in his district had been extracted away from the area, withdrawn from that duty, to present himself at Teen Murti Bhavan in a stationary and ceremonial position. He seems to have felt the frustration of his misplaced presence keenly.

It is not suggested that the summons to Pereira that pulled him out of his district were necessarily and conclusively some plot to stop him policing the area. But the fact stands that one of the officers most energetic in challenging the building unrest was called away from a post where he could continue to play his role. He wasn't the only one. In the north district, his junior ACP Keval Singh was pulled away from active policing, and in turn, his own juniors too, who had begun to confront the attackers.

The police commissioner allowed Maxwell Pereira to return to the district—but only on Pereira's insistence. Pereira appeared to have been insistent with a sense of urgency. He almost appeared to have confronted the commissioner, asking, 'What am I doing here?' (or its equivalent). In the face of this, the commissioner would have created a difficult record for himself to answer for had he continued to insist that Pereira stay on at Teen Murti Bhavan to help manage mourners and VIPs rather than handle rioters on the rampage in his district.

Note also that Teen Murti Bhavan is where the police commissioner had stationed himself while his city was burning—and killing. He did not on his own order his officer to do what he must in order to contain the violence, and to continue to do more of what he had already been known to be doing in countering the violence. In the end, Pereira told the commissioner he needed to go—he was almost informing rather than asking.

The commissioner of police would have known through internal communications, and he was informed by Pereira additionally, of the alarming situation developing around Sis Ganj. He would have known that his DCP North, S.K. Singh, was not on the scene to handle it. As Pereira told the commissioner, 'There's no one there handling the situation'. That fact was known also to the commissioner, who in any case does not appear to have challenged it. The commissioner issued no order for the DCP North to get to Sis Ganj in the meanwhile. Was there something more serious that S.K. Singh was handling? No report of more pressing duties for the DCP North at that time surfaced then, and none had surfaced in police records since, of some bigger crisis S.K. Singh was taking on elsewhere at that time than the saving of Sis Ganj.

Note also that the police commissioner seemed not to care whether Pereira had the necessary force to deal with the developing situation. He issued no command himself and offered no direction. Pereira had reports coming in of crowds assembling within sight of Sis Ganj, of people burning down Sikh shops. One of the biggest markets in Delhi was ablaze within sight of the gurdwara. To deal with this, Pereira returned with just the few men in his jeep, later backed by no more than three or four policemen from the Red Fort police post. And those would be unarmed constables.

Those few constables seemed to have done little more than send out wireless messages within the north district network. Those wireless messages they sent out would have reached DCP North S.K. Singh at the same time as they reached Pereira. S.K. Singh did not rush to Sis Ganj to save it, he didn't order his number two, Pereira, to get there.

And so, the only counter to those men gathering to attack that historic gurdwara was this brave little procession of the police led by this boy cop, with constables beating their short batons on the ground by way of announcing that effective policing was at hand. The fire brigade had been informed, it did not turn up. Police response to that rising danger looked more brave than effective, and neither the DCP North nor the police commissioner appeared to have issued orders, or offered reinforcement, that might make it any more effective.

~

To return now to the conversation with Pereira on what followed after that little march to Bhagirath Place:

> SS: Was this force enough to deal with the fires and the crowds at Bhagirath Place?
>
> MP: We had no more time for Bhagirath Place because there was a huge crowd assembling and coming down from Chandni Chowk side towards Sis Ganj gurdwara.
>
> SS: How big was the crowd? Hundreds? Thousands?
>
> MP: It was in hundreds, not thousands. And the crowds of a menacing nature were not that big compared to the crowds of a curious nature. But there was another problem. An intention

to attack the gurdwara was becoming evident, and the inmates of the gurdwara were not taking this kindly. They were coming out of the gates of the gurdwara, brandishing swords in the air, ready for confrontation. That was my first problem. The minute I reached the gurdwara, I talked to them first, I told them their protection was my responsibility, and they should not come out of the gurdwara.

In the meantime there had been many people hiding in the lanes and by-lanes, these were the nearest safe places for Sikhs who had happened to be on the road. They were making a beeline for the gurdwara. We spotted them, and escorted them into the gurdwara, and we asked them to remain within its safe sanctuary. These were local Sikhs, there were pilgrim Sikhs, there were lots of people. I remember there was a Sikh gentleman, a very distinguished gentleman, whose wife, a foreigner, came saying that he (her husband) had been in [the] Chandni Chowk area. I remember I had got hold of him and he was totally shattered. I escorted him personally into the gurdwara. I was able to unite him with her—that was three or four days later.

If you recall, in front of the gurdwara there was a police post called the Fountain Chowk police post. We had taken over that chowk because we had handed over the Kotwali police station building to the gurdwara ('kotwali' literally means a police station, but that police station that had come to be called simply Kotwali was located earlier within the compound of the gurdwara), as per some pact the government had with the Shiromani Akali Dal, because their guru was martyred in that kotwali. We needed a police presence there, and that's how we opened the police post there (at Fountain Chowk).

At the police post there was the SHO Kotwali (heading the police station) and there was the ACP Kotwali (heading that and also the Lahori Gate police station towards the Red Fort side on the east), and they had a small force with them. That emboldened us, and we could stand our ground and keep the two warring factions apart. We kept the Sikhs in the gurdwara and the crowds apart. One group of people was advancing from the Chandni Chowk town hall to one side and the other was coming from the railway station (to the north of the gurdwara).

SS: At this stage how many policemen did you have at your command?

MP: Maybe 20–25, what we would term a platoon. A platoon would be thirty strong, this was a small platoon.

SS: Were your policemen armed?

MP: We didn't have an armed party. An armed party was there for the district, and that was accompanying the then DCP, Mr S.K. Singh.

SS: Where was that armed party going?

MP: Apparently the forces were with Mr S.K. Singh, and he being the district police chief, must have gone around elsewhere when I reached here.

SS: You are being polite. We know that that armed force went nowhere.

MP: As far as I'm concerned, I can tell you what I did. I can't speak for others. They would be in a better position to say what they did or didn't.

SS: So then, what happened at Sis Ganj?

MP: We thought we had got it in our grip. But suddenly we got information that shops owned by Sikhs in Chandni Chowk (to the west side of the gurdwara on the Town Hall side; Bhagirath Place and Red Fort were to their east) were being set on fire. We immediately rushed there and dispersed the crowd initially. But they did not just go home. And we had no police presence to extend our policing impact up to the Town Hall or beyond. We had grouped our little force together so that we could control any situation in and around the gurdwara area.

But we did by then have a menacing crowd. Once or twice we did warn them of action, we set up our mob control banners, we launched our mob control drills and all the usual requirements, we had the shields, we had the long batons. We had by then a halfsection of a tear smoke squad from the district unit which was not with the rest of the forces that were at the DCP's command. I managed to bring that into the Chandni Chowk area from the district lines. There was half a section of the reserve (tear smoke squad) there.

So we fired tear smoke. We dispersed the crowds at least twice. But finally again their strength was gathering, and becoming stronger and stronger. They were raising slogans, they were coming down Chandni Chowk (towards the gurdwara from the west). At this stage we could not control them setting fire to Sikh shops. I had to give a very strong warning, and that is when I said I am opening fire.

Even then they did not stop. Then I ordered the firing from my personal revolver. I was not carrying the revolver, my gunman was carrying it. His name is still alive in my mind, Head Constable Satish Chandra. He was in my personal staff throughout. He opened fire, and one person dropped dead. That created a tremendous impact. I couldn't help myself. Then and there, on the microphone, I announced a reward of 200 rupees, a meagre 200 rupees, for opening fire. I told the crowd there will be more to follow if anyone ventures further. That is the sum and substance of what happened.

~

Comment again. Survey the scene as described by Pereira. To the east of Sis Ganj, Sikh shops had been set on fire, the biggest electrical goods market in Delhi was in flames. From the west, crowds were heading down to the gurdwara to attack it. A small rag-tag police platoon was unable to stop them from advancing. Sikhs from within the gurdwara had rushed out carrying swords, prepared to die for their gurdwara. They had been persuaded to go back in, but no one could tell for how long. If ever in the history of policing an armed force was needed, this was that moment.

Where was that armed force? It was right there, in that district. Potentially, it was even available. That force had been locked into the service of DCP S.K. Singh. A word from him, and the force could have been dispatched to Sis Ganj in quick time. It was never made available to Pereira's hastily assembled platoon.

Given the facts—and the fact that these facts were being communicated to S.K.Singh among other senior officers—it becomes obvious that the armed police unit was withheld from Sis Ganj for reasons that appear inexplicable in purely policing terms. Pereira, as number two, could not himself order relocation of an armed police unit then under charge of his boss. That had to be a decision for the boss to take, the boss knew just what the need was, and he did not take that decision.

What S.K. Singh knew, his own boss Hukum Chand Jatav knew, and given the alarming developments, the police commissioner himself was likely to know. All along the chain of command, the senior officers (a) knew just what sort of situation was building up at Sis Ganj, (b) knew that an armed force was urgently needed, and (c) were making sure it was not sent.

It was known to the police force that Sis Ganj was not just a target for the crowd, it was the only sanctuary available for Sikhs facing hostile crowds all around. They needed to get to the gurdwara for shelter, reaching it or not could be a matter of life and death. It was known that the police force present outside the gurdwara was too small to venture out into the lanes and other places around the gurdwara to rescue those Sikhs. It was by deliberate decision, if not by actually ordered command, that senior officers were placing Sikh lives at risk. These senior officers may or may not have wanted Sikhs killed—but they were doing nothing to ensure their protection either, in the face of imminent and life-threatening danger.

The small police force posted at Fountain Chowk was on its own until the little band led by Maxwell Pereira turned up—on its own without any direction from any top police officer other than Pereira himself. So it was this ramshackle platoon drawn from policemen in a single jeep, from a police kiosk, and then from an understaffed police post at Chandni Chowk, that Delhi Police had found to defend the most historic Sikh centre of worship in Delhi.

The top officers knew the situation was getting out of control particularly once crowds started to burn Sikh shops on the Town Hall side of the gurdwara. The little police force was just about holding its own in front of the gurdwara; it wasn't able to stop the crowd building up, burning shops, or attacking Sikhs all around the gurdwara. And this crisis had not erupted suddenly, it had been building up all morning, over several hours. The top leadership had all the time they could have asked for and more to send a new and stronger police force.

A district always has a reserve force available; police from many of the quieter or at the moment less demanding areas within the district could have been rushed to Sis Ganj; the administration staff within the police (and they are considerable) could have been summoned at a time like this—they are an informal reserve that active police units often draw upon in a crisis. The police had enough reaction time, they had enough reserves to draw on, they had within the district the armed unit under the command of its top officer. What the police did not have was the will at the top level to stop the violence, to do what it could to stop the attack on the gurdwara.

Were it not for one determined officer, nothing clearly was being done. Later, the top officers all got away with doing nothing. The only inquiry that could have confronted top police officers over this failure, and nearly did, was aborted. It was made sure that S.K. Singh, like other officers in Delhi, would not have to answer for their inaction.

Never mind armed police, or reinforcements, Pereira's little team was not offered even the minimal crowd control measures such as tear gas in the face of updates sent out on the district police wireless that the crowds were becoming dangerous and difficult to control. Pereira had to summon a half-unit waiting in the district lines as reserve that was in his powers to summon. Some tear gas was fired by this half-unit, but it was not enough to disperse the advancing crowd. In such circumstances, the last resort of the police was to open fire.

Open fire with what? The police weapon of choice at a time like this would appear to be the outdated but reliable .303 rifle. The .303 could fire single and targeted shots at considerable range. It was just the weapon that would be right for such a situation, rather than a weapon that might only spray bullets into a crowd. Certainly it would do better than a mere pistol or revolver. A .303 could have been used for targeted, and not necessarily lethal, shots at leaders in the crowd, such as shots to the leg. The sound of firing, the sight of policemen aiming rifles into the crowd, would without doubt have scattered the crowd. Delhi Police then had a strong armoury of .303 rifles. Whether reserve units were equipped with the .303 or with more automatic weapons, Pereira's platoon got neither.

The platoon relied on Pereira's personal revolver, in the hands of a head constable. This was fired, and one man dropped dead.

That one shot was enough—it stopped the advance, the crowds dissolved and disappeared. Under the circumstances, it was a risky move. It could so easily have gone wrong: a revolver is not the most accurate of weapons, it has only limited range—and it has to be fired from close range. The advancing crowd would have been very close to the police force for a single shot from a revolver to have killed someone. They would be close enough also for some in the crowd to see that the police were not carrying more deadly weapons. A signal here, a move there, and the police force could have been attacked and overwhelmed by the crowd— not unknown in riot situations in India.

We could have our own views on Pereira's announcement on the loudspeaker of a reward for the policeman who killed a man in the advancing crowd. That kind of move seems to pre-date all the new, and correct, standards of modern policing and human rights. But politically correct hindsight must have its limits. The intention clearly was to signal to the crowd a determination on the part of the police that they meant business, that they would kill if need be. What finally matters is that it worked, the crowd melted and the gurdwara was saved. That single shot followed by announcement of the reward saved a lot of lives, and more than lives.

~

SS: Was that shooting the end of the trouble at Sis Ganj?

MP: There is plenty more that happened thereafter, by which time I had mobilized whatever was left of the manpower.

SS: So you could mobilize a bigger force later?

MP: Mainly I mobilized plain-clothes people to infiltrate into the crowds, to go down the lanes, and get us information.

SS: How long had the confrontation around Sis Ganj lasted?

MP: I really cannot remember how long it took me to do all this … with all the jostling, where each [side] was trying to assess the other's strength, how much they can reach out, how much they can take advantage. We have been in any number of such situations where you can't really define an end time.

After the incident, I informed the control room immediately that I have opened fire and I have killed a person. These are matters of record, these are matters of importance that have to be known. Especially if you have opened fire, you need to inform the control room. And to bring this to the notice of my superiors, including my additional commissioner (Hukum Chand Jatav), and my commissioner of police (Subhash Tandon). What troubled me was that there was pin-drop silence. There was no response coming from the control room.

I kept asking them to confirm, that have you passed on this information to the superiors? I would not get a reply to that. There was total wireless silence on that score, and that is what surprised me, it troubled me all the time, it troubled me all the while. It just kept nagging me.

Later, I remember I was informed that my own additional commissioner, Hukum Chand Jatav, came to the Red Fort and went away; he did not come to meet us. We were the police force handling this. And he did not call me either. By the time we made up our mind to go and see him there, we were told he had taken off, he was no longer there.

SS: What was the control room doing?

MP: No one would bring these things on record. The firing was not brought on record by the control room.

SS: The control room is manned by juniors, but what about the officers heading it? Why was there no feedback given to you? Who, then, would have taken that decision not to give you feedback, and to not place the firing on record, after you informed them?

MP: I am unable to answer that. All I can say is that I did report everything factually and immediately and thereafter to the inquiry commission.

~

Consider the communication wall Pereira was describing. The Delhi Police had opened fire in which a man was killed. Supposedly he was a sympathizer of Indira Gandhi, out to target Sikhs and a place associated with them on the morning following the assassination. An officer of the rank of additional DCP had reported this to the control room, and he did not hear a word back. He asked for that information to be passed on to his seniors, and he didn't hear a word from them. It is inconceivable that the control room would not have communicated word of the killing in police firing to Pereira's senior officers.

The usual chain of command at the control room had been changed suddenly after the assassination. A senior police officer by the name of Nikhil Kumar was given charge of the control room, even though he was not actively a part of the Delhi Police set-up at the time. He was there, he said later—in an attempt at lightness that too many in the city could not share—as a 'guest artiste'. Could the junior staff that handles calls and communication at the control room have taken a decision on their own to block communication from an officer who was second in command of the north district police? They would have had to communicate that information, they could not have withheld it.

For the police to kill in firing is serious. Officers hesitate long before they order firing. It sets off strong reactions among the public, inquiries follow, it often leads to some sort of disciplinary action against the officers, if only to quieten crowd leaders and their political bosses. Coming on 1 November, the day after two men from the Delhi Police had killed Indira Gandhi, for the police to have killed an Indira Gandhi supporter was a serious development.

What kind of response could the senior officers have offered? Could they have censured Pereira for that firing? It wouldn't be easy to send out such a response in the face of such effective action in that situation. Certainly, Pereira had to face no disciplinary procedures, or even an inquiry over the firing. Could they have sent out a signal to the force that this had been exemplary action that had contained the violence and ended it, that others should resort to firing under such circumstances if need be? They did not. That option might be sensible policing but must have appeared politically indiscreet.

But once there is firing and killing by the police, it would be usual for senior officers to either commend or condemn. They would take note of it in some way, not pretend they had not heard of it after being told of it. The silence Pereira spoke of sounded chilling. Without doubt it was, as he found it, very odd.

Decisive orders delivered dramatically stopped a crowd in its murderous tracks—but not a word came from Pereira's bosses that he may have done the right thing, the effective thing. What came instead over the wireless had all the inaudible markings of silent disapproval. That undeclared disapproval was palpable in Jatav's strange visit to that area through the course of those developments. He was right there, but he only came and went, with no offer of reinforcements, or of an armed force backup, or any support to the struggling police platoon. And it was within his means to have ordered DCP S.K. Singh to divert his armed unit to Pereira. He chose not to.

Jatav had arrived on the spot—or the outer edge of the spot—but stopped short of driving up those extra few hundred yards right to the scene of confrontation outside the gurdwara. What had he come for? In plain policing terms he should have taken the lead in stopping the violence on the scene right before him; he had come close enough to spot it from some distance. He left without ever being confronted with serious questions that arose over what he did or not do at Sis Ganj—or elsewhere for that matter. The confrontation at Sis Ganj had been by far the most dangerous in the north district. Far more was at stake here than anywhere else. The attack on Sis Ganj was controlled—just about. At too many other places it was not. Scores of other gurdwaras were attacked, scores within killed.

~

SS: What was going on beyond Sis Ganj?

MP: I was kept busy in the district because there were things happening in Azadpur, there were things happening in Gulabi Bagh, and in Jahangirpuri. There were officers deployed, and I was giving directions on wireless to them. Reports were coming that people and places are being burnt, that kerosene is being poured at places, and I was just screaming on the wireless all the time, saying what are you doing, why are you not acting, saying I don't want commentaries, I was saying open fire, just open fire and stop this carnage. We were going berserk trying to keep things under control.

SS: And this was happening all over Delhi.

MP: I wasn't bothered what was happening elsewhere, I had no clue, I was bothered about my district, and trying my best, within the resources available, to control the situation and keep the situation calm within the limits of our resources.

SS: What were the challenging situations other than Sis Ganj?

MP: There was the case of my ACP at Ashok Vihar (Mahabir Singh). He was telling me he is seeing two Sikhs being caught, then he told me they are pouring kerosene over them, that now they have set them on fire ... he was giving a running commentary on the wireless. I remember screaming at him, asking him, what are you doing giving me commentaries. Just open fire.

SS: We know what happened at Sis Ganj in the north district—or what did not happen as a result of the action you led. But elsewhere in the north district, were the casualties relatively low, were things fairly well under control?

MP: I can't claim that because for me the trauma was not from what we did, the trauma was because the Sabzi Mandi morgue was in my area. I remember visiting the Sabzi Mandi morgue and seeing a mountain of bodies. There was nothing anybody could do about it. Half-burnt, fully burnt bodies piled one on top of the other. Bodies were coming all along, there were vehicles coming from Punjab discarding bodies all along the GT Karnal Road, there were bodies being recovered by us, there were bodies being thrown out of trains that were coming in, people were killed and thrown on to the apple trucks coming from Himachal Pradesh.

SS: Did some of your other officers take action?

MP: Yes, there was Darshan Lal Kashyap, my ACP in Kingsway Camp, in Jahangirpuri, an affected area; and in Gulabi Bagh my then ACP Raghubir Singh—he opened fire, Kashyap opened fire. These were all people who really worked. It didn't matter who worked, it mattered very much where people didn't work. I knew there were things happening elsewhere in the district, and you can't blame me for expecting the district chief, the DCP monitoring the situation ... and things like that. I'm sure he will be able to tell you more about it, and I'm sure he had done his bit in his own way.

SS: In Gulabi Bagh and Kingsway Camp, were there casualties in the firing?

MP: I expect so. When so many officers were in the middle of so much action, it is difficult to have tracked every incident, there were no accompanying scribes with the law enforcers, like in the Mughal era when they used to accompany people sent out to deal with such situations, who recorded what was happening. We don't have that kind of arrangement. Everything is after the event, and if there were records, they would come after a lapse of hours, and sometimes days. It was all on a colossal scale. It's easy to blame the police, but at some places what could the police do when things had gone out of control?

SS: Were there follow-up processes later?

MP: Who was there to record what was happening? There was total chaos about registration of cases—in 90 per cent of cases I found later that all sorts of things had just been clubbed. As the records go, there was, for example, just some event in Trilokpuri. The event was recorded in one FIR, and all bodies found there form part of that one FIR.

SS: So there just were no records from which to investigate?

MP: You can do any amount of this post-mortem of events and wanting justice to be done, but there is no record, no evidence, just hearsay; you have eyewitnesses coming forward but no evidence of such things being recorded. That is a problem in real-time investigation. I would like to believe there would be many officers who tried to do their duty—and many under me in the north district did do their duty—I'm sure there were people not able to do their duty, and were dumbfounded. Whatever could be done was done and I'm quite proud of my staff that rallied around me, and so we did whatever we could.

SS: Is a lot still not recorded, still not known?

MP: I would expect things to be known because there have been so many commissions of inquiry, there were so many investigation teams to go into details and recording of events. There was a riot cell of the Delhi Police which was created after the riots, there are eminent officers who have headed this riot cell, and they have struggled to put together a record of all that happened, to put incidents in perspective, categorize them differently and what not.

SS: But it wouldn't help for them to be men of integrity when the data was poor, when they ran into those gaps in the whole process.

MP: Absolutely. That is why you normally never allow any gaps in recording events. Every time there is any kind of delay in reporting, there is a problem. Questions like when an incident took place, when was it reported. These are pertinent matters in all investigations.

SS: Are we saying that police records do not cover all the deaths that took place?

MP: I have no means of knowing, I cannot really speak about that. Given the magnitude of the calamity, I would expect there would be any number of people who went unidentified. Who would have been able to identify bodies that were all along the Burari belt? Unless people came searching for them, practically most bodies, by the time they were recovered from different places and what not, were rotten. The stench of death is the worst, and this was worse than that.

SS: Bodies could have been lying for days before they were recovered?

MP: They could have been, and there were some definitely. We suffered the consequences of bodies in the north district. They could have come from anywhere along the road or railway route, they could have come from anywhere on the GT Karnal Road and landed in Delhi. There were bodies in cars from Haryana and Punjab, and were discarded in Delhi. At that time, areas like Burari were only sparsely populated. Often the bodies of people murdered outside the area, even in Punjab, would be found there. It was a known dumping ground for bodies.

SS: Were there post-mortems or autopsies?

MP: There were. Normally the police morgue attached to the hospital would have two or three teams. I have no clue what they did or what they didn't do, and how they managed the bodies.

SS: Were investigations launched? Or after the bodies were disposed of, were the investigations just dropped?

MP: I can only say this much: whatever we could record, we did. If we had picked up a body, we did record that we had picked up a body. And whether it was identified, and how it was disposed of later. If you recall, immediately after the riots, I was sent [off] as DCP South. I'm sure the north district people took over and they would have done all this. My knowledge of the after-action is not so full, because I moved on to south district thereafter.

SS: Whether north or south, was there no follow-up action based on the bodies found, over how the victim was killed, who this person was, whether there were witnesses and all that? Did such investigation take place?

MP: I'm sure that was wanting because many persons may have gone as unidentified. By that time the riot cell had been formed. This was a specialized investigating agency only to investigate the riot cases; every single thing that was on record was being passed on to the riot cell, and there was a lot of staff given to them. They were doing documentation, categorizations, trying to streamline the different information, gathering the detail needed to conduct investigation. The investigation unit was opened up, and I'm sure someone there would be in a better position to answer this because I cannot speculate and answer for things I do not really know.

~

A final comment. Here was yet more evidence of the police not taking action down the line from prevention to investigation. And we have this from the direct experience of the most effective police officer in Delhi at the time. The flipside of this officer doing the right thing presented itself as the picture of what other officers were not doing. Pereira was directing police action over the wireless, he was giving orders to open fire where necessary, and under the circumstances it had of course become necessary. Pereira was doing the exceptional; it should never have been exceptional, it's the sort of thing the other officers should have been doing, and so glaringly did not.

The police were not taking action everywhere but they could, and should have, on the basis of information and updates pouring into the wireless network; it appears from these communications that many police officers waited for directions that did not come. A very few acted without word from the very top, as did Pereira, but a lot simply seemed unsure what would be acceptable to do, how far it might be forgiven to act without orders.

By law and by requirement, no policeman needs orders 'from above' to stop a crowd burning a man to death before his eyes. But it appears that in most places in the city, an unsure force was waiting for what they would recognize as firm orders to stop the violence, and such orders did not come. Too many officers did not act on their own.

In the south, east and west police districts, no record arises of the district police chiefs directing effective action to match the gravity and extent of the reports coming in. Many officers from the Delhi Police, too many, have got away with culpable silence covering criminal inaction.

The police records themselves were limited—they would be if the ones responsible for taking action that they didn't were the ones responsible also for creating those records. One would lead inevitably to the other; it was hardly likely that the police would decide not to police, and then create an accurate record of the precise ways in which they failed. The police record is a record of gaps, and their failure corresponded largely to the gaps in the records. When the police took no action, they simultaneously did all they could to ensure no action could be taken against them later.

Rather oddly, Pereira compares the failure in police recording in 1984 wistfully with what he thought were better record-keeping practices in Mughal times, centuries earlier. Was Delhi in the late twentieth century, with its wireless network and all, behind Mughal times in its record-keeping practices?

The Mughal tradition of policing is not as distant from the present set-up as we might be tempted to believe. Some of the police recordkeeping practices to this day go back to Mughal times, and these practices can still work very well. At the heart of record keeping is the 'roznamcha', the daily diary, in which a police station records all incidents in its knowledge. The roznamcha system seems to have worked effectively through Mughal times, and for the British administration to retain intact later in its policing set-up, and it continues to this day.

These records in the roznamcha are meant to be studied to determine what incidents reported and recorded amount to which crimes under particular sections of law. That would then lead on to cases being registered, investigated and prosecuted. The first step is intended to turn knowledge into record; the second to make that record the launchpad for investigation and prosecution by way of the first information reports. In practice, of course all steps get corrupted: what may be known may not be recorded; what is then recorded might not then be registered as a case, what may get registered is often not investigated, and where investigations come, they often fail to gather sufficient evidence to lead to successful prosecution.

A record can for a start be as good only as the police force creating the record. The fact—and recorded fact—is that policing standards in Delhi those three days collapsed well below even the usually corrupt, and very far below mediaeval ways. The Mughal practice of sending scribes with active policing forces to return with their account to record in the roznamcha could potentially have created a fuller record than all the wireless-fed information in Delhi did those three days.

It might even have been quicker: a police scribe could return and record what he had seen at the end of the same day. In Delhi in 1984, several days passed, with no record to match the extent of the carnage. Once days passed, recording itself was abandoned. If you would go only by the sparse cases the Delhi Police registered, nothing very much happened in Delhi at all to match what we later discovered had. Within police communication, the cases registered were few in relation to the roznamcha entries, and those in turn were a fraction of the information floating about over the wireless and coming to the police from the public. This mismatch between communication and the cases that should have arisen as a consequence of the communication, that Ved Marwah noted in his inquiry, was colossal. As big as the injustice that inevitably followed.

Remarkably, that failure has also been caught out through the very process that created it. In the face of the gaps between police recording and police knowledge, the failure to create a record for the purpose of prosecution is itself a matter of record. Because there is one record of what the police knew and a separate record of what they did—or failed to do. This mismatch of itself sets up a basis for investigation with prosecution to follow.

Police cells were set up to investigate precisely this. But once the records they gathered were transferred to commissions of inquiry, they became material for some judge to take a view on—not facts for the police to act upon. In the end, cases of murder were not investigated because they only were cases of murder, not registered cases of murder.

Observations made at the end of commissions of inquiries mattered little. What those commissions eventually pronounced to be laxity was in law criminality. That criminality was prosecuted neither by the inquiry commissions nor by the police.

9

Central Steps

A simple statistic tells a story and asks a question. Hundreds of instances of assault on Sikhs and on their homes and businesses erupted in the central district area of Delhi Police, but all this led to only about twenty Sikhs killed. Twenty can never be only—one is one too many. But in one of the six police districts that Delhi was divided into, it is a small figure seen against the killings across the city that added up to about 3,000. The district managed to survive assaults but avoided large-scale killings. Something got done here that was right, or at least substantially right.

The DCP heading central district then was Amod Kanth. He was the officer I had run into at the Karol Bagh police station who stood up for his juniors against a Congress MP and implicitly against his own boss after the local police had hauled up looters. The looters had turned out to be members of the Congress party, for whose release Congress MP Dharam Dass Shastri had turned up at the police station along with other local Congress leaders.

That incident erupted a couple of days after the killings were over. But Kanth told me, in the course of a chat at his office in Prayas, a charity for children he has set up close to Tughlakabad in south Delhi, that he had seen the Congress hand much earlier, and that the violence had begun only after local Congress leaders gathered to organize it late on the night on 31 October.

Kanth set up that charity in 1988, late in his career as police officer, and now manages it full-time. We had talked about those killings in the days and weeks following the violence, but in January 2014 when 117 we spoke I was hearing more than I'd heard earlier Kanth speak about how the police prepared to deal with the aftermath of the assassination— and how local Congress leaders prepared.

Well after leaving the police service, Amod Kanth, I gathered, contested the Delhi elections in 2008 on a Congress party ticket. My conversation with him did not extend into his position in politics that came much later, or his work as social activist. Or even to his years in Delhi Police while I was on the crime beat. Our chat stayed confined to those few days of the attacks on Sikhs immediately after the assassination of Indira Gandhi. Over those days Kanth had been remarkably effective. The record speaks for itself, and Kanth spoke with me of the steps the police took that made that kind of record possible.

'The first thing I did when I reached office on the morning of 31 October was to organize a meeting of all officers,' he said. 'To my mind, to my imagination, to my fear, I thought we were going to face one of the worst times the country had known. The thought came to my mind that we might have a civil war. I called the police officers, I called the Home Guards who were attached to me, I called the civil defence officials immediately. By the time news of the assassination began to be displayed in the press area on Bahadur Shah Zafar Marg, I had already held a meeting.'

The press area he spoke of was Bahadur Shah Zafar Marg where *The Indian Express*, *The Times of India* and other newspapers had their offices, next door to the central district DCP's office in Daryaganj. The newspaper offices had a 'Spot News' board outside to display the headlines of the moment. A peon accompanied by a sub-editor would step up to the wooden board carrying slates of letters, Scrabble-like in a bag. These would then be slotted in by hand to add up to a headline for a passer-by.

The potentially quicker way of getting news would be All India Radio. But that was a government mouthpiece, and it could be notoriously slow (it was only by the evening of 31 October that it announced Mrs Gandhi had been killed). A newspaper copy would turn up at homes only in the mornings, and that made these Spot News boards about the quickest way of bringing news—but only to anyone who happened to be passing by on that road. In Delhi two others such boards had been set up outside the offices of *The Statesman* and the *Hindustan Times* in Connaught Place. People taking Bahadur Shah Zafar Marg or driving through Connaught Place became the most privileged in Delhi, in the news sense: they would invariably be the first to know the latest. Bus passengers on the wrong side would peer past other passengers to read these boards to assume the status of some of the best informed people in India at that moment. It was these few who learnt first that morning of Mrs Gandhi's death.

Those boards had announced fairly early that morning that she had been shot, and updated the news early afternoon that she had been killed. I myself was keeping *The Indian Express* office informed; the office was getting inputs also from the United News of India (UNI) and the Press Trust of India (PTI) news agencies. *The Indian Express* also produced a hasty sheet with the news, a supplement as it was called. Distribution of this supplement went only as far as the crowds that began to gather outside these boards to stop for the latest.

It was that morning that Kanth said a meeting had been called at the DCP's office next door in Daryaganj just as the first update on the Spot News board was announcing Mrs Gandhi had been shot.

'There were more than 100 people at the meeting,' Kanth said, 'This included some members of the public too, because the civil defence is constituted of important public figures. I talked to all of them, and I said that we are going to face one of the most difficult times in the city of Delhi. I said that there would be riots, and serious riots. I was fully convinced that this was going to happen.

'By about lunch time the information started spreading. We also learnt that a crowd had started gathering at the All India Institute of Medical Sciences. A crowd had begun to gather even before that at Bahadur Shah Zafar Marg in my area (around the Spot News boards), and they were getting restive. I said to the officers that let's prepare for anything that may happen. Towards evening, the situation began to get grim. There were no riots, but small skirmishes had broken out at some places in south Delhi, and at some places in my area also. But then those were very small.

'At that time this is what was going on, and I thought we could contain it. No big riots had begun. Not until 11 p.m. or a little later. The riots started later. I had to concentrate myself on my district because there was no meeting as such at the police headquarters, there was no direction from the police headquarters. That would have been where all DCPs were called, and discussions took place, and a plan of action drawn up. This kind of thought, which was coming to my mind, was probably not coming to the minds of others, they were not thinking along those lines.'

~

Pause a moment to reflect on just this stark fact. A district police team could see the trouble coming, and begin preparing for it straightaway, but the police headquarters made no such move, they were not 'thinking along those lines'. The facts were not such as to set off apprehension only in the central district; that district had no particular relation to the assassination. The top brass of Delhi Police was the one set of people who could have made a difference, who could have contained the anticipated unrest, and whose job it was to do so.

The central district had no freak premonition of trouble: anyone could see then that a degree of violence was likely, even if no one could ever have thought so many might be murdered. Fear of what might come was in the air, you could feel it. And if everyone could see it coming, surely the police officers in charge of law and order in the city could.

So much that proved lethal through those days of the killings in 1984 was what did not happen, what did not get done. The top police officers made no move to do the obvious that an officer was doing within just a district. As Kanth said, it would have been normal—had the top police officers wanted normal policing—to call a meeting at the police headquarters early to prepare against imminent trouble ahead, to draw up a coordinated plan for prevention of incidents and for dealing with them. And even more, to then communicate such a plan, and such an intention, clearly to the force. A half-hour meeting, an order on the wireless, would have gone a long way. The signal would have been clear: that some people might feel provoked but that lawlessness would not be tolerated.

Instead, the police headquarters was in shutdown mode. Closed to the police, closed to the public. Too many could not get through on the emergency number controlled at the headquarters. Calls couldn't come in, directions were not going out. Like Maxwell Pereira in the north district, Kanth too found no direction from the police headquarters. And these were officers looking for directions, they were out to do what they could to contain the attacks.

That failure to call such a meeting became of itself a message. A refusal to take extraordinary preventive steps, and to be seen to be so doing, was interpreted through the police force to mean that their leadership was less than keen to limit violence that would naturally be aimed at Sikhs.

No doubt every officer could produce some sort of record of some sort of meeting held. What counted was not naturally the mere holding of a meeting, but such a meeting as signalling will, and then producing a plan for substantive steps on the ground. Kanth was the top officer of the central district, and his orders could become effective right across the district. That was more than Maxwell Pereira could do in the north district. He was the number two man in that district force, he could do little more than his personal heroism would allow, or at most some limited intervention as the number two because the top man was not offering the district force the leadership it would need to fight the violence.

A sense of danger gripped us all. Kanth's fear of civil war might appear in retrospect an overstatement. It wasn't. Everyone in the city, if not in the country, was fearing some such thing. I certainly thought then, for the first, and fortunately the only time yet, that India was collapsing into chaos and might even fall apart. The very air was implosive. Normal living stood suspended for just about everyone. No one I knew did any of those things people do in normal times, like going to a party or to the cinema or even just hanging around talking about this and that. A political pall hung heavy over us.

My own fears were no different than everyone else's I spoke with. Who could ever think of an India without Sikhs within it and on its side? Whether Sikhs would stay that way was the first political thought on people's minds, it became the first and usually the only point of conversation. The fallout of an internal government conflict with Sikhs had gripped the country. Within the police, Kanth could hardly have been the only officer to think of civil war. Whatever anyone thought, there was nothing wrong in preparing for the worst.

That meeting in the central police district on the morning of 31 October was inspired by fear of a breakdown of a magnitude far beyond some mere district-level unrest. But to control the streets of Delhi those days would be to get a grip on India itself—no less. All eyes appeared to be on Delhi, certainly Punjab's eyes were on Delhi. That was the bold political underlining to the need for the police to keep peace those days, beyond the standard responsibility of maintaining law and order at all times.

In the paradox of the day, far-sighted political needs required short-sighted policing at street level. Given order on the streets, or even minimized disorder in the face of visibly firm policing, the politics would perhaps have a civilized mess to deal with, not mass murders. The police needed those days to be near-sighted in their actions if not in their awareness, to look no further than the streets under their charge, and to keep them quiet. Officers who failed to do this, and far too many failed, and who did not as much as try to succeed, were obviously failing innocent citizens it was their duty to protect. They were also failing India, and the very idea of India of holding everyone together. They were doing a very good job of rivalling Bhindranwale in rocking a shaken edifice.

~

Through the day on 31 October, not a lot arose for the police to deal with that looked serious. Scuffles and small incidents were reported here and there. These surfaced as isolated expressions of anger with an aggressive thrust—nobody was yet seeing signs of methodical murders.

'Then something happened which was really disturbing,' Kanth said. 'Some of the small leaders—and some of them from the CongressI, yes—started moving around. And then, small meetings in groups started taking place.'

These meetings began, he told me, close to midnight. The time when one might think people would be home and call it a day, especially after a day as traumatic as that. But it was at that time that reports came in to the police that these small groups had begun to gather, brought together by local leaders. The Congress party was showing its hand—the local police would hardly fail to have spotted the ruling party leaders in their area.

About the same time that night came another development—that I too witnessed around my home in Malviya Nagar in the south district. Delhi's water supply, we were being warned, had been poisoned by Sikhs. Here's our brief chat at this point:

> AK: Information started spreading, nefarious information, about 11.30 to twelve at night, that Sikhs had poisoned water tanks. I spoke to the municipal commissioner, I spoke to other senior officers, I was countering this. In fact, while I was on the move through the district that night in the walled city, Karol Bagh and other areas, this rumour was being spread deliberately. The point of this rumour was to suggest that Sikhs were becoming aggressive. On one hand there was a strong feeling developing against Sikhs, and then such rumour was being spread of poisoning of water tanks. Secondly, information was being spread about concentration of Sikhs in some gurdwaras, and that they were armed.
>
> SS: Who was spreading such information?
>
> AK: It was those small leaders of the area who were on the move. There is nothing wrong in being on the move, but the move was not to create a peaceful situation but to … you get the point. That was the kind of situation that was building up. It was at this time that small fights started. Then the bigger

fights started. I heard of problems starting simultaneously in many parts of my area, particularly in the walled city.

SS: What were these problems?

AK: That Sikhs were being attacked. People began gathering, in hundreds. And leaders from the Congress were addressing these assemblies at some places. And these kinds of gatherings started moving ominously. We were trying to protect Sikhs.

SS: Could the top party leaders have restrained their own local leaders?

AK: The leaders should have contained them in the interest of law and order. They did not do so. The leaders did not come out to contain them.

SS: You speak of community leaders. Did a lot of them happen to be Congress leaders?

AK: Obviously. Many of them would be Congress [leaders] for the simple reason that the issue was with regard to their leader. Today you will find some of them no longer in Congress also. I say this as someone who knows the city.

SS: A lot of the resettlement colonies, where the attackers came from, have been Congress vote banks traditionally.

AK: That's a fact. And they became active in those times.

~

After all these years, we have this DCP of a police district spell out clearly that it was local Congress leaders who were in the forefront of the gathering crowds that unleashed the violence. The fact emerges, starkly, that it was local Congress leaders who led the targeting of Sikhs, unrestrained by their seniors. There comes a point, and it comes early, past which the top leadership cannot dissociate themselves and the party itself from its members and workers. The top party leaders did nothing to restrain these local party men—even if you would accept that they did not signal lead. Scattered party men carried the culpability of killing, the top leadership the culpability of choosing not to stop them. At the same time, the Congress party was seen to bring no decisive leadership to bear on the police to prevent bloodshed.

Some particular facts arise from Kanth's account: one, that all day on 31 October, late into the night, till about 11 p.m. or so, only shows of annoyance had been evident here and there; scuffles and skirmishes, that's all. In the rawest period of provocation, through the whole day after the assassination was announced, and all through the evening after the news had spread, violence came by way of incidents scattered, isolated and minor. This was so all over Delhi, not just in the central district. The gravest incidents on 31 October were reported outside of the All India Institute of Medical Sciences where Indira Gandhi had been taken and declared dead. These incidents too were well short of murders.

It had been a long and traumatic day for everyone. People had struggled to put an end to it and get home. Delhi's streets would go quiet about 11 p.m., the city then offered few places open late in the night. Many millions in Delhi were back home, and stayed there.

So far so spontaneous, and so far so minor. The disturbing development Kanth spoke of came when groups of local leaders—he named the Congress—began to gather people about them. Congress workers had obviously been called together by their leaders—they could hardly all have just happened to run into one another on the streets in the middle of the night after a long day.

It was after these coordinated and organized groups began to gather that the attacks really began, and as Kanth said they began simultaneously. And they did not seem to have begun at places other than those where these groups had gathered—no reports anywhere, then or later, that just plain residents stepped out into some midnight meetings to then launch attacks.

Nor was the Congress hand hidden; party leaders had taken to the streets and begun gathering their men about them quite openly. It is a matter of record that these very crowds turned violent. Where they found the opportunity, they attacked. Where they couldn't, they merely looted.

The simultaneous gatherings, followed by simultaneous attacks, could not have been but organized. Nor the water poisoning rumour that was spread at the same time by those men. That rumour could hardly have come coincidentally where Kanth heard it in his district, where I heard it in Malviya Nagar a dozen miles south, and in scores of areas all over the city.

I had only just reached home about 2 a.m. or so when I heard a voice blaring out on a loudspeaker outside my house. Someone in a van driving along the road that separates Malviya Nagar from Panchsheel Park was warning us over a loudspeaker mounted on its roof against drinking water. The voice blared out that Sikhs had poisoned the water.

Many of my neighbours came out, everyone got talking about this, as they would. None immediately thought it the lie it later turned out to be. Everyone was scared that Sikhs were out to kill the rest. The water never was poisoned by Sikhs, but certainly the air had been poisoned by those spreading that rumour. In that charged atmosphere of those days, nobody thought such a rumour to be immediately impossible.

Who was making these announcements? Just some well-meaning people? How would they all come to know at once of a danger that did not exist? How would they all know of the same fictionalized danger in the middle of the night and set out to warn people all over the city? This communication was carefully coordinated—the simultaneous lies through the city that night could never have been broadcast otherwise. Kanth said the municipality was conveying denials that any such thing had happened, but in the middle of the night how would they communicate this? Only by the following morning was the lie countered through clarifications. Meanwhile that well-resourced lie had given the city a sleepless night and raised either some new fear of the Sikhs—or provoked aggression against them.

The organization behind the lie had ensured the means to deliver the same lie everywhere. It had found the means to acquire vehicles equipped with loudspeakers right around the city at very short notice— loudspeakers of the kind used at election rallies. Just plain people don't own such loudspeakers: it is political party workers who have them or know where to get them—through known stocks, familiar stores, or from party offices.

For some time, the poison move worked. That night and the next morning, every neighbour I ran into spoke of imminent attacks by Sikhs. I had heard that other cousinly rumour too in my neighbourhood that Kanth had spoken of in his area, that armed Sikhs had barricaded themselves inside gurdwaras, and were preparing to launch attacks. It was the kind of lie that could so easily be believed. People had by then seen terror attacks one after another originating from Punjab over the previous three years. Images of armed Sikh groups occupying the Golden Temple before Operation Blue Star had lodged themselves in people's minds; now that Indira Gandhi had been killed, many seemed ready to believe there must be something in these warnings.

Fears arose, suspicions soared—but no more. The rumours failed to turn the people of Delhi against their Sikh neighbours. Mass killings came at some places, carried out by particular groups that none among those who were targeted and who survived described as their neighbours. This was all very different from neighbours turning upon Sikhs down their street.

The pattern emerging through that night was clear—organized provocation followed by systematic killing. The organized attacks came after three developments surfaced almost simultaneously around the midnight of 31 October—when Congress-I groups began to gather, when rumours against Sikhs began to spread, and when the police then retreated from the streets.

In the central district, the police did not withdraw from the streets. The picture of just ordinary policing throughout that district, and not only by its top officers, is the most potent evidence on record of what the police could have done to counter violence had they been given the right signal.

~

And what signals came on the morning of 1 November? At last there was word from the police headquarters. And what was this order? That Sikh police officers should be disarmed and taken off duty.

Accordingly they were, across much of Delhi. In the north district, after an evening of remarkably effective management of riotous crowds, ACP Keval Singh and the Sikh SHO of Sabzi Mandi were among Sikh officers ordered off duty. Those orders went out right across the police force. It would be an order dangerous to enforce, and risky to ignore. The central district did not enforce it.

> AK: We got an order that became a matter of immediate concern. On the morning of 1 November, we had some sort of direction from police headquarters that Sikh officers should lay down their arms.

SS: What do we mean by some sort of direction? Was it a hint or an order?

AK: It was almost a clear direction, it came also on the wireless from police headquarters, that Sikh officers should not come out on the streets. The idea was that they should not be on duty. I contested this.

SS: This kind of order could have come ultimately only from the commissioner of police.

AK: Yes. That is correct. It came from the police headquarters. But there was a group of officers there. Mr Nikhil Kumar was there, he was a very important person. Mr Nikhil Kumar had been transferred out. But he was manning the police control room. And then among the senior people Mr H.C. Jatav was there, then Mr Gautam Kaul was there who was generally busy in his own area (he was additional commissioner of police, New Delhi range, that covered three police districts—New Delhi, south and west).

There were these loose and disorganized instructions coming in that I contested. Some of my best officers were Sikhs, and we had so many. The SHO Patel Nagar, SHO Rajender Nagar, ACP Daryaganj, these were all Sikhs. I told my Sikh officers, 'I will protect you, and you will be with me. You will not leave. Because if you leave today, tomorrow you cannot stand. This is a test for you.' And they did not leave. I had some serious problems, but I could manage those.

SS: What were these serious problems?

AK: Attacks. Whenever they came out with me, they were being attacked. I recall the face of Ajmer Singh Chauhan, a towering personality, a 6' 2" man, you remember (I knew Chauhan), he was in charge of the place where the cremation

> [of Indira Gandhi] took place, he was ACP Daryaganj. Some prohibitory orders were issued, but those nobody listened to. I was with him, and people started pelting stones at him. But Ajmer did not leave.

~

In issuing those orders were the police bosses out to save Sikh officers from angry crowds? That is certainly what they later argued. But no orders were issued to then protect these Sikh officers from the crowds. The orders from police headquarters had been to disarm Sikh officers. If protection of these Sikh officers was the prime concern of the police bosses, disarming them should have been about the last order to be given. The order would leave Sikh officers defenceless against attack. Not what you'd call a measure to protect them.

The message from the police headquarters was not that Sikh officers were at risk and that the rest of the police force must protect them. The orders seemed to point to Sikh officers as the risk—not to Sikh officers at risk. And the orders came from the very top of the chain of police officers in command in Delhi.

Some Sikh policemen were no doubt attacked in close scuffles on the streets, but these were not lone Sikhs abandoned to violent mobs. These were police officers, they had a police force with them, they had means with them to handle this anger aimed at them, and they did.

It's instructive to follow the tracks of a couple of Sikh inspectors through those days, as recorded by the central district police. As word of the assassination spread on 31 October, Inspector Hardeep Singh, then SHO of Rajender Nagar, led extensive patrolling of his area and kept it quiet. The big challenge came the next day when reports came in of a crowd heading to attack a gurdwara in

Inder Puri, a slum-like resettlement area close to Rajender Nagar. Hardeep Singh led a police force to confront the crowd, and dispersed them with a cane charge.

Soon, reports came that a gurdwara nearby had been surrounded, with hundreds of Sikhs trapped inside. He then rushed there, and with the help of the locally posted Sikh sub-inspector, Babu Singh, dispersed that crowd as well. Sikhs inside the gurdwara were rescued.

Inspector Hardeep Singh suffered head injuries and injuries to one arm in those confrontations. He was taken to Dr Ram Manohar Lohia Hospital near Connaught Place along with his driver Ved Prakash, who had also been injured. The injuries were not serious, he was discharged. He came straight back to his area to scatter gathering crowds out to target Sikhs.

Or consider the track record of Inspector Amrik Singh, the Sikh SHO in charge of Patel Nagar. As recorded by the police, he led his team into the Anand Parbat industrial area close to Patel Nagar and fired into the air to disperse groups trying to burn down Sikh-owned factories. Some from this crowd dared later to surround the police station itself. Amrik Singh returned and dispersed this lot as well. Such confrontations continued all day on 1 November, and records show he fired into the air more than once to scatter the crowds.

In the course of one such confrontation, he was attacked. Following that, DCP Kanth gave him the option of staying indoors. But Amrik Singh was back on duty within an hour of facing the attack, and by 5 p.m. that day he was again leading his force in dispersing a crowd building up on Military Road within his area that had been setting fire to houses and shops. He is reported to have led the rescue of more than 600 Sikh men, women and children.

Orders had come that morning to disarm Sikh officers and to take them off active duty. But that very day these Sikh officers were deployed, and they were deployed effectively.

The central district saw several cases of firing by trapped Sikhs, in self-defence, desperation or anger. Usually these were Sikh officers from the armed forces who had service revolvers with them. In one instance, Group Captain Manmohan Singh fired on a crowd from his house in Patel Nagar area. Three persons in the crowd were killed, this provoked the crowds more, and a confrontation built up. Inspector Amrik Singh rushed there with his force and joined the DCP in keeping the crowd back. Group Captain Manmohan Singh was taken into custody. Later that evening Amrik Singh led his small force in challenging a crowd building up at a bus stop near Guru Arjun Nagar within his area.

Inspector Hardeep Singh from Rajender Nagar too had had to deal with firing by Sikhs. The house of Kripal Singh had been surrounded by a mob in Inder Puri. Jagjeet Singh Chawla, who had a licensed gun, opened fire into the crowd from within, killing five men in the crowd, and injuring about ten. Inspector Hardeep Singh was deployed, and he assisted the DCP both in keeping the crowd back and taking Chawla into custody.

Despite the injuries suffered, Sikh officers out on the street managed to contain threatening crowds, and going by both local and police accounts, saved hundreds of lives. These were officers who knew their areas, and were therefore simply the best men for the job at the time. At no stage were non-Sikh policemen in the force disloyal; in the end it mattered little whether they were Sikh or not.

~

The central district demonstrated far more than the effective role Sikh officers could play out on the street even at such a time. The district force demonstrated that had instructions been given to police firmly, just a handful of even very junior policemen could have scattered away those bands of killers and looters on the loose. These groups indulged in criminality where they had the police on their side; where the police actually policed, they disappeared.

Inspector Ranbir Singh, SHO Karol Bagh (not a Sikh), lives on as a legend among Sikhs in the area for keeping looters away and for keeping Sikhs in his area safe. He was the inspector who later rounded up looters that turned out to be Congress party men, for whose release party MP Dharam Dass Shastri then came to the Karol Bagh police station. He had done a great deal earlier to save one of the richest streets in Delhi where a very large number of the businesses were owned by Sikhs.

Within hours of the assassination he had mobilized all the men he could within his police station, and deployed pickets in the shopping area and at local gurdwaras. The day of the assassination passed without incident. The next day instances arose all over of Sikhs being attacked. A mob gathered to attack Ajmal Khan Road, the weddingshopping street of Delhi. Ranbir Singh dispersed that crowd; he had to rush there on foot because his police jeep ran into engine trouble. Hardly a Sikh shop was attacked in Karol Bagh, and this, said Kanth in his police report at the time, was 'entirely due to him'.

These junior officers had demonstrated what was possible—and possible with far from insurmountable difficulties. Those small bands of looters showed themselves invariably to be a cowardly lot when they were confronted. A show of police force, even a show of police intent, and they would vanish. The few policemen who did confront those bands of men demonstrated the paralysis of the rest of the force.

Opening fire, and killing too, can actually save lives in such a situation. We saw that when Maxwell Pereira opened fire outside

Sis Ganj gurdwara. Inspector Ranbir Singh did so in Karol Bagh area. Rioters had descended on a Sikh-owned batteries shop and set it on fire on Abdul Rehman Road. Firing was ordered, and one of the rioters, a man by the name of Hukum Chand, was killed. But that firing ended the rioting, and saved potentially scores of Sikh lives.

Another group had advanced to loot jewellery shops on Bank Street, and here Ranbir Singh opened fire with just one assistant subinspector by his side. That was enough to send the looters running. The inspector saved all the markets in his area. This he did, Kanth's report noted, 'with practically no force at his command'. All twentyfour market associations of the area wrote a 'thank you' letter later to the local police—something quite unusual.

A simple but clear signal that the police must maintain the law and policemen stepped beyond normal limits to become dramatically effective. An inspector from the reserve police force in the central area, Jagpravesh Chandra, set out with a few men to control crowds without waiting for orders. His mission took him to the local tyre market to stop further loot—those days a tyre saved could mean a life saved. He prevented loot in Paharganj, firing four rounds in the air to save a group of besieged Sikhs in one building.

Officers far junior to inspectors, just one or two of them, were enough for those crowds. Sub-inspector Ram Singh stepped out of his police post at Prasad Nagar close to Patel Nagar in central Delhi to rescue a Sikh family. He fired in the air to scare a circling crowd away—without waiting for orders from above. He did not need such orders under the law. The claim by some that they had no orders was an excuse without basis in law, though firm orders from above would undoubtedly have helped.

Sub-inspector Dharam Pal almost single-handedly confronted the crowd descending on the industrial area in Anand Parbat at one point. Just one sub-inspector kept hundreds of those advancing looters back. And yet across almost all other districts, policemen and police officers sat in their police stations, kept track of all that was going on all around them, and did nothing. And, in not doing, in effect enabled loot and murder.

These unsung policemen created, in their own way, possibly the most telling record then for the police and the Congress government of the day; their actions came as evidence that the police did not have to be overwhelmed by the crowds even if the imbalance was something like a couple of policemen before a crowd of hundreds. The mass killings came in areas where the police demonstrably did nothing to stop the killing or encouraged it.

~

SS: So it was possible to control those crowds?

AK: This is the point I'm trying to make. Sikhs were attacked, yet the situation was controlled.

SS: How many such situations erupted in your district that were then controlled?

AK: I think not less than hundred in a matter of two days. What happened in some areas like east Delhi and west Delhi that you saw, and your colleagues saw, was never allowed in my district. The moment we learnt that there was someone to chase, we did. The crowd was not such that you could not chase.

SS: How many Sikh shops were attacked, how many Sikh homes were attacked?

AK: Thousands.

SS: So there were attacks on that scale, but not killings on that scale.

AK: The total number of deaths (in central district) was not very high. A number of Hindus were also killed.

SS: What was the total death toll in your district?

AK: Not more than thirty. That included those who died in firing. In my district, firing and police action also resulted in deaths.

SS: So this is the total number of deaths, including Sikhs being attacked, deaths in some cases of firing by Sikhs, and some cases of police firing?

AK: Yes.

SS: All this added up to about thirty?

AK: Yes.

SS: How many were killed in police firing?

AK: Three or four.

SS: Where?

AK: Paharganj, Patel Nagar.

SS: Were there Sikhs killed in police firing? Or Hindus?

AK: Both. Clashes also took place in which Sikhs opened fire and Hindus were killed.

SS: How many Hindus were killed in such firing?

AK: Eight or ten.

SS: So, a few killed in police firing on crowds, eight or ten killed by cornered Sikhs who were firing, and all this adds up to about thirty?

AK: Yes. The number of deaths in central Delhi was very small, despite all that happened.

SS: What did you do to prevent everything from getting any worse?

AK: You know the tyre market near Filmistan cinema? That tyre market took a lot of my time. All those tyres, you have seen those tyres on the roofs of those shops …

SS: Yes, huge numbers.

AK: Those tyres were taken to burn Sikhs. But in my area we did not allow them to loot those tyres. They were trying, but we went and chased them. As you know tyres were used heavily for surrounding these people and killing them individually. We chased them away, we stopped people [from] taking [away] tyres to be used as a weapon of offence.

SS: Did it help to get the army in later?

AK: The army was deployed. But the behaviour and conduct of the army in containing the crowds was no better than that of the police. The deployment also took place very late. That is a serious complaint that I have.

SS: How late was late?

AK: On 1November, there was no deployment. They were deployed on the evening of 2 November and the next day. When the army did come, and faced [the] crowds, they would not open fire. I am clear on this, and am on record on this.

SS: Was there a pattern to the killing? Khushwant Singh wrote that people of a certain class and from certain neighbourhoods, particularly the resettlement colonies, came out to attack well-off Sikhs. Did you see such a pattern?

AK: This is a fact. It's a very harsh fact, that underprivileged people—I don't wish to name the communities although I know the communities—who were in the neighbourhood of affluent communities invariably came out to attack.

SS: This was a pattern throughout?

AK: This was a pattern throughout. It was a clear pattern, an absolutely clear pattern. The entire Karol Bagh area was attacked by communities in the neighbourhood that were the not-so-rich people. The attackers came from these communities everywhere; you go to Paharganj, there is a community; go to Patel Nagar, there is a community.

In Delhi these now affluent colonies had been refugee colonies from the Partition, they had become established colonies by 1984. These colonies were created by settlers coming from outside in which the number of Sikhs was very high. They became affluent over time. Next to those colonies were those who rendered services. And they set up their own colonies, unauthorized colonies, which belonged to a certain class and community. This is near Patel Nagar, this is near Paharganj, Daryaganj. Inder Puri is a huge area, for instance, near Patel Nagar. There were jhuggi jhopri colonies (hutments), there were resettlement colonies, slums, villages converting into slums, dense and congested colonies. These are the kinds of people and colonies that were underprivileged and poor.

They had the opportunity to attack because Sikhs were there. Even within those colonies they attacked Sikhs. There was a big conflict going on inside Inder Puri. Some casualties took place. We had to tackle this pattern.

SS: What led the Karol Bagh police to make those arrests later?

AK: On the evening of 2 November we had a grip on the situation and we thought we must make recoveries. On 3 November we started making recoveries. We knew who the people were who had taken truckloads of items from the affluent families, from shops.

SS: You knew from the police on the ground, from your own force?

AK: Yes. We were trying to follow it up. We knew to which places the looted items had been taken. We started making recoveries of these. On the morning of 3 November we recovered goods worth Rs 65 lakh. These were items taken to the colonies around Karol Bagh. We had the courage to enter those homes and get [back] the items. We just told them to give back these items, and they started to return some of them.

When the items were brought to the police station that was the time Dharam Dass Shastri came. And not just he, all the Congress leaders of that area came. All of them started demanding from us why we have recovered the items from them. They wanted the items back. We had also arrested these people. It was difficult to apprehend these people, let me clarify. It had appeared almost impossible to apprehend these people in that charged atmosphere. But we still arrested many people.

We arrested these people, we made a case against them. In some houses killings took place. So when you carry items, and killings have taken place, you can make out a (murder) case. Later in the police headquarters, we had a discussion on this with the additional police commissioner, Mr Jatav.

SS: What was that discussion?

AK: The discussion was very clear. I was told that this was premature.

SS: You were told that this was premature action?

AK: That was the general feeling at the police headquarters.

SS: Was the commissioner of police present?

AK: No, the commissioner of police was not there at all. Generally he was not into activities. But then those who were then the important people were there. Generally, they thought that the action that I had led might create more problems. The idea was not to let the police act. The idea was that in a situation that was totally out of control, if you do this, you are creating more problems. The idea was that you are creating a situation by recoveries, by arrests, that the time was not right for that.

But I did it, and we withstood the ground. I think it was proper. After all, when a crime takes place—and we took it [the thefts followed by recoveries] as a crime, we thought each incident was a crime—that crime must be brought into regular FIRs.

SS: Did you have any meeting with Subhash Tandon (the police commissioner)?

AK: We had a couple of discussions.

SS: One on one, or in a group of officers?

AK: One on one also. Mr Tandon came from a background of intelligence operations. He was in the Intelligence Bureau (IB) throughout. He was not a man from public policing, he was not a man from law and order policing. Their approach is different. It is not to contain frontally. Their approach is not to tackle a situation, [but] to investigate and work out. He was of that profile, and he was a gentleman. Where I posed a problem, and wherever I said I am doing something, he said all right, carry on. Unlike the others who had opposed me. The general view was that I am becoming extra proactive. Tandon never stopped me from doing whatever I did.

SS: But isn't there a culture of silent signals? Nobody is going to say actually, actively, don't do this. But people give out non-verbal signals, by way of what they don't say. And if you turn this around, was there any direction from Tandon that you should do something? Or were you acting on your own?

AK: In any situation of law and order, when the police find that it is not able to contain a situation, and the crowd appears to be of the majority, very few police officers will have the courage to counter the majority view. You can't counter it on the ground, you are bound to fail. That was the situation that arose for Delhi Police. Delhi Police did not gather courage or muster resources to counter the situation, which, according to them, was created by the overwhelming majority. And that since they are from the majority, you can't do anything.

But I will not buy the theory that the Delhi Police deliberately and intentionally connived. Or that they actively led in the attacks.

SS: Not actively led, but realizing that this kind of thing may have majority support, that there is a certain environment created, so stand back? Or sit back?

AK: Yes, in some areas.

SS: Was this not an abdication of responsibilities?

AK: In some areas, and probably in outlying areas, this happened more, where the police were in small numbers and could not contain the crowds, they probably decided not to go out and confront. Because with a violent crowd, they have no option but to confront. When the crowd is aggressive, either you try to negotiate with the crowd, and if that does not work, you have to prevent, physically, with lathis, firepower. If you fail, you get injured, I got injured several times. At least 30–40 times I was inside the crowd. I could have been shot; in firing, a person six inches away from me died.

~

That last was a reference to an incident in Paharganj that came a couple of days after the killings were over. An exchange of firing took place involving a group of Sikhs inside a building and the police, along with army men. In that firing, some of the Sikhs within the building were killed, as were some people they had fired upon. A Gurkha soldier from the army who was with the police, and standing close to Kanth at that time, was shot and killed. Kanth did what he could to save the soldier, and was later given a gallantry award by the army for it. The incident dragged Kanth into dispute, some accused him of joining an attack on Sikhs inside that building, and then getting a medal for it. That Kanth had acted against Sikhs was not an accusation I would make; I had seen much the opposite. Whatever I had or hadn't, the record is clear.

Oddly, the two most effective police officers at the time, Maxwell Pereira and Amod Kanth, both told me they thought that they were failing then to handle what had arisen. Maxwell Pereira had saved Sis Ganj but felt he had failed in the face of much else in his district. And so did Kanth—before discovering what failures really were like in some other districts.

'I felt,' Kanth said, 'looking at my own record of containing law and order situations successfully, that I had failed. But when I learnt about [the] other districts, I was aghast. Mine was the one district where we had managed to control things. Of course, it was a riot situation. But it did not go out of control. I thought then that it had gone out of control, I am being very frank, very truthful with you. I thought I had not been able to contain the situation, I thought that I should have. But then the findings around the city were very different.' 'Did it all impact you personally?'

'It had a traumatic effect on me. My whole thought process changed. I was deeply disturbed by this whole chain of incidents. I had never seen anything like this. I was always in the districts, and those were bad times. I consider the 1980s as the most difficult, the most violent time Delhi has known. It has never witnessed again what it had seen in the 1980s.

'I was always in an important position, heading, west, south and then the central districts, and then the crime branch. I handled some of the biggest cases of Delhi Police in those years. But those few days [in 1984] have gone down in my memory, in my psyche, deeply. I can never forget all that happened. I remember every incident, it is a picture, an image settled in my mind. What I was before those few days, what I was afterwards, are two very different men.'

Had the record of the police district, which Kanth headed, been replicated across Delhi, the death toll in Delhi would have been about a hundred. Think of the lives that would have been saved in that scenario. 1984 wouldn't have become what it has; among other things, this book would never have had to be written. And yet Amod Kanth became a much-disliked figure among the Sikh leaders of Delhi.

This sharp unpopularity arose from that incident at Paharganj on 5 November 1984 after most of the killings were over. What rankled clearly was that Amod Kanth was given a gallantry medal over his handling of that incident. Perhaps understandably so. Within days of those thousands of killings, here was a police officer being awarded a gallantry medal for taking on some Sikhs who had fired on a group they had felt threatened by. Whatever the particular circumstances of that day, the award of a medal over such action at such a time was an ugly move from the government. But which police officer refuses a medal that comes his way?

A petition was made to the High Court to strip Kanth of the gallantry award. The court turned down the petition on the grounds that it had no jurisdiction to order such reversal, but not before Justice Muralidhar noted that 'the State ought to display sensitivity to the feelings of the victim community and be circumscept in hastening to award gallantry medals to the officials of the law enforcement machinery soon after the events'.

It isn't Kanth's record in the district that Sikhs look at now, it is that misplaced medal.

10

DETAINING THE POLICE

A few shots were fired into the air on a street in east Delhi the same morning of 1 November that Maxwell Pereira ordered a single shot to be fired into the men gathering to storm Sis Ganj gurdwara. Those shots in the air in east Delhi had a different consequence. They killed nobody; what they killed was a police officer's will to control the violence. Collateral damage came with the message this sent out to other policemen, that violent crowds must not be challenged, let alone stopped.

It took only one shot from a revolver in the end to save Sis Ganj. That shot from Pereira's revolver had killed, but more, it had fired a message that minimally strong action would bring calm to the streets of Delhi. That shot went home to the crowd, and the message that rang out should have gone home to the police. That message simply was that this of all times was a time to open fire, maybe even just in the air for a start.

The rest of the police force did not hear about Pereira's shot, tragically. Word of it was silenced, the police control room and the police system answered the communication of this action with silence— the police bosses decided that so far as the rest of the force was concerned, that firing had not happened. That shot at Sis Ganj could have signalled an example for action the rest must take—if the police leadership had wanted such action. It was the firing in east Delhi that showed what the senior police authorities really wanted.

The Delhi Armed Police, a large and separate unit of Delhi Police, had sent a truckload of policemen into east Delhi from their 140 headquarters at Kingsway Camp in north Delhi, with the intention of backing the local police with armed force, Shamsher Deol, then DCP attached to the armed police, told me at his government home in Chanakyapuri in the course of a chat in January 2014. Deol had only just retired after completing his last stint as police head in the Andaman Islands.

He remembered that mission well:

> There was one inspector who was sent from the armed police into the east district on the morning of 1 November with a force of twenty or thirty as reinforcement. On the way, he saw a mob out on the streets, attacking places, and so he fired two or three shots in the air.
>
> He was going to the east from the Kingsway Camp centre via Wazirabad and Nand Nagri and those places. And it was effective. The crowd saw the police and heard the firing, and it disappeared.
>
> The SHO (from the local police) landed up. He said (to the inspector from the armed police), 'Tu marega! Who do you think you are, coming to my area, causing problems for me?' When the inspector returned to the lines, he was worried. He was worried that he had fired three shots in the air. He immediately reported sick, and he spent the next three days hanging around Delhi Cantonment. He managed to replace the three bullets fired from the .303 rifle. He wanted to show he had actually never fired, he wanted to collect proof that all his bullets were intact.
>
> It was a little later that he told me all this. I said, 'You should have said you fired, you didn't kill anybody.' But he was in a state of paranoia, he said he was afraid he'd done it, he was saying

he had acted against the nation. He thought they would come down on him heavily, that he would be suspended.

What this inspector had done sounded good, or should have; looters dispersed with firing in the air, without injuring anyone, let alone killing. But that was only the beginning of his troubles. So he bought his way out of his troubles in his visit to the Cantonment area. Delhi Cantonment is home to large army units, and he obviously managed to buy three bullets, and what he thought would be his safety, from someone there. Through that expedition, on sick leave taken for that purpose, he managed to keep his record clean: the replaced bullets sat as evidence that he had not fired, that he had not dispersed any crowd in any firing.

Such was the level of fear among the police over taking action against the killers. The junior police officers feared disciplinary action from their seniors if they stopped men targeting Sikhs—a fear that the seniors did nothing to dispel. Pereira was senior enough, and bold enough, to get away with it; not so almost all the juniors right across the city.

That truck sent out from the Delhi Armed Police wasn't the only one available for dispatch, those twenty to thirty armed men were not the only armed force available and ready to be deployed. Several truckloads and busloads of armed police sat in the Kingsway Camp lines, all ready to be called out. They never were made available to Pereira, who badly wanted an armed police unit; other officers simply didn't seem to have wanted an armed force around.

Deol was not then with the armed police; it was his wife Kanwaljit Deol, also a police officer, who was then posted with the Delhi Armed Police, in addition to heading the recently created cell handling crimes against women. Shamsher Deol was with the Police Training School near Delhi, he had been seconded to the armed police just the day Indira Gandhi was assassinated.

He had been with the top officers of Delhi Police when news of the shooting came in.

'That day was the CRPF raising day. The entire top brass, VIPs, everybody was at Jharoda Kalan at the CRPF group centre (about an hour's drive west from the centre of Delhi) ... the commissioner of police, the chief of the Intelligence Bureau, the home minister (and later Prime Minister) P.V. Narasimha Rao.

'The wireless operator of the police commissioner came up to me, he was a little shy of going up in front of all those great guys sitting out there. He told me there has been firing at the PM's house. He said the commissioner of police has to be informed. I said I'll tell him. I wasn't immediately alarmed, there would be instances of accidental firing sometimes. Anyhow, I went up and told [the commissioner]. He somehow had the sense that this was not accidental firing. He got up and tried to leave discreetly.

'By then other wireless staff had got through to the other people, and everybody began to leave one after another. That's when I realized something had really gone wrong. Soon after, there was a wireless message that all police officers who were not in the districts should go to the Kingsway Camp armed police lines. So we all landed up there.

'There we got all the force together within the DAP (Delhi Armed Police), whatever was available. We had about six busloads of policemen—they were sitting in these buses, waiting to go out. The total strength of the armed police then was about 4,500, but most had been deployed routinely to their various posts as personal security officers and guards and for other duties.

'But whatever reserve we could get together was substantial, we had a few hundred armed policemen with us. And there were about seven or eight of us DCP rank officers sitting out there. We were with Mr Kulbir Singh, who was the additional CP in charge of the DAP.

'After some time, Qamar Ahmed, one of the officers with me, and I got a little restless. We were hearing that crowds were building up. We said to Kulbir Singh we should go out. He said no, he told us that they may ask us for force later, and if we went out, the force would already be committed. Stupid arguments. So we just sat there.'

And that, through all the killing, is about all that this police force did, and the officers called to lead it could do.

~

The top police leadership had moved fast, in a way. Orders for police preparedness had come swiftly after news of the shooting of Indira Gandhi—police officers not posted in the local districts headed to the armed police centre where units of the armed police were available, and from where these armed men could be led by these newly transferred officers.

To deal with what? They were never deployed to deal with the city cracking up all around them. So what was the perceived threat for which they were so hastily mobilized and kept on the ready within a few hours of the assassination?

The instant deployment of DCP rank officers to the armed police could only have been ordered by the police commissioner. He knew the city was in flames around him, that men were out killing—he saw that for himself on the morning of 1 November at Rakab Ganj gurdwara, which was attacked, a few minutes' drive from Teen Murti Bhavan.

The police commissioner had visited Rakab Ganj briefly from Teen Murti Bhavan, where he had positioned himself around the VIPs filing past Mrs Gandhi's body. Early reports from the gurdwara area had spoken of Sikhs within the gurdwara hitting back at advancing crowds. That brought the police commissioner there—he was quick to go to places where reports arose of Sikhs hitting back.

After setting up an armed police reserve so rapidly, and moving senior officers there to command it, the police commissioner did not then order their deployment around the city. Were they kept in preparation to deal with aggression from the Sikhs? Because they certainly were not called upon to stop aggression against the Sikhs.

The officers with the armed police knew they were needed, they had asked to be sent out. This was refused. The unit that went out to east Delhi led to a fearful inspector buying bullets from soldiers to show he had done nothing when in fact he had. Other units stayed put.

It was known to the top police officers that besides these hundreds of armed policemen waiting to be deployed, some at least among the thousands of other armed policemen on routine duties could be available for redeployment from their scattered posts in an emergency. Some of them were posted close to the trouble in the districts. So, many more armed policemen were available than these waiting busloads.

To this huge force of the Delhi Armed Police add a large force from the Central Reserve Police Force (CRPF), at whose raising day the top officers sat on the morning when word came of the assassination. This was an armed force available for the police to summon whenever and wherever the Delhi Armed Police might not be enough. And they were called up—a full platoon from the CRPF stood at the Rakab Ganj gurdwara doing nothing to stop mobs advancing there; they stood as witnesses to the scene and to the fact that an armed force was available to the police, should the police have wanted to stop the killers. They should have.

~

And what could Kanwaljit Deol do as a DCP on a regular posting already with the armed police? She was asked to go home. She was then nine months pregnant, and her boss undoubtedly was kind to suggest this. None of the other DCPs with the armed police—and several had been stationed there—was pregnant. As it turned out, Kanwaljit Deol could in any case not go back to find any rest.

'Kulbir Singh said she should go back and rest, so she left,' said Shamsher Deol. 'Our house was in East Kidwai Nagar, opposite the All India Institute of Medical Sciences (where Mrs Gandhi's body had been taken on the morning of the assassination). From our house, you could see the main road. She reached home and went to the roof. She saw a bus being stopped. She saw passing Sikhs being taunted; they didn't even know what had happened.

'Then they started stopping buses and pulling out people. They pulled out one sardar, and roughed him up, his turban fell off. He grabbed it and started running, he jumped over the nullah. After a bit he stopped and started putting his turban back on. But three or four men started running towards him again. Mrs Deol saw this, walked out and stood between them and the sardar. She spoke sharply to them, told them "What are you doing?" They stopped, looked a little uncertain, they turned around, and they went back. And she was just one pregnant housewife.

'So that was what you needed at that particular time to stop people from doing anything. I think if these 200–300 armed cops we had with us had been at the AIIMS, it would have had an impact on these men. It would have taken very little to put the squeeze on.'

As a top police officer of the armed police, Kanwaljit Deol could do nothing. In her capacity as a pregnant woman, she came close to saving a life. The men she confronted didn't need even to hear a shot from a revolver, she just shooed them away; and away they went.

Word of strong police action on that evening of 31 October would have gone out to the entire police force. They would have known that they must stop these violent gangs. That evening those violent groups were allowed their way unchecked at one place; later they had their way just about everywhere. The police had been informed, without being told, that if men were running riot against the Sikhs, they must not be stopped.

Late that night Shamsher Deol got deployment orders, he was ordered to move with force. But not to deal with the attacks and all the killing that came that night. He was ordered to head for the five-star Ashok Hotel in Chanakyapuri in south Delhi. That is where VIPs arriving to attend Indira Gandhi's funeral would be staying. His force would be posted to protect them and to manage VIP movement. It was there that the officer sat uselessly over the next couple of days.

~

SS: Through all this, what did you know of [the] events in the rest of the city?

SD: Incidents went on throughout the night. There were a lot of phone calls to the police, and a lot were unattended.

SS: The police simply were not answering distress calls?

SD: Many people did not get through to the police. Later one Sikh told me that he had realized that if we phoned up and said we are Sikhs and we are feeling insecure, you weren't going to get any kind of response at all. So he said he called to say that Sikhs are gathering around here, they are gathering around us. He said he told others too that they should call and say this. Once they said that, he said, they got such a good response. Calls saying that Sikhs were the ones attacking got a lot more response.

SS: How many such calls might have been made?

SD: We really don't know how many because everybody wasn't in the know of what was really happening. People (in the police) were suppressing [information], they were not recording, they had just put the phone off the hook, because you can just imagine how many phone calls were coming through.

SS: And you were sent to Ashok Hotel?

SD: Yes, that night I was asked to go out to Ashok Hotel, where the VIPs would be gathering for the funeral. There they gave me force.

SS: Did the force include Sikhs?

SD: Two of the officers were Sikh, Inspector Shamsher Singh and another guy. When they were coming for work on 1 November, they barely managed to make it. They were in civvies.

SS: Were Sikh police officers attacked?

SD: Yes. We had called a force from the Police Training School, I had a lot of people there doing courses. Those trucks were stopped at Uttam Nagar (in west Delhi) when they were coming. Look at the boldness—these people stopped police trucks, with policemen with arms inside them. They saw three Sikhs inside. They said, we want them to step out of the trucks. They were not handed over, but look at the audacity.

SS: In Ashok Hotel did you have an idea what's going on in the city?

SD: We didn't know what was going on, except that here and there we would see smoke going up. We didn't know why it was like that.

SS: Did you encounter any of these crowds directly?

SD: The next morning I was going to Ashok Hotel from home, and I saw four chaps carrying iron rods, one had a sword. I told my driver to stop. I challenged them, and they just ran. There was a time when the slightest show of intent would have had the desired result. I was in plain clothes but I had a pistol in my hand. I had got myself a 9 mm that I then kept with me.

SS: What was going on within the police force?

SD: I did turn up later at the police headquarters. You see, a lot of the time what happens is that when you do something wrong, you start defending yourself, and then you start believing that defence. And then you find all sorts of reasons why you couldn't handle the situation, you say there were no clear-cut orders. But you don't need, you didn't need, orders.

SS: Did you have any direct dealings with the police commissioner?

SD: Subhash Tandon was the CP (commissioner of police). He earlier had a very good relationship with the Nehru family. He was from the Rajasthan cadre. That was before he became commissioner.

SS: But were there clear orders from the commissioner that the police should go out and stop this?

SD: Well, he is a nice man and personally a gentleman …

SS: Yes, personally a gentleman, but we're not talking about that.

SD: On 1 November he landed up at Ashok Hotel to make sure all was OK. There was blood on his uniform. He told me, 'Shamsher, people have gone mad.'

~

It was to be Deol's fate to be everywhere he could have made all the difference—and then make a difference nowhere. He was with the armed police that sat in their buses with arms crossed when they were needed across the city as never before or since. Later, he was posted to support the police inquiry led by Ved Marwah—that was terminated before its findings could be written into a report.

> SS: What happened once you took over the investigations with the Marwah inquiry?
>
> SD: It wasn't [an] investigation. It was only a recording, after asking officers, after looking at their records based on wireless dispatches and other records, and their reports for the day. Because a daily report does go out, we were looking at what they had mentioned, what they had not mentioned. Marwah was very particular about where they were at what time. And they themselves gave an account of what they did, and what they said happened. So it was a recording to determine at most who should face a departmental inquiry, who should face major penalties, who has done what, who has not done what.
>
> SS: Did this cause problems within the police?
>
> SD: The police became two sets of people—those who felt vulnerable that they could get stuck in this thing; and those who had nothing to do with it or, like Maxwell Pereira, who did a good job. Then the usual politics started. Some said you are getting after people of a certain caste, or you didn't like so and so from the start, that you are victimizing so and so. This was really not true, because those people [the officers in the districts] had fought tooth and nail to be in those positions (coveted postings in the districts), and it backfired on them. Otherwise it used to be a great thing, being in charge of a range or of a district. All of a sudden they saw the downside of it.

SS: Other than the inquiry, what about the investigations?

SD: There were never any real investigations.

SS: If not on the basis of records, then on the basis of the bodies found?

SD: Many bodies simply landed in other districts. Many were thrown into the Yamuna, so they would float into somebody else's jurisdiction. Or some people just went and left them on the Ridge. The guy in charge of the Ridge complained later that bodies from all the districts had been dumped into his district overnight. So that those officers [who had dumped the bodies] could say nothing happened in their area [where those people had been killed]. The bodies on the Ridge were mostly from [the] west district.

SS: What did police records show?

SD: Police records show very few deaths.

SS: There were about 3,000. The police records admit only a small fraction of this. Has this ever been resolved?

SD: That discrepancy can never be resolved. The police just made catch-all summaries—that mobs attacked in various localities. They didn't record specific complaints, they would register just a general FIR. All the police records went into so many inquiries. Marwah did not finish, all records were sent to Justice Ranganath Mishra. Then came the Justice [G.T.] Nanavati inquiry. The records were going from one place to another. Eventually what happened to the records one doesn't know.

SS: The records were handed over, and for that reason they were not available for the police to act on?

SD: First, we were scrutinizing them. Then, when our inquiry was put on hold, they were lying with us, under lock and key.

And then, these were handed over to the next inquiry. All the FIRs, logbooks, control room information coming in, the roznamchas, the duty rosters, who was on duty at which place, movements, communications ... all those things.

SS: So the police could not investigate later because they did not have records in their hands to work with?

SD: The first thing is, which police officer would want to say that 300 people died in his area.

SS: But there was a riot cell set up for investigations.

SD: There was a riot cell, [but] they found it difficult to get hold of records. In any case, at the recording stage itself, there was no mention of names or numbers of deaths. Later you cannot correct it. Many of the cases failed in court because of this.

SS: So, first, the record was not created. Second, it was transferred out of the reach of the police, and that was the end of it. And then bodies were thrown about, got rid of.

SD: Yes.

SS: So we are living with a situation where the police records show something, and have to go on showing something far different from, and far less than, the final death toll.

SD: No authentication ever took place. Many people did not get compensation, the FIRs did not mention the name of the man who died. The one looking for compensation would have a composite, general FIR, he would run around, and get nothing. The FIR had no name. That was a wrong which was never righted. And it cannot be.

SS: Why not?

SD: That first record has to be of so-and-so complaining in relation to so-and-so. Or of the police finding out. So that they would register one complaint, and then on the basis of the next, register another. Those complaints would have to say which is the locality, who are the witnesses, and so on. It can't be just general. The FIR is such an important document, it is that which can set the ball of justice rolling. The wheels of the criminal justice system rest on this. Without an FIR, it's difficult. Even if an FIR is delayed, that is a very big lacuna.

SS: Three thousand people murdered in three days in Delhi, and no investigation?

SD: There was never an investigation. Never. Whatever investigative follow-up came was in cases where the court ordered the police to look into a few cases. Independently by the police, there was no effort to try to identify culprits or to arrest them. Finally, there were hardly any convictions. And even these few were not convicted on the basis of police investigation, but because NGOs and activists rallied people around and managed to find witnesses that they brought to court. And here too these were not witnesses who would say they saw somebody murdering someone. The NGO route is well meaning but it's not reliable.

SS: It seems that so far the Marwah inquiry had come closest to delivering justice.

SD: If the Marwah inquiry had gone through, it would have set a record for all that happened. All statements, records, logbooks. It would have shown up the discrepancy between claims and records. You have vehicle logs also. Marwah had them seized and sealed very quickly. These could have pointed to differences between claims and what really happened, and who was doing what and where. It's difficult to fudge records, because there is one record by the control room, a separate one maintained by the district control room, and there is the record of the driver.

If you change one, you would have to change those recorded in the other places.

SS: Did the Marwah inquiry face pressure?

SD: There was a lot of pressure from a few officers. Others were affronted that all we were doing was a police inquiry, they said you need a judicial inquiry. People thought police inquiring into the police was unconvincing, little knowing that Marwah would have hung a lot of people.

~

In some ways like the inspector from the armed police who made the mistake of firing shots into the air to scare away looters, Assistant Commissioner of Police Keval Singh may have made a mistake on the evening of 31 October. He stepped out on the streets in the Sabzi Mandi area of the north district, stopped looters, rounded up many, and arrested some. For a Sikh police officer, that was a courageous thing to do that evening.

He went on to make a bigger mistake—he sent out a wireless message asking for permission to shoot at looters if needed. He got his reply shortly after sending that request: he received orders to hand over charge. Inspector Gurmail Singh, the Sikh SHO of Sabzi Mandi police station, received similar orders. These officers had quickly become active against looters. They were deactivated immediately. In the central district Amod Kanth had stood up against orders to disarm and deactivate Sikh officers; here in the north district, nobody did.

The police wireless records tell a little story for that evening. At 8.32 p.m., the records show, Keval Singh was describing the situation at Shora Kothi in the Sabzi Mandi area as bad, and asking for permission to shoot at sight. At 9.22 p.m., fifty minutes after Keval Singh's message, the DCP North, S.K. Singh, ordered that all messages meant for the ACP, Sabzi Mandi (Keval Singh), be passed on to the ACP, Headquarters, an officer of similar rank to Keval Singh posted in the district police headquarters.

The next morning, the ACP, Headquarters, came personally to Sabzi Mandi to relieve Keval Singh of charge. As the wireless messages show, Keval Singh was removed from his position almost immediately after seeking permission to open fire.

The next twist to this story was to come later, before the Justice Mishra Commission. Additional Commissioner of Police Hukum Chand Jatav, who according to police records had asked for Keval Singh to be relieved of his charge, submitted a statement that Keval Singh and SHO Gurmail Singh were 'guilty of abandoning their positions of duty during the riots'.

An officer doing his job was stopped from doing it, and later accused of failing to do it. The facts from the wireless record were clear well before this accusation was made before the Mishra Commission. If there was anything at all to the charge that Keval Singh had abandoned his position, no one ever followed it up. On the other hand, nobody ever challenged Jatav for making such an accusation.

Now that he is retired, I could speak with Keval Singh at last. I did, over an evening at his flat in Vasant Kunj in south Delhi.

SS: What happened in your area after the assassination?

KS: On 31 October, during the daytime there was nothing. All day there was absolutely nothing. As soon as evening came, the streets started filling with crowds. It happened quite suddenly. And then the loot started.

SS: Where?

KS: I saw that in the streets around Hindu Rao Hospital [close to the Delhi University campus]. People started looting Sikh shops and houses as if they have been selected. They just knew who owns what shops, who lives where.

SS: Did you think of opening fire?

KS: Under such circumstances, if there is firing, and if you fire a .303 bullet into the crowd, it could pierce ten chests. It was difficult to order firing in such a situation. So everybody wanted to ascertain that we could give orders to fire. We would have needed very clear instructions and guidance. The people on the top are supposed to guide their junior officers, and the junior officers are supposed to move in the field with that guidance, what they should do, and how to react. Unfortunately, that guidance was missing.

SS: Did you ask for permission to open fire?

KS: I asked for permission, but it never came.

SS: When did you ask?

KS: That very evening. When the situation started deteriorating.

SS: Did you ask over the wireless?

KS: Yes.

SS: Who would have seen the message?

KS: This was a message to the north district control room. Which means the message would have gone to the DCP (S.K. Singh) and Additional DCP (Maxwell Pereira).

SS: There was no response from the DCP?

KS: Nothing, no order came that day. An order came the next morning, that I must not go into the field, and that another officer will take my place.

SS: Did others fire at other places?

KS: The only one who gave orders was Maxwell Pereira. He was just a straight police officer respecting his uniform.

SS: Was there any leadership at all?

KS: The police became almost leaderless. Many police officers began to side with the crowd, or they just became disinterested in taking any action. It was not that the police were not there, they were there. Many police officers sided with the crowd at many places, and did nothing.

SS: What did you do, without permission to open fire?

KS: We tried anyhow to disperse the crowds.

SS: How did you do that?

KS: We did what we could with whatever people we could collect from the police station.

SS: How many people could you collect?

KS: About ten to fifteen, no more.

SS: And you went out with them?

KS: Yes, I picked them up from the police station.

SS: As a Sikh officer did you have any particular fear?

KS: There was a lurking fear that these very policemen may either not follow your orders, or they may even attack you.

SS: Your own policemen?

KS: My own policemen. That was a real fear.

SS: Was there a fear that your police station might be attacked?

KS: We were in an area close to the Clock Tower [in Sabzi Mandi area], and one man came rushing to me. He said some people are planning to burn your police station. So we rushed back to the police station.

SS: Was there an actual attempt to burn down the police station?

KS: No.

SS: But that evening you went out into the streets. As a Sikh police officer, did anyone say anything to you? Did anyone try to attack you?

KS: Not at that time.

SS: So you were out in the streets, leading your ten to fifteen men, and trying to control the situation, and nobody got after you.

KS: Nobody tried to attack me personally. We were the police after all, we would hit back if attacked. The target was not the police, the target was the Sikhs in the public.

SS: Where was the worst of it?

KS: The worst was in the area known as Kabir Basti, close to Hindu Rao Hopsital, very close to the Delhi University campus. Kabir Basti is a very low income area, we learnt that people had been burnt alive there. On the night of 31 October. But that we came to know subsequently.

SS: The looting began that evening?

KS: Yes, there were no immediate killings in the area that we saw, but there was a lot of looting. Many deserted their homes and took shelter where they could. Those who could not get shelter were physically attacked.

SS: Were the police successful in controlling the crowds?

KS: Not very. The crowds were overwhelming. When a riot takes place spontaneously, it's different; someone is bold, someone is scared, it's different. But when the rioters are motivated and organized, it's another ball game.

SS: What makes you say this was not spontaneous, and that it was organized?

KS: Well, understand the situation. Of course, the Prime Minister of the country had been shot dead, but the man on the street is not immediately affected by that. He cannot be so much provoked, and that too everywhere, that he should react in such a violent manner. And why just in this case? Mahatma Gandhi was shot dead. A few scuffles may have taken place, but there were no riots to such an extent because nobody provoked them. Subsequently, also, Rajiv Gandhi was brutally killed. But it [the public's reaction] was controlled, the instructions were very clear, leadership was in place, nothing happened. But this time [in 1984] [the] leadership was either not in control or the leadership sponsored it, so we had the violence.

SS: Indira Gandhi was the Prime Minister of the country, not of Delhi. All over the country almost nothing happened. And there are Sikhs all over the country. Why just in Delhi?

KS: Barring Bokaro and Kanpur, where there were small and scattered incidents, and one or two in Indore, there was nothing. If this was sentimental reaction, a psychological reaction, a spontaneous reaction, if this is what it was, it should have happened everywhere. But since Delhi was under the control of certain people, it happened in Delhi.

SS: Was there a pattern of crowd behaviour and not just individually expressed anger? Riots have their patterns.

KS: Basically, it was not a riot. In a riot, two parties feel aggrieved, they clash. Here it was a one-sided attack; the other [side] did not have the time, capacity, or the mind to retaliate. Their properties were looted, others were thrown into the fire. Had it been a riot, some from the other side too would have suffered. The non-Sikhs did not suffer.

SS: But was there something in the actual movement and conduct of the crowds that suggested organized motivation? If some angry people come out on the street, it will be one kind of conduct. If they are a part of an organized group, it will be a different dynamics. What was the pattern, if there was one?

KS: At the street level, it was the local goons, or the party workers, they led the people. And provoked the people.

SS: Local Congress party leaders?

KS: Let me say local leaders. They provoked people. There were those looters, and behind them were the executors. There is not a great deal of difference between the local goonda and the local politician. And this is true of all parties.

SS: That evening, that night, what happened?

KS: We arrested thirty to forty people. We recovered looted property from people seen carrying it, we did that on the evening of 31 October itself. A case was also registered. Whatever we could do with our small resources, we did.

SS: What did the local police do through the night?

KS: Without any guidance, nothing much could be done except moving around. We would see who is suffering, whom we could help, whom we could catch. We were doing this throughout the night. My SHO and I were on duty. We were making arrests and recovering property.

SS: And in the morning?

KS: There was an order from DCP North. That Mr Raghubir Singh (not a Sikh) is coming to take over from me. He was ACP, Headquarters, in the north district. And then SHO Gurmail Singh was also shifted. Orders came on wireless to hand over charge.

SS: What did you do then? Were you given another charge?

KS: No, for more than quite a number of days, maybe a couple of weeks, I was not given any charge. I only remember that subsequently I was shifted to Traffic. For a few days I remained without a posting. Because formally the transfer order did not come—those orders were verbal, not on paper. My written order came after a few weeks.

SS: Once you had that order on the morning of 1 November to hand over charge, was there anything you could do?

KS: I could not do much. But local people knew me as the ACP, Sabzi Mandi. The affected people didn't know who has been shifted and who has not been shifted. So many came to me, contacted me, and helping them was my responsibility. My vehicle was with me, my driver was with me, one or two constables too I had with me. So I would send them out to pick them up and bring them to safe places.

SS: What were the safe places?

KS: To many affected people the Sabzi Mandi police station became a camping area. Some of the affected people stayed there up to a year. If nothing else, I could at least save some lives and tell them to come and find shelter. I sent my jeep out to rescue trapped people. Otherwise people would not dare venture out. [For] the next few days this is what I did.

SS: What action was taken by Raghubir Singh who replaced you?

KS: I can't say. He might have done something, but I'm not sure.

SS: And after 1 November?

KS: By 2 November, the army was called, so all that happened was on 31 October and 1 November. But in Delhi the worst was on the night of 31 October.

SS: Did the Sikh leadership step in with any help later?

KS: Today the Akalis project themselves as sufferers. But to my mind, they are equal culprits. You see, nothing happened to any Akali leader.

SS: And they didn't speak up for the poor Sikhs?

KS: Those who died were poor, like the Sikhs from Alwar, they had small jobs like making keys for bicycles, weaving charpais, and things like that. They were poor, they had no mai-baap [godfather]. The Akalis would talk about them, but they did nothing for justice for these people. Even their cases have not been fought by the Akalis. They offered only lip service.

SS: So who spoke up for these people?

KS: Nobody owned these people. Not the police, not the Akalis, not the government, nobody. But if 3,000 people have died, and nobody is responsible for that, it's very strange. The killers got away, the police got away, everybody got away with it.

III

THE KILLINGS

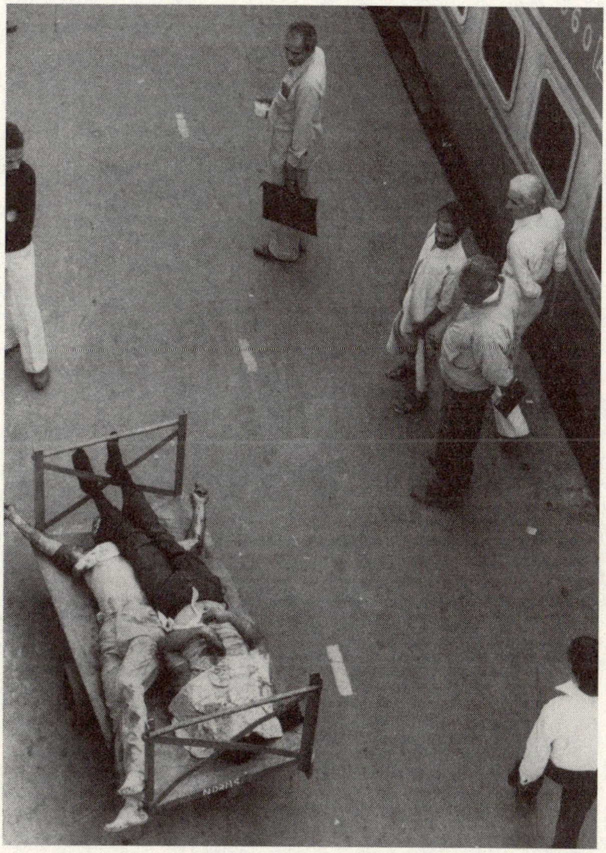

11

Assassination and Before

As dining tables go, the one in our simple house in Malviya Nagar was forgettable. Who remembers tables anyway? But a vision of that table froze in my mind on the morning of 31 October 1984, and it's a vivid picture. The morning sun was setting little hexagonal islands on a plastic sheet over the table through a concrete lattice when the phone rang. It was a friend in the police. 'Pata kar,' he said, 'Indira nu goli vajji ay.' (Find out, Indira has been shot.)

I must have been looking at that table when I took that call, memories of moments that stun do freeze pictures in the mind that never go away. Odd that the visual snapshot of that moment turned out to be that table settled uncertainly over an incompletely cemented floor. The momentous attached itself to an image of the mundane, and stayed that way.

Mrs Gandhi had been taken, my friend said, to the All India Institute of Medical Sciences (AIIMS). I abandoned the table where I might have settled down to the usual breakfast, kick-started my Vespa scooter, and headed out. I had no hope at all of getting anywhere near where she might have been taken to within the hospital, or anywhere near her home at 1 Safdarjung Road, then the official residence of the Prime Minister, where I guessed she had been shot.

My friend from the police had called within minutes of the first reports of the shooting flashed on the police wireless system. I could not 'flash' the news with similar speed. That would be for news agencies such as UNI and PTI to do. I was with *The Indian Express*, which would only come out the following day. That early in the day hardly anyone would be around in the office to take a call, and there's not a lot they might have done if they did. Whatever UNI or PTI was flashing was only into newspaper offices, and the papers would only come out the next day.

In those pre-Internet days, the only television broadcaster was the government-controlled Doordarshan; the only radio broadcaster the government-controlled All India Radio. Those would make an announcement as approved, and when approved, by the government. They eventually did, only much later in the day.

The fastest we could have reported the news would be under the banner, 'Spot News'. There would be a 'dak' edition of the paper that would go out late afternoon for dispatch and delivery in towns around Delhi, but nobody took those editions seriously. That day *The Indian Express* produced also an early supplement sheet with the news for circulation to anyone who happened to be around the building.

I'd made an early start, but I could see it would be a difficult day ahead. I was the crime reporter of *The Indian Express*, and the report on the attack on Mrs Gandhi would be for me to file. I'd have the day, until about midnight, to gather all the information I could on the assassination. It was going to be, and it turned out, about the hardest day's reporting I'd ever set out to do.

It was also the most disturbing. Routine reporting is fairly businesslike, but reporting the events of 1984 was never quite reporting as usual. It wasn't for anyone. Politically induced nausea had gripped us all, and that morning it had me in a gut-wrenching grip. The shooting of Indira Gandhi was a 'big' story, but it wasn't in its 'bigness' that it had felt different. It was more in the shock, the feeling of sickness it brought.

As anticipated, I didn't get anywhere near where Indira Gandhi had been taken within AIIMS. When I reached the hospital, I saw some policemen posted at entrances, though not too many. It was perhaps too early for heavy deployment. A degree of police presence wasn't unusual at the VIP hospital, and that early not many people at AIIMS had any idea what was going on. No word came from the hospital, unsurprisingly. But a couple of policemen there did tell me that Indira Gandhi had been shot in her house and that she had been brought to this hospital.

I didn't even think of going towards 1 Safdarjung Road where she lived. That early in the day on 31 October we knew for certain only that she had been shot. Something ominous hung heavy over that morning, I knew in the gut she would have been killed; I didn't think for a moment that I'd be reporting a story that day of some assassination attempt that Indira Gandhi survived.

The question of the morning was to find out exactly what had happened—the circumstances and the details of the killing. The report would have to come from police sources, not from the scene of the killing, or from the hospital. I began to prepare for this. I also 'knew', though my friend from the police had not mentioned this, that it would be some Sikh or Sikhs who would have killed her. No great deduction required here. Anyone who heard of the shooting knew that it would be a Sikh, and we soon got confirmation that it was a couple of Sikh policemen who had shot her.

After Operation Blue Star in June of that year when the army stormed the Golden Temple in Amritsar, after years of violence in Punjab that led up to Blue Star, India looked like it was coming apart. And ever since Blue Star, everyone knew that sooner or later, probably sooner than later, some Sikh would get Indira Gandhi. No retrospective claim this; an assassination had always looked inevitable.

Indira Gandhi herself seemed to have seen it coming. Just a day earlier, on 30 October, she had delivered a speech in Bhubaneswar ahead of the elections due in December. The speech has been translated and reported here and there with minor variations. 'If I die today, every drop of my blood will invigorate the nation. I do not care whether I live or die. I have lived a long life and I am proud that I spent the whole of my life in the service of my people. I am only proud of this and nothing else. I shall continue to serve until my last breath and when I die, I can say, that every drop of my blood will invigorate India and strengthen it.' Those were among the very last words she ever spoke in public.

She was so wrong. In the days that followed the assassination, India was not invigorated, nor strengthened. It cracked and crumbled. Her blood provoked bloodshed such as India had never seen before. The very state of India, the custodians of India, were to assault an idea of India that had been dear even to Indira Gandhi.

Inevitable as it was, the assassination shook us all. Whatever one's politics, whatever one's views on her responsibility in creating the Punjab crisis in the first place, she didn't deserve to die like that—to be shot dead by the very men who had sworn to protect her. With that shock over the assassination arose fears, fears over India itself.

India had come to feel like a person I had a close relationship with and who was now in a state of near collapse. The very sense of India with Sikhs as its proud emblem had changed after Blue Star, and now this assassination was upon us. How much could India take that year? This now seemed too much—and this was before the killings were to begin later that very night.

These thoughts came and went, but my immediate worry was of a more working-class kind: how would I report the assassination? Where would I get information on just what had happened? Officially, not a word could be expected. The police headquarters had a press office of sorts, whose job it was mainly to say nothing, or to say how much they couldn't say.

A tired, almost retired constable would be sent out in the evenings carrying a handout, listing sparse summaries of cases of minor crime that the police had solved. Nobody took much notice of this sheet, you couldn't be a crime reporter for a day if you were to rely on that sheet. On this day we were never going to get a sheet delivered to us telling us all exactly how two men from the Delhi Police had shot the Prime Minister.

It would have to depend on who within the police could say what, speaking unofficially, of course. We crime reporters had made it our job to look for information this way. We would make contact with police officers, in the headquarters, in the districts. We would circulate among them, offer a platform for publication of information it suited them to share, and ensure discretion in checking and then publishing leaks. We were in a leaky business.

My own efforts over years in this direction had delivered in the morning—it was such building of relationships that was behind that morning call. But of course other crime reporters were well-connected too, and they would be putting everything into this story. We would be competing to get the fullest story out. So through those fears about India that were churning the gut, my mind was searching for officers who might know what had happened, who could be reachable, and who might want to share information.

I got to office and started working the phone. I had a fairly clear idea whom I would call, and began to call everyone I could. And prepared to call again and again. Because later in the day more details could be expected to emerge.

On a day like this nothing was certain. Not everyone in the police was in a position to know a lot. Every detail wouldn't be on the wireless, and only very few policemen and officers were at 1 Safdarjung Road that morning. It was from these that other officers would make it their business to know what happened. We would all try to get information through these officers. That worry over just how much I could hope to find out, and from where, overrode the more fundamental political fears. That's just a reporter's life. Those fears over India wouldn't go away, but there was a job to be done.

~

Essentially what happened on the morning of 31 October became known fairly soon. Some details we didn't get to know, and as I discovered, we still don't know. We know how Indira Gandhi was assassinated. But we still don't have an authenticated and precise account of just how and when her assassins, Beant Singh and Satwant Singh, were shot.

Indira Gandhi was assassinated around 9.20 a.m. She was walking down the straight paved path from 1 Safdarjung Road to her office in adjoining 1 Akbar Road where she was to be interviewed by the British actor and film-maker, Peter Ustinov, who was making a documentary. Indira Gandhi's personal assistant, R.K. Dhawan, was with her, walking by her side. Along that path lay a wicket gate where sub-inspector Beant Singh and constable Satwant Singh had positioned themselves side by side.

As Mrs Gandhi approached, Beant Singh fired three shots into her with his pistol. She collapsed to the ground. Satwant Singh then emptied thirty shots from his Sten gun into her as she lay on the ground. Both assassins then dropped their guns to the ground and surrendered. Beant Singh said: 'Assi jo karna si kar lya ae, hun tusi jo karna ay, karo.' (We have done what we had to, now you do what you want to.)

Incredibly, no ambulance was around or near the PM's home. She was taken to AIIMS, about four kilometres away, in an Ambassador car through crawling Delhi traffic. The level of immediate medical aid available at her house was no more than first aid, and with no particular skills around for that either. It's doubtful that medical intervention right then could have saved her, given the way she had been shot. A medical report later confirmed that she had died on the spot, well before she was brought to hospital.

Post-mortem and forensic reports revealed that thirty-three rounds had been fired at her, three from Beant Singh's pistol, and thirty from Satwant Singh's Sten gun. Of the thirty-three shots fired, thirty had hit her. Of those, twenty-three bullets passed through her body, seven bullets lay trapped within. Thus ended the life of India's most controversial Prime Minister.

Indira Gandhi was formally declared dead at 2.20 p.m. Word of the killing had spread well before then. A government announcement that Indira Gandhi was dead came through Doordarshan only in an evening bulletin, about ten hours after the assassination.

Troubling questions hovered over the killing. What had gone wrong of security? And with intelligence? The fact emerged soon that Satwant Singh had managed to switch duties that morning to secure a posting alongside Beant Singh at that spot, after complaining of some stomach problem. Just how he might have explained that standing at that spot would help his stomach problem, we still don't know. But clearly, Beant and Satwant had been looking for an opportunity where just the two of them would face her—just one of them along with another policeman would have risked timely intervention by the other. It proved easy enough that they were the only two at that spot carrying guns as she walked up.

What happened after they shot her is only vaguely known. Just how were Beant Singh and Satwant Singh shot, and on whose orders? After they had dropped their weapons, they represented no immediate threat to anyone. The little information that has crept through suggests there was some sort of argument or scuffle between the assassins and commandos of the Indo-Tibetan Border Police (ITBP) that had been roped into VIP security services in Delhi. By one account, Beant Singh and Satwant Singh were captured and taken to a police room, and the ITBP men fired at Beant after he tried to seize one of their weapons. The suggestion is that Beant Singh provoked the firing in order to die, to escape interrogation and torture.

One account from a couple of senior officers was that some hotheaded ITBP men discovered what had happened, and just fired at both the Sikh policemen. What we do know is that after the firing they both fell to the ground. A senior Delhi Police officer came quickly to that spot after he heard firing. Beant Singh lay dead, and it was presumed that Satwant Singh was dead too. The officer then saw a slight movement of Satwant's finger. Satwant was then taken to hospital. He survived, and was later hanged in 1989.

Officers told me that senior police officers were furious with the ITBP men who shot Beant and Satwant. They were asked to explain who gave them orders to shoot at the two assassins after they had surrendered. The ITBP men said they were commandos, they did not need orders to shoot.

The oldest unwritten code for soldiers and the police is that you never shoot someone who has laid down his arms. But never mind the moral code—that has never much been honoured fully by the police in India. The shooting of Beant Singh was a fatal mistake for the police— he was the senior of the two policemen, a sub-inspector. Satwant Singh was only a newly recruited constable. It would be through interrogation of Beant Singh that the police would have wanted to unearth a conspiracy behind the killing.

Beant Singh had been in Indira Gandhi's security for some years, and through that period had become close to the family. He was known personally to Indira Gandhi and also to her children and grandchildren. There never is any final confirmation of intelligence reports, but credible accounts suggested that there had been intelligence warnings about Beant Singh, that he was removed from his post for some time, but posted back on Indira Gandhi's insistence. Later an uncle of Beant Singh, Kehar Singh, was sentenced to death for conspiring with Beant Singh in the killing.

Satwant Singh was then only twenty-one, and had been recruited into the security service just a few months earlier—around the time of Operation Blue Star. At the Prime Minister's house, he too had been removed from close access to the PM at one stage, but finally got himself posted in Mrs Gandhi's way with a loaded Sten gun in his hands without much difficulty—and in the company only of Beant Singh. In the end, the two assassins had the motivation, the will, the weapons, and the access. No police security arrangements or intelligence systems could stop them.

~

A buzzing, if inconsequential, debate arose: was this more of a security failure or an intelligence failure? We know that Indira Gandhi had refused suggestions to remove Sikh officers from her security—and that included particularly Beant Singh. But whose decision was it to change Satwant's duties that day in order to post two armed policemen together at the same place, with nobody else around, after both had been listed by the intelligence earlier as suspects?

An inquiry led by Justice Thakkar later said 'the needle of suspicion' of complicity in the assassination pointed to R.K. Dhawan. I found it very odd that an inquiry could have produced such a self-evidently irresponsible conclusion. A 'needle of suspicion' can start off a police investigation, and even lead to an arrest; but it cannot be the conclusion of an inquiry commission—

insinuations are not for an inquiry committee to make. It would need to back any finding with evidence; without evidence it cannot speak of having found anything. If it hadn't found evidence against someone, why name that someone?

Needles of suspicion were spinning wildly around those days after the assassination. One theory mushroomed after another, with no reference to the earlier theory quietly abandoned. Everyone wanted to crack some grand conspiracy behind the assassination; it wasn't just an inquiry commission that ventured and failed.

The newspapers wanted to unearth a conspiracy from day one. My editors would wait every day for me to produce a report revealing some sinister conspiracy behind the killing. Understandably the conspiracy angle was now the big overhanging question over the killing. It was not a story I could chase in the days just following the assassination: Sikhs were being massacred in Delhi, and that was what I first went out to report. I would keep checking with senior officers about any firm indications of some revealed conspiracy. They could not tell me what they did not know—and what there wasn't to know.

It didn't help me at all that some of my colleagues in the other newspapers began publishing stories unearthing new conspiracies by the day—those were stories guaranteed to land on the front page. Editors wanted to know why I didn't have this story here, that one there, that purported to reveal the conspiracy. As these stories went, we in *The Indian Express* were falling behind.

I remember one such story that suggested that a CIA man had handed Beant Singh a brief case with $50,000 to carry out the assassination. I was hauled up again that morning. How could we have missed a story like this? Such stories kept coming up, and I kept on 'missing' them. These stories later turned out to be non-stories; no conspiracy that went beyond Kehar Singh was ever unearthed. But over the weeks, I was failing as a crime reporter because I had not dug up any conspiracies at a time when other front pages were running rich with them. Nobody ever told me later that I had been right to not report these non-conspiracies. And that too, understandably. The business of newspaper reporting doesn't work that way.

Kehar Singh was hanged for his part in such conspiracy that emerged. But nothing ever was seen of some high-profile mastermind, no sign appeared of the hand of 'outside agencies'. What I heard added up to nothing. Some police officer would say what some intelligence report had to say, that Beant Singh had been approached, that suggestions had been made to him, that he was told he was in a position to take revenge for Operation Blue Star as no one else was. But any hope of unearthing a conspiracy bigger than Kehar Singh died with Beant Singh.

Satwant Singh, only a lad, was never likely to be the first point of contact in a conspiracy. Undoubtedly, he too had been motivated by some persons. Again, it was unlikely to have been powerful political people. Interrogation of Satwant over the years yielded nothing.

The interrogation would certainly have included torture. The police

did all they possibly could to extract something out of Satwant. A very senior officer from the Delhi Police told me that the police team working on Satwant could not extract information of a conspiracy because they had not interrogated him properly. And how would you have interrogated him? I asked. 'I would have hung him upside down from the ceiling and said, Now tell me the conspiracy.' This is how mindlessly brutal some senior police officers could be. No doubt other interrogators had worked similar techniques on Satwant, and found nothing. We all would hear occasionally about the trial of Satwant Singh. But no other names emerged through that trial.

In the absence of a productive investigation, police officers began pointing fingers at one another and settling scores. Top security officers around Mrs Gandhi had been hated for the proximity to power that their posts had brought them. They were now hounded, and themselves interrogated.

Everybody who had anything to do with Mrs Gandhi's security did all they could to explain themselves and accuse others. They were all thrown out of active duty—their removal was made to look like a throwing out. But this was inconsequential. Indira Gandhi had been assassinated, and they had failed to prevent it.

~

What came to be dreaded as the Punjab problem was just about to erupt when I started off as journalist in 1978. I encountered it first as a chap who also read the newspapers, and not as a journalist. I'd just finished an MA in English literature, and my mind was more full of George Eliot and T.S. Eliot than it was of anybody called Jarnail Singh Bhindranwale. But April 1978, just as I was finishing my MA degree, brought the first shock wave that shook the position of Punjab in my mind as some happy and prosperous place. Thirteen Sikhs were killed in firing in Amritsar by men from the Nirankari sect. The Sikhs had come to oppose a Nirankari congregation. That killing triggered the start of a bloody decade for Punjab.

Some milestones I saw as a newspaper reader; down the road the milestones began to edge nearer and nearer my work within the newspaper, first as a desk journalist before I became a reporter. Sure, sitting within a newspaper office far from the realities of an ever more troubled Punjab did not of itself bring any more information or understanding of the problem, even if some people still imagine that journalists somehow necessarily know more than others do. But inside a newspaper office, those developments outside felt closer, they carried perhaps more immediacy. Then, of course, the Punjab problem was to become work itself.

I had joined *The Indian Express* in 1978 as a sub-editor. For the first few months, I was sent one floor downstairs from the main newsroom to train as proofreader. The proofreading desk was located next to huge machines that poured molten lead into moulds cast into the typeface of the text punched in. So, beneath each printed line in a newspaper sat a single lead mould, about an inch deep, and naturally of the thickness and width of a column-wide line on a newspaper page.

To assemble a report, a chap would pick up these moulds and place themselves physically in an iron tray the size of a newspaper page. How and where you placed them determined the layout of the page. These assembled trays would finally be inked against paper in machines that would then give us the newspaper pages.

Proofreading demanded sections within the iron galleys to be printed separately. Fixing a proofreading error meant marking it on a printout and then composing that whole line again to create a new mould. This would then be carried to the tray, the old one pulled out and the new one slotted in. It took hours usually after a report had been filed and edited to then slot it into a newspaper. After a reporter had sat on one of those Remington typewriters upstairs and typed out a report, after a sub-editor had marked changes and corrections on to a typed page, the typed text along with handwritten changes on it would be punched in by someone else on to one of those lead machines to create the mould line by line, and then proofread, and then the corrections recast.

Close to printing time, there often wouldn't be time to get a print for proofreading; confronting deadlines late at night we'd peer at the type cast on the pieces of lead upside down under a light to see if the spellings were right. For breaking news that came late, we would assemble newly cast lead moulds where needed, stop the printing machines, lift out the old moulds on the tray, replace them with the new, and then resume printing. None of us then had heard of anything called a computer. Lead was as far as we technologically got. The fumes from the molten lead all around were far from healthy; to deal with that risk to health, we were paid ten rupees a month as milk allowance.

In the end, the newspaper we all teamed up to produce was a lengthy process. That process set its leaden weight on the speed at which we could handle news, the extent to which we could update it within the newspaper office—after accounting for the limits to communication speed in an era where the Internet existed in some scifi world. These base facts impacted what a newspaper could report, and how. Reporters, sub-editors, the men working on the lead downstairs all worked fast, but we still worked only a twenty-fourhour cycle.

Past my proofreading spell, I finally made it upstairs to begin work as sub-editor at the general news desk. Following on from that I joined a senior editor some time in 1980 at an independent desk for handling city news. It's through these years that I began to process reports that started to come in of the fallout of Punjab-based terrorism upon the streets of Delhi. For me as a journalist working in Delhi that fallout advanced remorselessly from peripheral awareness to take up place as the centerpiece of my work.

~

About the first attack that shook Delhi was the assassination of Nirankari leader Baba Gurbachan Singh, in clear revenge for the killing of the Sikhs in Amritsar in 1978. He was shot dead in Delhi in April 1980, two years after those Amritsar killings. Jarnail Singh Bhindranwale was named as a conspirator. That was about the time when every other day—and soon just about every day—Bhindranwale's name began to appear. He'd be in the news as one the government was attempting political dealings with, as one linked by the police with one case of violence after another, as one who dared the government in Delhi and was getting away with it.

September 1981 brought the assassination of Lala Jagat Narain, editor of the influential *Punjab Kesri* newspaper. He was shot in Punjab, but that killing shook us all. The *Punjab Kesri* was also published from Delhi. Over those years of violence, scores of journalists working with *Punjab Kesri* were gunned down and that included Jagat Narain's son, Ramesh Chander. Journalists were much on the 'hit list' of terrorists we kept hearing about. My friend and colleague in *The Indian Express*, Sanjeev Gaur, was later stabbed inside the Golden Temple complex.

Bhindranwale was arrested as a suspect in the murder of Lala Jagat Narain. He was soon released, and turned up in Delhi to celebrate the release. We were reporting that he came in an open jeep, garlanded by his supporters along the way. The open jeep was followed by busloads of his men, many sitting on the roofs displaying Sten guns openly, and even firing into the air. The convoy drove right to the Parliament House in Delhi. The police were seen waving the convoy along and clearing the way for it.

These were strange sights to see through the reports coming in. The Sten guns his men were carrying were obviously illegal weapons, and they were being displayed defiantly from the tops of buses outside the Parliament House. Everything began to look wrong. Punjab did not appear as it should, the government did not appear as it ought to. The newspaper was full of commentaries analysing this situation.

At the end of that year Santokh Singh, a top leader in the Delhi Sikh Gurdwara Prabandhak Committee, was assassinated in Delhi. He was a Congress party man who had once been close to Bhindranwale. Now there was no let-up to the violence that had begun and started to spill over into Delhi.

So much of the future of Punjab was being decided in Delhi. My senior colleagues covering politics would write analysis pieces, they would talk knowledgably about the latest mess. I understood neither what they said, nor what they wrote, and for no fault of theirs. It was a confusing picture, and just as confusing for the players themselves in that political game, and gamesmanship.

I don't believe I made much sense of Punjab politics at the time— I don't know anyone who did. The broad, and hopelessly confusing, picture was that Indira Gandhi was variously supporting and opposing Bhindranwale, that the Congress was opposing the Akalis, who were opposing the Congress right back. The Akalis were at times dealing with Bhindranwale and then rivalling him. In the shadowy but influential midst of all this sat Zail Singh, Mrs Gandhi's home minister after 1980 and President of India from July 1982.

The Akalis launched a morcha (mass protest) that threatened to descend on Delhi and disrupt the Asian Games of 1982. Orders went out to throw a protective ring around the stadium, around Delhi itself, against Sikh threats. That set off cases of harassment and humiliation of Sikhs coming in and out of Delhi, and of some high-profile Sikhs at that. Militant Sikh groups hit back, more and more through 1983. In March 1984, H.S. Manchanda, a Congress loyalist and critic of the Akali morcha, was shot dead in Delhi. The spiralling violence led up to Operation Blue Star in 1984.

I was given charge of crime reporting in Delhi late in 1982. Delhi was then being targeted in one terrorist attack after another. As I wrote one such story, I'd wait for the next. What and who would the militants pick on next? The known targets began to be ringed by commandos, police checkpoints sprang up all over the city for the first time. Privately, police officers would say that not all their checkpoints could stop the killers without some form of political solution to the problem.

The checkpoint solution had only made everything worse, most damagingly around the Asian Games of 1982. Police officers would admit for years that they had only provoked alienation and opposition. That provoked alienation threw many into the arms of Bhindranwale politically, if not actually among the arms his men handed out.

All that led to the assassination of Mrs Gandhi would keep going back to one name—Jarnail Singh Bhindranwale, whose house in Punjab I was to visit the day All India Radio announced that his body had been found inside the Golden Temple complex during Operation Blue Star.

I was not then covering the seamless political mess between Delhi and Punjab, I only reported its fallout on the streets of Delhi, and later from Punjab around Blue Star. The capital was very much on the map of terrorism originating in Punjab—Delhi was not far from Punjab in any sense. The Punjab situation everyone spoke of was just as much a situation in Delhi.

You had to be very senior in a newspaper to presume to have a political view that anyone would listen to, let alone publish. Political commentaries were the business of the political pundits within the newspaper, and of these there were many. Nobody sought the views of lowly reporters on matters of state, or on anything else. K.N. Pandita, the editorial assistant who used to put together the prestigious opinion page, was fond of telling us, 'The reporter is only a porter.'

Porter as I was of information intended to be newsworthy, I couldn't import those hierarchical walls within the office into my mind. I could not make that distinction between my reporting and some sense of the political source of the violence I was reporting. No one could; the political storms of 1984 left nobody untouched.

Politics and violence became inseparable; the politics was about the violence, the violence was over the politics. There could simply be no reporting of the violence without awareness of the politics being played out in Punjab. Everyone had a view from the street, and I had mine.

As I reported one terrorist attack after another in Delhi, it was plain to me that the government was getting it badly wrong in dealing with Punjab. It became clear, inescapably clear, that the government was in fact doing more than just a little to build up this Punjab crisis rather than resolve it.

This hardly stood as a unique assessment. And by no means did I as a reporter gain some unique insight that led to a conclusion that millions and millions shared. Just about everyone seemed to think the government was getting it wrong, except for the government. Or at least, the face of the government that actually was being expressed through policy. Perhaps a population of wise heads spoke against such policy within the government. If they did, they didn't prevail.

We could all see a coming collapse. We could sense in the air as much as we could see on the pages of the newspapers that worse was to come. That sense pervaded my humble crime beat. I must have had endless conversations with the police officers whose responsibility it was to handle the advancing violence. Not one police officer ever once said in off-the-record conversations that the police could solve the problem at their level. Every one of them blamed the government—not once can I remember one officer saying the government was handling this right. Officers I remember fumed for long over the proud display of illegal weapons that Bhindranwale had led in Delhi, that they had been asked only to facilitate.

I remember an afternoon in the office of an assistant commissioner of police who was investigating a terrorist attack that had taken place a couple of days earlier. Two or three others were in his office, we were all sitting around his desk. He pulled out his pen from his shirt pocket and placed it near the edge of his table. This pen is India, he said, and it is also a truck reversing. He play-acted a truck cleaner giving the driver directions for reversing. He slid the pen closer and closer to the edge, with the 'cleaner' giving directions: 'Aan deyo, aan deyo.' (Let it come, let it come.) As the sliding pen approached the halfway place over the edge, the 'cleaner' changed directions: 'Jaan deyo, jaan deyo.' (Let it go, let it go.) The pen dropped to the floor. An unsophisticated representation of the way India was seen going at the time. But not inaccurate.

Police officers admitted that the intelligence they were getting on actual operations being planned was scarce. None of them was confident they could rely on what they would hear from the Punjab Police. The best they usually could do was to catch the killers from spot investigations. Some attackers were caught. They would then be 'interrogated'—standard police euphemism for torture. They then fed the government whatever information they were gathering. The focus of the interrogations was clear: the Delhi Police were always after the bigger conspiracy—to trace the men behind the men carrying out the attacks at street level.

These investigations of conspiracies pursued two lines: who had motivated the killers, and more, who armed them. Anger needs arms to express itself in terrorism. Punjab had found plenty of both. A sufficient body of young men was angry enough to kill someone associated with the government, or with Indira Gandhi's party, and increasingly, just innocent people. Bus passengers were particularly targeted. Increasingly, headlines began to appear of Hindus picked particularly in these bus attacks in Punjab. Terrorist attacks became a constant feature of the calendar through 1983.

The second line of investigation was the more pointed one. More than information, the police would want to know where the killers got their guns. They did not get far enough with those investigations, some isolated unearthing produced no grand design. Police officers said the reach of their investigations was limited, that such information they had would only bump uselessly against a political wall. They needed political sanction to proceed if not a political solution.

That political solution was not coming from the government. Who knows what the police's cousinly intelligence agencies were telling the government? It would be a safe guess that they didn't know enough, and to the extent they did, they were disregarded. Or, perhaps the top men in the intelligence services themselves politicized in their own way, were only telling the leaders what the leaders wanted to hear.

For me, two kinds of questions hung heavy over that period of reporting the fallout of Punjab-based terrorist attacks in Delhi. The questions went unreported, and were, so far as anybody might care, inconsequential, given that a reporter is just a reporter. These were only questions I would ask myself, I admit vaguely rather than definitely after each attack: First, why the Congress government was taking steps certain to provoke a backlash from the Sikhs? And second, if the backlash was coming, why the government wasn't dealing with it differently?

Every now and then reports surfaced of progress towards a solution, and then something would happen to undercut it all. I always thought that that something was really a someone—Zail Singh. My private one-line punditry on Punjab politics was that Zail Singh was on the face of it, and obviously for the face of it, with the government. But that he was discreetly, but surely, behind Bhindranwale. It was a woolly thought, never quite worked out. I believe this more firmly now—that the man seen as the number one enemy of the Prime Minister was being backed by her President. He appeared to have found a way of being supportive of Bhindranwale under cover of loyalty to Mrs Gandhi.

Unburdened then as a reporter is by the weighty demands of political punditry, and far as these few shared thoughts are from any retrospective punditry, I recall only my news desk and street sense of the origins of the troubles whose fallout I was reporting. I won't be unduly defensive of the street view either; if you look straight enough, and simply enough, streets say a good deal.

Street after street where a terrorist attack came was saying one thing at the least that no one could doubt—that this situation could not go on and on. We saw the violence in Punjab, and in Delhi, rising and rising. We could see that India couldn't survive that spiral endlessly. None of us could be sure what would change, what would give.

~

Early in June 1984 the government announced curfew across Punjab. Transport services were cancelled. Punjab came to a standstill, actually so; it was sealed off from the rest of the country. People shut themselves in at home, and waited. We all began what felt like a countdown to doom.

That announced curfew took me reporting now into Punjab. The curfew had paralysed the Chandigarh office of *The Indian Express*. Now, when the world wanted to know just what was developing within Punjab, the government choked information getting out. My editors decided that I should try to make it into Punjab through the curfew since the Chandigarh chaps were rendered immobile.

I tried first through that old Grand Trunk Road, the historic artery through Punjab. I took a taxi from Delhi, we drove up to Ambala and then turned into Punjab along G.T. Road. I did manage to drive through Haryana and cross over into Punjab, and a crossing over it felt. I was a little surprised I could cross into Punjab at the state border unchecked. We drove past a couple of groups of army men who stood by on the side of the road. They made no move to stop me; perhaps they had not been given firm enough orders by then.

Unusual orders they would have been—that nobody must go in and out of Punjab and anywhere within any more. Maybe an Ambassador car carrying a lone passenger looked official, I don't know. But I remember that we had that road eerily to ourselves, G.T. Road at that. A tight curfew seemed in place all around, even though I had driven right through it up to a point. I was stopped at Rajpura, inside Punjab, by a police unit, about 30 km from Ambala. From there I was turned back.

The next day we tried another entry route. This time there were three of us; my colleague Rahul Bedi, our photographer, R.K. Sharma and I headed out together in a taxi. We were going to try a more roundabout entry this time. We first headed to Chandigarh. We had a bit of a laugh along the way; Sharma said his wife had seen him off that morning like he was going to the front. In Chandigarh we hired a local taxi, a local driver we thought might know better where to take us, and how.

We headed into Roopnagar district past Ropar and drove to the head of Sirhind canal. But this foray too couldn't get us past a short distance into Punjab, and we had to turn back. The taxi driver had a word of friendly warning. 'You've come here to take pictures of others, make sure others don't come here taking pictures of you.' But he himself had been up for the drive; the taxi business couldn't be much good in a curfew.

Within a couple of days came Operation Blue Star. Our limited attempts from Delhi did not take us far in reporting the build-up to Blue Star, and to covering Blue Star itself as it unfolded. My colleague Kanwar Sandhu from the Chandigarh office was the one who was clued in. He seemed to know about the coming army operation well before anyone else I knew did. He knew also the name of the operation well before it became public.

Kanwar Sandhu had far better inside information from within Punjab than I could ever have hoped to find as a 'visiting' reporter from Delhi. It was a time when one needed well-placed sources within Punjab and Kanwar had those. His reports of those shattering operations in Amritsar through Blue Star were amongst the most immediate and accurate then.

I didn't envy colleagues trying to report Blue Star. The journalists even right within Amritsar were up against the near impossible; no individual could have tracked the many moves and countermoves of that bloody battle, especially through the night of 5 June when the army entered the Golden Temple complex. Immediate reconstruction of the whole operation would be a formidable task. I marvelled how so many of my colleagues, in the *Express* or outside, managed to dig out whatever information they did to report that battle the next day and over the days following.

Blue Star was a nightmare and also a nightmare to report. No information was forthcoming from the army; the police were not in the picture at all at first. Eyewitnesses to the operation sat trapped mostly within the complex, each eyewitness saw no more than a fraction of the battle. They could then not be reached physically or on the phone. Residents living around the Golden Temple all saw only bits of the battle, though they heard much of it. But each had only a fractional idea, and certainly no idea precisely what all happened.

After Blue Star, Rahul Bedi and I headed to Amritsar again from Delhi. Amritsar presented a shattered sight. From the streets around the Golden Temple we could see that the tall water tower in the complex had been shelled and had mostly collapsed. From some buildings around we could see that the Akal Takht stood demolished. Harmandar Sahib, the Golden Temple itself, was intact, an island of almost entirely untouched purity amidst the demolition all around.

For days after the assault, journalists were trying to piece together accounts; access to the Golden Temple complex remained blocked for a long time as the army cleaned up the place, and the evidence with it. Rahul got excellent reports out of Amritsar to assemble a picture of what had happened.

A friend in the Delhi Police had put me in touch with a senior officer in the Punjab Police. The Punjab Police, cast aside during the attack, had now been involved in the follow-up, and that included collection and disposal of bodies from the complex. This officer told me that they had collected 521 bodies. That would be excluding the number of army men who were killed. I'm aware that this number was contested—all numbers ever put forward by anyone in relation to that operation were contested. Given the disadvantageous position of the assaulting force, army casualties were bound to be high.

Operation Blue Star did not happen just in Amritsar though. Army operations were conducted simultaneously around thirty or so gurdwaras in Punjab. We heard in Amritsar that there had been particularly violent attacks at gurdwaras in Tarn Taran Sahib and in Moga. From the Delhi *Express* team, Rahul focused on Amritsar, and I headed out to Moga and Tarn Taran. The curfew had been eased, and Punjab was being allowed some movement.

Reports of army operations at Moga and in Tarn Taran, I found, had been exaggerated. The army did carry out operations there. But given the scale of the actions at Amritsar, these were minor, and nothing like the rumours sent swirling around over these attacks. Army men were carrying out a rapid repair and paint job at the

Moga gurdwara when I visited. In Tarn Taran, I saw no signs of any significant damage.

A political bombshell dropped just as I was checking out these other operations. All India Radio announced on the morning of 7 June that Bhindranwale's body had been found within the Golden Temple. Within hours of that broadcast, rumours arose of a massive uprising in Rode, Bhindranwale's village in Faridkot district. I put a trunk call through to my office in Delhi from Moga that I was heading out to Rode.

~

Getting from Moga to Rode turned out to be a long haul. I could not find a taxi. The bus services were still jagged. I found a bus that took me to Faridkot. After a longish wait, I found a tempo that took me further towards Rode. That ride still ended miles away from where I was told Bhindranwale's home was. I wasn't stuck for the lack of an address though—who in that area wouldn't know Bhindranwale's house? I just couldn't find anyone to take me there. On that sizzling afternoon in June, not many were around at that small kasba—a sort of village town—where the tempo had dropped me.

Some people by the roadside told me Bhindranwale's house was not far and pointed the way. I began walking. As always, kindly estimates of distance fell far short of the real distance itself—the Indian compulsion to be kind at such times always overrides any approach towards accuracy. I walked for what seemed a long time along the side of a road, confirming with anyone I could that I was headed the right way. Maybe the distance felt longer in that heat than it really was. I was getting close to exhaustion along the way when I found an unexpected lift.

A youngish Sikh chap I asked directions for said he'd take me to Bhindranwale's home. He wheeled out his bicycle from under a tree, and I hopped aboard on the carrier at the back. He rode on to some track in a field, then on to a small road of sorts. I had no idea where I was going. I asked politely if I should take turns doing the cycling, or that he could stop and let me walk the rest. My guilt rose with every passing minute that he should be sweating away lugging me as burden through that afternoon heat. He was impatiently dismissive of my polite offerings.

It felt like a long ride on the bicycle—allowing again for the certainty that it would always feel longer than it was. And then, suddenly, I saw where we were headed. I heard before I saw. It was the roar of a helicopter. It was circling a spot in the distance above some houses. That would be Bhindranwale's house; I didn't need directions any more.

My friend, the cyclist, soon stopped. I thanked him extensively, he responded with near contempt for the profuseness of my thanks, and turned around to cycle back the way he had brought me. I walked on towards the spot the helicopter was circling. As I walked up quite close, I could see the house must lie behind a wall along which I was walking. The helicopter was now overhead and very loud.

I remember the moment I turned right at the end of the wall. A very large number of Sikhs stood gathered around a house where some construction had recently been taking place; this then was Bhindranwale's house. The men standing around saw me approach, and seemed to freeze. Every one of them I thought was looking straight at me, at this stranger from nowhere walking up to them.

I was hit by a sudden consciousness that there wasn't a single nonSikh among them, the only Hindu-looking chap around was me. The events in Punjab then had brought that kind of consciousness sharply upon us. I walked up and introduced myself to a couple of them as a reporter from *The Indian Express*. They asked me to wait and went inside the house.

I must have waited a long minute or two. I just stood there. Nobody among that crowd spoke to me or to one another. Everyone stood still and silent under the eyes and the roar of the helicopter overhead. It kept circling round and round, very low.

After a bit the two men I had spoken to at first reappeared, and called me into the house. I was led into a room—I can't remember anything in it but a high charpai. The newly cemented walls had not been painted yet, they stood grey and unfinished. The two men stood in the doorway as I sat down.

One of the men asked me why I had come there. I said I'd heard there had been a lot of violence at this place, that I was there to check that out as a reporter. He told me there had been no trouble—and I had seen no sign of any. He asked me to wait in the room, and both men went out. I sat alone for a bit. Through a window I could see the men outside still standing silently, and all the while the helicopter was going round and round overhead.

In a bit one of the two men reappeared, the one who had spoken to me. He came carrying a thali with food on it—roti, daal, pickle and vegetable. I remember well what was on that thali; a meal I was offered at Bhindranwale's house on that of all days was not a meal I would forget. The kind host, because that was what this man had become, asked me if I had eaten anything through the day. I said I hadn't. He spoke with some concern, he asked me as though he could see that I hadn't. He probably figured I was more in need of food than information, and in any case he had no information to give. It was just rumours of trouble at that spot that had spread far. Those rumours had brought me to the place, and also presumably the army helicopter.

The rumours had been wild and dramatic, we had heard something along the lines of an armed rebellion. The rumours also brought, as I sat finishing my meal, my colleague from Chandigarh, Kanwar Sandhu. He too had heard of some major trouble here, and had made his way to Bhindranwale's house. Kanwar and I had always got on well when we met at the office; this was now an unusual place and time to catch up. We shared notes and produced a jointly bylined story in the *Express*. But there really was no story here. The rumours, like the helicopter, had been circling over nothing. Nothing remotely like an armed rebellion had erupted, but it was important to report this non-story if only to silence rumours.

For me personally there was another story here, and it was not the story I filed for the *Express* jointly with Kanwar. It was a story told by myself, to myself. The story was that I as a Hindu stranger had gone to the house of Bhindranwale the day it was declared that he had been killed inside the Golden Temple complex. This Hindu stranger that was me had faced no hostility. I was an alien Hindu when suspicions around alien Hindus around Punjab could have been at a peak. But I was offered rest, care and a meal. That dinner was to me the story. That, on that day, Bhindranwale's family did not forget the age-old traditions of Punjab of welcoming a stranger, looking after him, making him feel at home.

I haven't drawn romantic conclusions from that dinner that the hostility was any less than it was, or that Sikhs on those days in June had not been traumatized by Operation Blue Star or the announcement of Bhindranwale's death. The Hindus around Bhindranwale's house, if any still were living in the neighbourhood, had all vanished. It is true that men loyal to Bhindranwale had picked out innocent Hindus and killed scores of them in terrorist attacks.

My experience that one evening wasn't in tune with that of the multitudes of Hindus across Punjab terrorized by Bhindranwale's men, and this didn't make their experiences unreal or untrue. And not just Hindus, Sikhs too were targeted by Bhindranwale's men, according to some reports more Sikhs than Hindus. I don't for a moment extract any all-embracing conclusions from my experience of that day. But in that limited personal experience, I had found a touch of longed-for innocence amidst the violence all around. This was not all of the truth, but truth this too was. And no small truth either. Because it was true that other than small bands of killers, Sikh neighbours never moved to hound Hindus out of Punjab. A lot had to be right in Punjab still for me to have found such warmth in Bhindranwale's house that day. I found a better Punjab than the headlines in the newspaper I worked for had led me to expect. Maybe it was that touch within Punjab that had kept it sane and together. The goodness and giving I found weren't just mine for that evening.

The dinner brought a feeling of faith that rose above the wider political disputes of the day. Oddly, among the experiences I remember most about 1984 was that meal. My gut told me, even if not all of my brain could, that if this was how I could be welcomed at Bhindranwale's house that day, Punjab would be all right.

I didn't suggest this as a story for the paper; in the face of collapse all around, who would think of suggesting a story about that dinner? I didn't think of this as a story for the newspaper not only because newspapers did not take a lot of such stories then. Naïvely perhaps, I thought that the extraordinary circumstances of that warmth must remain untainted by any parade of public assertion arising from it. The thought of selling that experience for publication felt like it would be disrespectful of the moment. It was enough that I should carry the meaning of that visit within myself. In any case, there was plenty more to pursue by way of reporting the usual.

I had felt the undeclared force of the meaning of that dinner straightaway. That meaning was to deepen later that year. I compared my position at Bhindranwale's home with that of Sikhs in Delhi in those days after the assassination of Mrs Gandhi. I hadn't killed Bhindranwale—that was plain to that crowd of Sikhs around his home that I had walked into. I hadn't launched an attack on the Golden Temple. That was the work of others, even if it was others with a mostly Hindu-like look in line with my appearance.

It's just as true that no Sikh who was killed on the streets of Delhi later that year had killed Indira Gandhi; only a couple of chaps with some similar identifying features to theirs had. But in Punjab—and in Bhindranwale's home that day—this Hindu-looking stranger, to all appearances like those who had attacked Darbar Sahib and killed Bhindranwale, was cared for and looked after. In Delhi a shared similarity of appearance between Sikh assassins and other Sikhs had brought death by burning tyres around the necks of innocent Sikhs. In Delhi then the Sikh look spelt death, and brought death.

Three thousand Sikhs were killed in Delhi in just a couple of days. And still through those days, as through Blue Star earlier, hardly a Hindu was attacked across Punjab. In 1984 I grew proud of Punjab, and ashamed of Delhi.

12

ASSASSINATION AND AFTER

The story in Delhi on the morning after the assassination stood written in the sky. The moment I stepped out of my house in Malviya Nagar I saw columns of smoke rising in the sky, dozens of them. Smoke was going to be my guide through the city that morning.

I had tried calling the press office at the police headquarters several times that morning, with no expectations of getting through, and I didn't. The only reason to call was that it would have been odd not to. I hadn't got through either to any of the officers I had called. On a couple of numbers someone answered to say that 'sahib' was at the 'mauka' (spot), the standard way of avoiding calls. If they were at the mauka, I had no way of reaching them in that era before mobile phones.

As I made those calls, I switched on our black-and-white television set, which meant watching Doordarshan. It brought home an alarming picture live from Teen Murti Bhavan where Indira Gandhi's body lay. On the television screen I saw one group of men after another being directed through the Bhavan. To a man, they had taken up a single cry: 'Khoon ka badla khoon' (Blood for blood).

Those men were not there mourning with hands folded, they were crying for murder with fists raised. It was a frightening sight. What would these men do to get their blood for blood, what would they get up to once they left that place? And what might others do, around the country, watching this call for blood go out? And to see that policemen were only directing the men making that call, not stopping them. And further to know all the while that this call to kill was being broadcast by the official mouthpiece of the government? The air thickened with foreboding of terrible things to come.

These are no retrospective thoughts: the sight of those baying men was frightening then and there. Something was going badly wrong, and being seen—and shown—to be going badly wrong. Mourning had turned into a call for murder, the police were managing the men raising that cry deferentially, the government had placed a megaphone to it.

What was all this leading to? I called a couple of reporters I knew. None had any idea, except to say there must be trouble brewing. None of us knew what, where. There would be no one to call in *The Indian Express* office that early. And so I decided to chase the smoke signals to begin my day's work. They were all I had to go by.

One column of smoke swelled into the sky thicker and blacker than the rest. It rose in the direction of IIT-Delhi, Munirka and Vasant Vihar that lay along Outer Ring Road to the west. That looked like the column to chase first. I kick-started my scooter and headed out in that direction.

That such a directed route belonged to the era of cave days was no retrospective thought either. It came to me right then as I turned the scooter handle to chase that heavy column of smoke. Cave days as some metaphor arising in later anger might have been more comfortable to absorb, as an image through which to see the breakdown of civilized structures. But I wasn't applying metaphor later as an inroad to understanding. The smoke signals were guiding me on the ground, they gave my scooter direction. They had become a reporter's sources in the sky.

What did occur to me later was that this smoke-led choice was really worse than cave-day experience. Because I was not looking at controlled signals sent out as measured message. These were signals of the loss of control; together they signalled that the city as I knew it was falling apart.

We had all been afraid from the previous evening that some such thing might happen. My colleague, Joseph Maliakan, had reported on the violent flare-ups outside AIIMS and around on the evening of 31 October. Sikhs had been dragged out from buses and cars and assaulted. It was always likely that more of this would follow. The sky was saying we would see worse than we'd feared.

That was not how I had planned to start my day. After filing my report on the assassination late at night on 31October, I was expecting to, and was expected to, file a follow-up report on the assassination. I had planned to get to the office, work the phone, and see whom I could speak to for that story. But now this new scenario arose above an assassination follow-up. That would in any case have to be filed, but that wasn't the first thing on my mind when I set out in the direction of that biggest of the smoky spirals.

I'd gone no further than the Malviya Nagar corner, as it was called, when I stopped by the side of a few men talking to a Sikh chap from the area I didn't know but whom I'd seen around for years. The men were suggesting he go back home. He was arguing against this. I felt supportive of the Sikh chap on principle; it seemed outrageous that he should not step out of home only because a couple of men who happened to be Sikhs had shot Indira Gandhi. Despite the smoke signals, this was still a morning of at least some innocence.

Yes, some Sikhs had been attacked the previous evening, but should all Sikhs now go into hiding? Who could think of the streets of Delhi as 'Sikh-free'? I thought at one level that the chaps around him were rude. But the smoke in the skies set a sinister frame around their words. I could see the principle, but wished anyway that the Sikh chap would simply listen to the men, go home and stay there. Mixed thoughts, mixed-up thoughts, but such they were. I didn't wait to see if he did actually go home. That column of smoke to the west looked like it was thickening by the minute and rising higher and higher in a billowing black tower above the others. And all those other columns of smoke rose too. Delhi looked like it had just been blitzed in aerial bombing.

~

I saw soon enough that this billowing pillar of smoke was rising from Vasant Vihar. Traffic along the way had flowed ominously light. I saw only small groups of men here and there, none of the normal buzz you'd expect on a Thursday morning. Two petrol stations I passed were both closed. I remember feeling reassured that my Vespa had a full tank—in those days of living on an *Indian Express* reporter's salary of a few hundred rupees a month, such was not always the case. That full tank made all the difference to a day's work in a city without open petrol stations or public transport to be seen.

I knew a moment before I got there what was on fire. The blazing base of that smoke was the otherwise elegant red-brick building of the Guru Harkrishan Public School. The school was named after the youngest of the ten Sikh gurus who had died when he was only seven. It was one in a chain of such schools that drew primarily, but not only, Sikh pupils. Fires had broken out at several places within the building. The biggest blaze had gripped one section of the school building. I parked my scooter on a bridge over a nearby nullah on Outer Ring Road. A man I spoke to told me that the blazing base was the school library.

A group of maybe a hundred or so men stood watching the blaze by that bridge at the junction of Outer Ring Road and Poorvi

Marg, looking, it seemed, at their handiwork. Almost certainly it was this lot that had started the fire. They stood watching that blaze approvingly, none showed any signs that someone ought to do anything to put it out. Of the fire brigade, I saw no sign. Nor of the police. The school compound was deserted. It wasn't the morning for children to go to school, certainly not Sikh children.

I drove on further along Outer Ring Road. I ran into a bigger crowd gathered outside Malai Mandir, a couple of minutes' ride away along the road. I saw a crowd there stop a rare bus that came along. They searched it, looking obviously for Sikhs. They were stopping almost every passing vehicle to survey passengers for Sikhs. None of the vehicles that was stopped while I was there appeared to have been carrying a Sikh. I didn't stay there very long. I wanted desperately to reach the police. I headed for the Vasant Vihar police station, just round the corner from Malai Mandir behind the C block market.

The policemen were sitting inside the police station compound, in full force. They actually just sat, in scattered groups in the front yard of the police station. A few stood around, in twos and threes, chatting. None looked like they thought any policing was required anywhere around them.

I stepped up to the office of the SHO who would be in charge of the police station. He wasn't there. I told a junior officer I ran into about the burning school. I didn't have to—he could see that smoke from the police station. The police had to know about the attack on the school. I can't remember what this officer said to me, but he was dismissive, looked the other way, and walked off.

I went back to the front yard. None of the policemen would look at me or talk to me. I spoke to another junior officer, he must have been sub-inspector or assistant sub-inspector. I spoke about the school fire, the men on the main road stopping vehicles.

I wasn't saying anything he didn't know; he just didn't want to know. Sitting around inside the police station doing nothing wasn't the decision of the junior chaps I had spoken to, they just hadn't received orders to move out to do anything. They didn't look like they were in a state of alert either where any orders to move might arrive imminently.

The sight of these policemen presented an early discovery that morning of 1 November—that the police had switched off. Groups were out on the streets to attack Sikhs and their institutions, and they knew already that no one was going to stop them. The worst of those 1984 attacks certainly did not come in Vasant Vihar, but it was here that I discovered that Delhi was now a city without a police force. Gangs on the move looking for Sikhs had the city to themselves, and such Sikhs as they could find to themselves. What followed would lie between the will of these gangs and the fate of the Sikhs they would encounter.

All the killings I ran into later reduced the burning of that school in Vasant Vihar to a minor matter, one of the later paragraphs in the news report of the day. But if the sight of those Sikh-hunting gangs was frightening, the stillness of the police was unsettling, deeply and disturbingly so. Gangs can come and go and break the law along the way; the stillness of the policemen declared suspension of law by the government.

The law of the jungle had come to Delhi then, friends said later. But Delhi hadn't surrendered to the law of the jungle, because jungles do have some laws. Creatures that inhabit them know more or less where the dangers lie, they have an idea what their odds are, they live in preparation to face dangers, they adopt strategies to protect themselves, and to deal with an attack when it arises. Delhi's Sikhs were unprepared for the gangs; more, they were unprepared for this abrupt abandonment of the rule of law by its custodians. Delhi was plunged into a state far, far worse than the law of the jungle. Sikhs became defenceless quarries in familiar territories that now looked unfamiliar.

~

So far I'd only followed the smoke I saw, with no idea about the rest of the city. But clearly the rest of the city would be seeing a similar breakdown or worse.

From Vasant Vihar I headed for office, to find a phone and to team up with the rest. Not forgetting a follow-up to the assassination would have to be filed, no matter what else happened. A shock was waiting for me when I reached office. It was Mohan Singh. He had escaped the killings that had begun in Trilokpuri that morning to come to our office. Rahul Bedi and Joseph Maliakan decided to go to Trilokpuri.

From the office on Bahadur Shah Zafar Marg, I called the police headquarters to get a picture of the unrest around the city. There never was a day that brought up more to talk to the police about—and when the police had less to say.

Officially almost nothing was forthcoming from the police about any violence at all, except that someone at the press office said they had some reports of some violence—that's all. Officially and unofficially, not a word came of any breakthrough in investigation of the assassination. The editors were keen on that follow-up, it would be a major front-page story again. It was my job to fill that space. Not an easy task, because as it was to turn out, there never really was a followup of any significance—not that day, and never later. I spoke with everyone I could reach who could possibly know anything, but I found very little to add to what had been reported on day one.

But all the while that day, the police officers I spoke to were filling me in unofficially on some of the widespread and serious violence breaking out across the city. Within the office, three among our reporters team of about ten or so were at hand for reporting the violence: Rahul Bedi, Joseph Maliakan and myself.

In a short while I heard that Rakab Ganj gurdwara, right next to the Parliament House was being attacked. I was told some people had been killed there, that Sikhs were being attacked and burnt alive. This was no longer a moment, then, to work the phone any more to chase some ghostly follow-up to the assassination. I looked for a photographer to accompany me to Rakab Ganj, but couldn't find one. No office transport was available. I headed out once again on my scooter.

I reached the gurdwara, and I could see that the road in front of the gurdwara facing the Central Secretariat had filled up with a crowd that kept surging towards the gurdwara. At least two Sikhs had been burnt alive. The crowd kept advancing in waves towards the gurdwara, on occasion held back by Congress-I MP Kamal Nath. An armed contingent of the CRPF under the command of Additional Commissioner of Police Gautam Kaul stood by and watched. The police made no move to stop the crowds, or to drive them away. The situation raised troubling questions about the involvement of Congress leaders and its government in the unrest (Chapter 5).

Later that day, an office car became available briefly. A short drive out from the office around Daryaganj and surrounding areas, I could see groups on the street looking for Sikhs. One group stopped our car to check whether we might be hiding any Sikh in it. I could not stay out in the city long. It was getting close to deadline and I returned to the office to file my reports for the day.

The next day I went to Sultanpuri where I discovered hundreds had been killed (Chapter 6). In the evening, I got word from a police source that Prime Minister Rajiv Gandhi would be visiting east Delhi. I learnt that Rajiv Gandhi would visit an area close to the Durgapura Chowk gurdwara. I headed out to the gurdwara along with my friend and colleague Joydeep Gupta from *The Statesman* who had also learned of the PM's planned visit.

The usual preparations had been made for a VVIP visit. The route to be taken by the new Prime Minister was lined with policemen—the district was evidently not short of a police force to deploy in strength, to add to whatever security force might have been brought in from outside the district. Delhi Police never do run short of policemen for VIP duty, or VVIP duty, as this would no doubt be.

Hari Pillai, who was in charge of Mrs Gandhi's security earlier, and had not yet been removed, together with Ajay Aggarwal, another senior officer from the security, were overseeing arrangements. We were told when we reached that Rajiv Gandhi would still be some time coming. Joydeep and I decided to walk up to the Durgapura Chowk gurdwara, around which we had heard earlier from police sources that Sikhs had been attacked.

The gurdwara was a simple two-storey structure amidst tiny tenements linked by patchy roads. It looked eerily quiet that evening, we could see nobody there, nobody around it. We entered through the front gate leading to the main hall; the hall was deserted. Then we saw some movement towards the top of a staircase to a side. Someone was calling us upstairs. We climbed up, and here the space was packed with a large bunch of Sikh men and some women towards the back. Most of the men had made some attempt to shave their beards off and had cut their hair, roughly and hastily.

We had just about come into the sight of these men and women when two youths, both smouldering in anger, advanced towards us. An elderly man stopped them firmly before they could reach us. Whether they meant to attack us I couldn't say, but they did seem to come at us in great anger.

Joydeep and I introduced ourselves as reporters. The elderly man, joined by some others, began to talk to us. They told us that gangs had descended on their homes, dragged men out of their homes and burnt them alive. These few had survived the attacks and then fled to take shelter in the gurdwara. But they had been pursued. At the gurdwara, they said, they had been attacked but had managed to defend themselves. Some internal reports from here had apparently been sent to the Prime Minister's office and so Rajiv Gandhi had decided to visit.

The Sikhs within said they were expecting more attacks. And meanwhile they faced other difficulties. The elderly amongst them almost begged us to arrange for some food for them. There were children in there, they said. These survivors in hiding in the gurdwara were exhausted, they were famished, they had seen people, their own people and families killed. Some had been killed in an attack on the gurdwara. They said they didn't know if they would live to see the next morning.

Barely 50 yards from that truck and still very close to the gurdwara, the DCP in charge of the east district police, an officer called Sewa Dass, had driven up. He was standing by the side of his official white Ambassador car. The scheduled visit of the Prime Minister had brought the police to the area in force. Sewa Dass was visibly unhappy seeing us there.

We asked Sewa Dass about violence in his area. He told us attacks had been launched from the gurdwara. He said the men inside had attacked an innocent crowd outside, killing a girl. So naturally, he said, the crowd had hit back. He said one Sikh inside the gurdwara had been killed.

Sewa Dass said that all day there had been only two deaths in the district. By then a thousand had died in east Delhi. Soon, Sewa Dass turned around, got into his car and drove away. We waited there for a bit, and in a while the police force in the area melted away. Rajiv Gandhi's visit had been cancelled.

It was getting late in the evening and we returned to file our reports. We could not arrange any food for the people, for the children within the gurdwara. To this day, the memory of that failure brings pain. Looking back, I still wouldn't know how we could have arranged food for them under those circumstances. Everything was closed all around. We were nowhere near a telephone, we wouldn't have known whom to call anyhow. That was only another moment among so many those days when I did so much less than what I should, and perhaps could, have done.

Worse, we couldn't be sure that the Sikhs within were safe after we left. Who could be sure the same men wouldn't attack again, or that the police would protect the people within the gurdwara. We could only hope that the planned visit of the Prime Minister followed by media attention to the spot would alert the police to now protect the gurdwara and those within. But I admit we left the place without being sure of this—those days no one could be sure of anything. Who could be sure of protection from what the police had now become?

The Sikh survivors I met right across east Delhi in days to come all blamed H.K.L. Bhagat, the Congress MP for east Delhi. Bhagat was known to be particularly close to Mrs Gandhi.

We could see that east Delhi had seen the worst of the killings. We could see also that the police were switched off right across the district. True, one could never suggest guilt from putting such a circumstantial two and two together. But right across the district, victims and witnesses would speak again and again of Congress party men among the attackers, and often leading them. Many local Congressmen were named in affidavits filed before inquiry commissions.

No evidence appeared in court to convince any judge of Bhagat's involvement in any murder. One or two affidavits filed against Bhagat were later withdrawn. Some coercion over withdrawal of these affidavits was alleged but never established in a court.

Months later, around Diwali of 1985, an Ambassador car drove up to my house in Malviya Nagar. Fortunately, I was home at the time. Two men stepped out, they unloaded large gift-wrapped cartons and carried them to the front verandah. They said these were Diwali gifts for me from Mr Bhagat. I insisted they reload these gifts into their car and take them back. I conveyed my thanks to Mr Bhagat for the gifts, and said I could not accept them. I have no idea what was within those boxes.

Mr Bhagat phoned me later. He said he had sent those gifts in goodwill, and that he had noted that I had sent them back. I was polite, and thanked him for sending them. I didn't refuse the gifts, I admit, because of any evidence in hand of Bhagat's involvement in the east Delhi killings. As a journalist one doesn't accept such gifts, that's all.

~

As reporters, we could only report. But did we?

Quite an unsuspecting bunch of reporters we all were. On the morning of 2 November, I reported in the *Express* that hundreds had been killed in violence across the city. It emerged later that by then, close to 3,000 people had been killed. By the evening of 1 November, when I filed that report, I didn't know how many had died, or that many had died. Nobody did. Not even the government, I suspect. By the next day it had become clear that the number of those killed was far higher than just a few hundred. How many had been murdered? I still didn't have that number. All I could then say in my report was that murders had turned into massacres.

The question did arise later why the extent of reporting had not kept up with the extent of killing. And why hide behind any collective 'we'? I was the crime reporter for the *Express*, the responsibility for that reporting fell first on me. Through my career as a journalist, and it has by now stretched fairly long, I've never got it so badly wrong: at a moment when 3,000 people had already been killed in the city, I thought it was around 300. Some others even thought that an exaggeration.

The error followed exceptional blockages to the usual pathways of information. The prime route for that information would have to be the police. But that never does happen in a riot-like situation. The first efforts of the police invariably are to under-report deaths. This time the police had become complicit in the killings; in a few cases actively, and for the rest by looking the other way—which in effect was not that far removed from active complicity. The police were not then going to keep the public updated over their extensive guilt.

That we had reported first that hundreds had been murdered, and then that murders had turned into massacres, followed from our visits to some of the areas that saw the worst. That assessment still was not informed by the police, whose word would be called 'official' and therefore reliable. By 'we' I mean just a couple of us reporters in the *Express* and Joydeep from *The Statesman*.

We made such assessment as we could on the basis of what we found. That we in the *Express* had spoken of massacres at that early stage was still a lot more than most other newspaper had suggested, or what the police or any government agency had admitted. But our visits to the violence-hit areas of Delhi were limited. Among a few of us, we could not in the space of a couple of days have gone just everywhere. We were severely restricted logistically.

As it happens, the final death toll is still disputed—and not by conspiracy theorists alone. The Ahuja Committee set up by the

Justice Mishra inquiry determined the death toll to be 2,733. The reason to round that estimate off to around 3,000 is the input from police officers about very large numbers of unclaimed and dumped bodies. The reason for an estimate around 3,000 is that the total is likely to be somewhat more, though not very much more, than the number determined by the Ahuja Committee. The government's own records admit wide divergences in varying totals—and those were all in their way official.

The root of the difficulty lay in the failure of the police then—or its unwillingness—to record the number of deaths accurately. The Mittal inquiry notes the reported police numbers and then makes its own estimates on how many actually might have been killed within a police station area. The gap between police records and the Mittal estimates is at places very wide. It would suggest that the number 2,733, precise as it sounds, might not be the last word on the death toll.

Through the reporting those days, the kind of information we relied on would be considered unofficial—and the unofficial is usually considered a synonym for unreliable. But all our unofficially fed estimates were still closer to the truth than any official admission in those days. The police headquarters could not tell us because they wouldn't want to, but at the police headquarters itself they might not have had the full picture. That central pool would have to be fed by the districts, and when the districts were hiding deaths, they had that much less to report to the police headquarters and to admit in their own records.

The police wireless was buzzing with reports of incidents and attacks, but not with accurately reported numbers of deaths in the violence. The police failure to stop murders, and consequently to fail to record the number of people murdered, restricted the extent to which we could report the killings accurately then. Because officially, these murders hadn't happened. Our failure to report the death toll accurately then was nothing before the greater failure this led to— denial of justice later. Which officer would investigate a murder of which there was no record?

True, it never can be sufficient defence for a reporter that he got it wrong—or not right enough—because he was clueless. I do think as a reporting team we could have done more to take our reporting closer to the full picture. Perhaps the entire reporting team could have been divided across the city to check out and report violence that was erupting all over, with one or two chasing each police district. I was hearing of violence all over, and between all of us more of what we heard from both police and public sources could have been checked out.

I did come to know there had been killings in the Cantonment area, in Jahangirpuri in the north, and at many places in east Delhi beyond Trilokpuri. These all went unreported—none of us got to those places. Our photographers wouldn't venture out into the city.

I remember Rahul Bedi fuming about this in the newsroom. He was asking the editor for more reporters to be sent out. One senior colleague said he couldn't go because he was 'manning the telephone'. Another senior colleague would tell us knowledgably about what he was hearing—but not think of heading that way to check it out.

Thirty years later some blame game is not for me now to play. I share those thoughts and experiences because a question hangs heavy— it has ever since: how could so many murders have taken place in Delhi and gone unreported?

Rahul Bedi and I later both received the Delhi Crime Reporters Association award for our reporting in those days. This was never an award to boast about. And not only, and obviously, because such killing could not become an occasion for handing out awards. The association took its decision, but certainly there was no ceremonial awarding or acceptance of any such award.

But more, this was no occasion for an award because the 'award' was a reminder also about all that had not been reported. All that Rahul and I did cover was still a fraction of the killings—though Trilokpuri and Sultanpuri, which we visited and reported from, were the two biggest fractions then, Trilokpuri more than Sultanpuri.

It is usual for reporters to boast of stories they break, to exaggerate their impact without embarrassment. But we in the *Express* did not think of those reports as 'stories' we were 'breaking'. Rahul, Joseph, Joydeep from *The Statesman*, and I myself—none of us ventured into the city looking for material to secure byline egos to advertise. Reporters chase bylines in normal times. Those were not normal times.

We were encountering horrors beyond any we believed we would ever witness, we were responding to the horrors by reporting them, which is all we could do. Together with these, we reported from wherever we went the precipitating horror of seeing the failings of the police that had made all these killings possible. I wish someone had reported the killings we could not get to.

In the *Express*, we took our decision to go out into the city at just our level as reporters. Nobody told us to go, and nobody stopped us. That was simply the way it was in the *Express* newsroom: we were a healthily independent lot, to put it politely. We did not wait for any word from the top, the newsroom was chaotically free of any culture of control. We were doing what the *Express* has always done, what our editor-in-chief George Verghese would have wanted us to, even if he didn't actually tell us what to do, or send word down a hierarchical line.

This sort of newsroom culture showed in the newspaper. The *Express* had always been a reporter's paper, and it was heartening to see it continued so long after I left it, under editors such as Shekhar Gupta, himself a pukka reporter, and so it continues into the present. It is that culture within that made the *Express* the bold newspaper it was and brought us the reputation it did.

It was this reputation of the *Express* that led us to discovering what had happened in Trilokpuri. Mohan Singh had escaped Trilokpuri to take word of the killings to the police headquarters, a fairly short distance across the river from Trilokpuri. He was turned away at the entrance to the headquarters, or PHQ as we called it. He then walked on from PHQ to the offices of *The Indian Express*, which were at the very furthest end on Bahadur Shah Zafar Marg. He did not think of going to the offices of the *Patriot*, *National Herald* and *The Times of India* newspapers that fell on the way. He believed it was at the *Express* that he would get a response, and he did.

Rahul and Joseph reported the massacres from Trilokpuri—hundreds had been killed in just Block 32. They followed up with further visits and reports. They confronted the police and the army with facts they found. Rahul and Joseph were the first to expose the massacre and the police failure that led to it, even police connivance. If ever Delhi had needed such tough and incisive reporting, it was now.

Mohan Singh had walked into our office with information, that we then followed up. But all along, police officers—sometimes very junior officers—were giving us information discreetly because they trusted the *Express*. They could be sure that we would respect confidentiality in the first place. But they also believed that if anyone, we would step out and check out the information offered, and report what we found factual and newsy. Those days many officers wanted the facts on the ground to surface—and these were not Sikh officers. They were shocked in their own way, they wanted some things that were happening to be known. They believed that if anyone, the *Express* would do it.

Pity we could not follow up then on every one of the leads offered, we ran out of time and we ran out of—us.

The editor-in-chief, George Verghese, supported us in quite unexpected ways. It was he who had sent us reporting into Punjab in June 1984, and now he fully backed the efforts we were making to report the killings across Delhi after the assassination. Exactly which reporter should do what, he did not specify; that wasn't for him to do. In any case, this was no planned reporting operation; we were stumbling upon the growing extent of the killings only as we went and encountered what we did.

I think it was the evening of 3 November, after a long day out. Those days of reporting must have been exhausting for us; we didn't think of this then, but Mr Verghese evidently did. Soon after I sat down at the typewriter late that evening, Verghese entered the newsroom with fresh hot food prepared in the guest house in an adjoining section of the building, where the owner of the newspaper, Ram Nath Goenka, lived.

The editor-in-chief was far elevated above us junior reporters and the formidable Ram Nath Goenka a remote figure. I felt a bit overwhelmed that dinner had been prepared for us in the kitchen of the owner of the newspaper and that the editor-in-chief was actually serving it to us; he came himself carrying the food to our desks in the newsroom. I remember him coming around a second time to my desk where I sat at my typewriter, carrying a bowl with more dal for the rice. Later he insisted I had a banana. Mr Verghese died in December 2014. I was at his funeral in Lodhi Road in Delhi and the day brought back memories from the newsroom of 1984. They don't make editors like him any more; they don't make men like him any more. When he died we lost our best.

The resident editor of the *Express* then was A.N. Dar, a fine gentleman and fine editor. But a disturbing dispute arose with him in his office. I had gone to Trilokpuri for a follow-up report along with our chief reporter then, Devsagar Singh. Block 32, where almost every Sikh had been killed, appeared deserted. But in the front yard of one of those little houses, we saw a lone Sikh sitting on a charpai. That front yard stretched only a few square yards, the houses were no more than two small rooms, one behind the other.

As we approached, a lady came to the doorway. She looked at us, lowered her face, covered her head and went back in. We joined the elderly Sikh on the charpai. He sat there, like some ghost of himself. He told us that hardly a Sikh had been left alive by the killers on that street and all around. After talking about the killings, he began to tell us about the rapes.

He pointed within to his own house. He said there had been thirty men, and they had all raped. He spoke of more rapes that had taken place in other houses, in which now nobody was left. Perhaps as a reporter I should have asked for more specific details. Questions about how many women and how many men and where. But I didn't. I was not sure whether we were going to report this. Devsagar wasn't sure either. I admit I was in no hurry to throw precise questions demanding more details from the frail old man. What more could he say about his own home, how much could he say of what he had heard happened in the houses of his neighbours that we could report on the strength of what he said?

Where, at such a time, could anyone look for 'confirmation' of what he was telling me? Not from the police certainly. Not from other Sikhs there, hardly anyone remained. Not from any women we could find, none were around. But by instinct—and with no evidence in hand—I believed he was telling the truth, that he was not making it up. I did think though that this aspect needed to be verified and reported after further checks.

As advised by Devsagar, I reported this to Mr Dar back in the office. He was firm that the rapes must not be reported. He then mentioned a reason for not reporting that I've never forgotten.

'Three hundred have died, let not 3,000 be killed,' he said. Neither of us knew then that the figurative numbers he spoke would turn out to be the actual figure for those dead. We were reporting massacres, but not the number 3,000. Neither of us thought it possible as we spoke that by that moment 3,000 Sikhs had actually been killed in Delhi.

Mr Dar's decision was no doubt controversial. My gut feeling was that we should report the rapes because if they had happened, then report we must. I tried to argue the point for a bit, but the decision was that we should not publish a report on the rapes.

Hindsight brings unfair advantages over such decisions. I abandoned that report with some reluctance. But I did recognize then that Mr Dar had a point. He no doubt thought that in that knife-edge atmosphere, a report on rapes could become extremely provocative, and lead to violence and clashes, in Delhi and who knows, in Punjab. So we blanked rapes out of our reporting. The incidence of rapes through those days was to emerge in reports by an independent group a good deal later.

~

We didn't see it those days but it wasn't much later that we figured in the *Express* that other reporters and newspapers hardly went out to report the killings. This is not a comfortable comment to make. The unwritten code is that we should get on with our own work and not point fingers at others. But the question that arises here is far too big to smother under politeness. That a few thousand are murdered in Delhi and most newspapers do not send a reporter out to report from where the murders happened? I do not raise this question to make some implicit claims about ourselves in the *Express*: it wasn't about this then, and it isn't now.

Reporters from the other papers, other than Joydeep Gupta from *The Statesman*, simply were missing from the scenes of the worst of the killings, in Trilokpuri and Sultanpuri, for instance. Or Jahangirpuri, the Cantonment and other areas in east Delhi that we could not get into. Consequently, the other papers reported almost nothing on those few days of the killings from where they had been taking place. Delhi all around us was burning, its people were being killed, and most city reporters were not reporting this. And who was taking photographs?

Very few, hardly a couple of them all over the city. Those 1984 killings produced very few photographs, and none at all from the areas where the worst happened.

I have no wish to turn these pages into a launchpad for retrospectively rude remarks about others, my colleagues. But a by-product of those days remains the story of the stories not told, that those whose business it was to tell those stories did not go out to hear them and report them. There does come a time when reporters must talk also about nonreporting.

It's not to brag that I say that if it weren't for Rahul, Joseph, Joydeep and myself, the worst of the killings might simply have gone unreported then. Who knows, the scale of those killings might have remained unknown, given the failure of the police to lodge cases, and given the scale and speed with which the police were destroying evidence? When Delhi was witnessing some of the worst violence in its history, the worst anywhere in peaceful times, why were only such few reporters on the move?

The other newspapers appeared not to have asked that question, then or later. I certainly have no business to presume to answer that question on their behalf, or even ask it of them. But I can't stop asking myself. Guessing between one newsroom and another, several possibilities could lie behind that non-reporting. Perhaps the reporters had taken the static position of waiting to hear from the police headquarters; having taken that route, they did not realize the extent of the killing unleashed across the city—just as we had not at first grasped the full extent of it within the *Express* office. But when we heard of the killings, we went where we heard the worst of these were happening. If others heard, they didn't go. We could not see what was going on within the newsrooms of the other newspapers; we did see that no news came out of them.

Why they didn't report should, I believe, not be a question for me alone. Those turned out to be the days of the most serious underreporting Delhi has known in modern times. Surely we must ask why.

The obvious logic against such an attempt is as familiar as it is inadequate. That if a good deal at the time went unreported, why speak now about reports never filed? That logic can be extended further into the question: why say anything about those killings at all any more as they're long over and best forgotten? This suggestion does often arise over the 1984 killings. Eventually, this then begins to overlap with the broader question: does the past matter, does history matter?

Yes, it matters, and it is as true to say, as it appears trite in the saying of it, that the past shapes the present in all sorts of ways. But it matters over 1984 in more immediate ways. What happened is not all history yet—people are still living with the consequence of that injustice; murderers who have lived long enough still savour the freedom that suspension of law then brought them. This injustice is not unrelated to the questions that need to be asked of the media.

The media silence proved deathly—it very likely led to deaths. Quick and comprehensive reporting could have saved lives. In an environment when policing stood suspended, and just about everyone was looking the other way, a few newspaper reports stood as the only public expression of the truth unfolding on the streets; these reports were the only public window into the unfolding horrors.

Forty reporters tracking the violence all over the city instead of just four could well have drawn the police out of their closed-eye position. In the face of immediate and extensive reporting of the violence on the streets, the police could simply not have continued to look the other way as comfortably as they did. The police could do as they did at least partly because very few were looking at them and reporting their act of looking away.

Sadly, all this is now conjecture, but in the face of any immediate and extensive reporting, killings in the Cantonment and in the rest of east Delhi, besides Trilokpuri, could never have lasted as long as they did. Bold reports splashed across the front pages of all newspapers backed by telling photographs would have brought firm pressure to bear on the police. That does raise a disturbing question: that just as the police were in unspoken collusion with the killers, were most of the media in unspoken collusion with the police?

The way newspapers were structured, three levels would be involved in taking decisions: reporters, the chief reporter and the top editors. I'm not sure whether the editors would have given specific instructions that the violence across the city must not be reported. But so far as we could see from the newspapers, they did not send out instructions either that the violence across the city actually must be reported, and fully—had such instructions come from the bosses, the outcome on the pages of these newspapers would have been very different.

The chief reporters would have stood as the key persons behind the silence. As chief reporter myself of *The Indian Express* later, it's clear to me how central the chief reporters would have been in shaping such a decision. They would have known in their newsrooms of killings taking place across the city. No sign ever appeared that they sent their reporters out.

It was normal practice in all newspapers for reporters to get their daily assignments from the chief reporter. At the *Express*, the chief reporter would write out the daily assignments in a register kept in the newsroom on his desk for all to see. The practice in other newspapers was similar. The chief reporter was the reporters' link with the top editors; he or she would attend daily meetings called by the editor and brief the editor and other senior editors on the city story plan. I wish I could have had some idea of who said what at those meetings in those days. But given the facts and given those pages, the blanking out of the worst in those newspapers was indication enough that those chief reporters got no direction from the editors, and that they did not give any to their reporters.

In a strange way this paralleled the structure of silence and inaction within the police. In the police there had been no firm orders from the top, and so the police force stayed put, it gave up its force at the time Delhi most needed it. The police became complicit in the killings through their knowledge of the attacks and failing to stop them when it was they, and they alone, who could have, and were bound by law to, stop them. In parallel, the media became complicit in the killings through failing to report the killings, and the linked police inaction over these, which was asking to be reported. The 'not-doing' by the police became lethal; the 'not-reporting' by most of the media nearlethal. Those were the days of the killings of Sikhs, of course; they became the days also of the killing of information. Of information that could have saved Sikhs.

In any history of the media in India, the pages marking those days must number as perhaps the most shameful. In the years of the Emergency during 1975–77, the media, as the jurist Soli Sorabjee famously said, were asked to bend and they crawled. In November 1984 the media could have spoken at least a little, and it shut up. Through the Emergency the media shut up over principles of free speech; in 1984 over murders on the streets for them to see, if only they had looked.

~

The story of the Sikhs attacked in Delhi didn't end with the killings, it continued with the survivors. Tens of thousands became homeless, none who emerged alive from Trilokpuri or Sultanpuri or other such areas could think ever of going back. Delhi became a city of refugees once again, as it had just after Partition in 1947.

Sikhs all over were worried sick over their loved ones in Delhi. Most victims were poor, they could not be reached because they had no telephones. Others had left their homes to find shelter with neighbours and friends—and this was a very large number. Sikhs could not step out themselves to check. They sat as prisoners of their circumstances where they could find shelter, and waited, and worried.

In the early days after the killings had ended a Sikh friend I went to college with could not get through to his sister's family in Faridabad— Sikhs had been killed in that area and also around Tughlakabad to the south of Delhi. The family could not be reached on phone.

I headed out to look for them late one night after finishing work. It wasn't going to be easy because a late night curfew was in force along the way to stop more crowds gathering to kill. A curfew was at last being enforced. Maybe it stopped yet more killings, but it did seem to have come too late. I borrowed a car and used my newspaper identity card to get past security points along the way. Once in Faridabad, I lost my way; I had an address and some general directions but didn't know the area at all. For a long stretch nobody appeared that I could ask.

Eventually I spotted a local policeman along a deserted road I had taken. He pointed to a row of houses across some open ground.

I could not see a road to those houses from where I was, the road I was on curved the other way. I figured I could drive across the ground; I did, and drove into a ditch. I was lucky to come out of it with the car intact. Once across, I knocked on a few neighbours' doors till someone pointed to a house the family had moved to.

Luckily I found my friend's family in there, all safe and well.

In Delhi people offered all sorts of places to shelter the homeless. Many thousands left to join relatives in Punjab, but a lot of those poor Sikhs had no relatives in Punjab. They faced a long winter ahead. Across Delhi, school buildings, gurdwaras, even police stations were turned into refugee centres. Once the violence that the police had enhanced receded, it was still the police that many frightened refugees had to turn to for protection. Police stations did now offer protection— their holiday from policing was now over. At last they had been given firm orders to ensure peace and protection.

I became closely familiar with this follow-up crisis not primarily as a reporter but because my wife, then pregnant, and many of her friends got together to do what they could to look after some of the refugees. Sikh groups themselves could not step up openly in those early days after the killings. The fear among Sikhs lasted a long time after the end of the violence; I think it lasted years and years.

My wife used to go to Seemapuri in east Delhi every day from Malviya Nagar in the south, changing buses along the way, and returning quite late. As did her friends. On a lucky day someone would produce a car. And these were only the people I knew. All over the city people came up with help at hand. Homeless Sikhs needed the help, they saw the warmth behind the help, and it made a difference.

Much was needed; food every day, clothes and bedding for the advancing winter, a little money people could use, medical care, so much for the many needs of the children. Not least, all the time, to be around someone who cared, whom the refugees could speak to about their needs, about how they could now hope to survive, where they would now go. The refugees had questions about their loved ones they could not find any more. The volunteers had no answers to those questions: the police didn't want to hear about the missing and they had nothing to tell.

In those early days, these supporters who gathered around were all that the refugees had. The tradition of giving in gurdwaras had taken a blow; many of the gurdwaras were themselves struggling to recover from the destruction brought upon them. But many gurdwaras still raised volunteers to prepare langar (a meal offered as prasad) for the refugee camps, and to raise such resources as they could. It did appear that more money from Sikh philanthropists came for repairs and rebuilding of gurdwaras than for the Sikhs struggling at these refugee centres.

The refugee centres had their needs but they had also their anger— how would it be otherwise. So many of us were angry, very angry over what had happened. And certainly every Sikh I ever met was. I remember some weeks after the killings, the Sikhs at the taxi stand across from the *Express* office returned from hiding, to our great relief. We used to look at that empty stand and fear for them.

One morning our photographer R.L. Chopra and I hired a taxi from their stand across the road for an assignment. We recognized our Sikh driver. He would say only one thing as we headed out, he said he wanted to get at someone in revenge (he used the Punjabi word, 'vad'). Chopra replied that he could 'vad' whom he liked as long as he didn't 'vad' us. The driver said nothing. A little way along the road the taxi had to stop at some point. The driver turned around to speak to us. 'How could I ever "vad" you?' he said.

Anger no doubt fed the revenge attacks by an extremist group. Congress MP Lalit Maken was assassinated in mid-1985; Arjan Dass, a Congress party councillor close to the Gandhi family was shot dead a little later. That year also brought bombs planted in transistor radios that went off all over the city. These attacks came from fringe extremists; the anger among Sikh people was real but never was directed simply at non-Sikhs. The Sikhs separated the Delhi killers from just the people of Delhi.

The silver lining of those post-killing days, and it was a broad one, appeared by way of those countless people of Delhi who looked after the Sikhs in those refugee camps. Theirs was a healing touch, their touch healed also political wounds.

I attended a meeting at a hall on the Delhi University campus early in 1985, addressed by Harcharan Singh Longowal, the Akali Dal leader who had once rivalled Bhindranwale in confronting the Congress government of Indira Gandhi. He had then launched and led a lengthy morcha against the government. At this meeting on the university campus he would have had more reason than ever to speak in anger against the Congress government of the day. But he appeared on stage before us with hands folded. He thanked everybody in the room, the 'soney sajjano' (lovely people) as he called them, for standing by the Sikhs in the city. The healing touch brought emotional insulation against anger.

I did not report the refugee story much, though I visited many of these centres with friends who volunteered support there. The rebuilding of lives was 'not news'. I remained under pressure to file reports that might present some conspiracy behind the assassination of Mrs Gandhi. And then, elections were coming up by end-December that I was assigned to cover. The election became the story. Everybody wanted to forget the killings and the survivors.

13

Commissions and Omissions

An inquiry commission was set up in 1985, to be headed by Justice Ranganath Mishra. I decided to hand in affidavits based on what I had seen. I imagined my affidavits would be of some significance—they related to two members of parliament I had run into through the violence, they presented a face of policing I had seen for myself.

I could present, I thought, independent eyewitness accounts. Very few had seen the violence who could now claim to be independent eyewitnesses and who were also testifying to what they saw. Otherwise the affidavit game was all between the killers and the victims. The killers, needless to say, were not now going to present an honest picture. Many of the surviving victims would, and did. Tragically, such accounts were submitted under an overhang of doubt—that these were 'interested' accounts and therefore not 'objective'.

No one had seen more than the surviving victims had, and no one else had seen it so tragically close. But the testimony of eyewitnesses to actual murder, who saw and could identify the killers, was dismissed, their accounts discounted. Or they were silenced by fear and threats.

In ordinary circumstances police accounts would be accepted as authoritative to a degree. But they couldn't be over those killings of 1984. The police became prime agents for a cover-up, quite the opposite of any expectation that they would uncover facts. They couldn't be expected to produce independent eyewitness statements through investigations or say anything credible themselves.

Given my front-line viewing of some of those events, I had to submit affidavits because, important or not, here was an opportunity to join a process of justice, to say what I saw. That seemed straightforward enough, but some well-meaning lawyers suggested a chat with one of them so that I could be prepared for what to expect; I had never appeared before a judge.

A couple of days before I was to appear before Justice Mishra, I met Nandita Haksar, a lawyer who took up social causes actively. She instructed me just how I should present my evidence before the Mishra Commission. I have no recollection exactly what she suggested I do or don't, but I do have a clear recollection that this advice left me confused. I had thought it would be straight and simple—I had reported what I had seen, and now I would tell the commission what I had seen and reported, that's all. As it turned out, that wasn't all, at all. I was to discover why Nandita thought I needed to prepare myself.

~

The appearance before Justice Mishra was much like my idea of appearing before a judge. The judge sat tall and austere-looking in a high pulpitlike space at an elevation to appropriately Supreme Court-like level, he actually sat 'up there'. Some lawyer or court official or some such figure directed me, at our ground level, to explain the circumstances in which I had filed my affidavits. I spoke about what I had seen and reported in the course of my work as a reporter with the *Express*, which I had then summed up in affidavits placed before the commission.

Then it came to cross-examination by two lawyers, one representing the Central government and one the Delhi Police. I cannot remember which was which and I doubt it matters, they spoke the same language. The first of the two asked me if I could produce eyewitnesses who could testify that I had been there at these places that I had reported from. I didn't understand immediately what he was saying. But the demand became rapidly clear: I was being asked to produce independent eyewitnesses who could testify that I had been there as eyewitness.

I could hardly believe this demand. I asked why they were asking me to produce a witness and did they think I was not there at all, that I was making this up? I remember well the advice from the lawyer. 'Don't get excited,' he said in what I recall as an educative tone. 'You must never get excited.' Justice Mishra nodded in agreement, he said I should not get excited when presenting evidence.

No, I could not produce any eyewitness to testify that I had ever been at Rakab Ganj and at other places I had mentioned, never mind to then bring them up to testify that I had indeed seen what I was saying I had seen. Or even just that they had seen me seeing. So they would have to see me seeing, and also see for themselves what it was that I was seeing, if such evidence was to carry. The impossibility of this demand was immediately evident to me. It also occurred to me, right there, that had I taken an eyewitness along with me, he could not then have been considered independent at all. It was apparent, and apparent also then, that this business of finding an eyewitness to an eyewitness could go on indefinitely.

The second lawyer gave me a second chance. He spoke kindly, to calm me down presumably. If not eyewitness, could I produce a logbook from *The Indian Express* that would list exactly where I was in the city at what time and could such a logbook confirm that I was indeed at those places I had given my eyewitness accounts from? I explained that no newspaper keeps such logbooks and that this was not the way city reporters worked.

That's it, evidence dismissed. I had produced no eyewitness to testify that I was an eyewitness, nor a logbook from my newspaper office tracking my minute-to-minute movements through the day. No credence could therefore attach to what I was saying—in the end, none was. I emerged from that hearing some poor sod, and what does he know about legal matters.

I could see why a police lawyer would have to defend the police somehow and so attack a witness seen as against the police. I was not sure why the government lawyer had taken the position he had. Call it naïve, but I couldn't figure out why the government representative wanted so much to smother every word spoken on behalf of the victims.

Surely this was a government of the people and surely it was justice for people we were talking about. Wasn't this their government as much as anyone else's? Why would the government not want to be on their side? Surely there was a difference between the government itself and erring officialdom? Why did there even have to be two sides in that hearing—one speaking for the government and the police, the other for the victims? Why would the government have chosen to defend failing police officers and suspect leaders, and not defend people's right to justice?

Why was the government viewing officials as more its own than the people who died and suffered as a consequence of the actions or inactions of its officials and its political leaders? It wouldn't be right to expect uncritical sympathy from the government, or any support for a position that might be separate from facts. But the government position before the hearings was not to seek to ascertain facts for the sake of justice for its people—it was a position of denial, by default, of any suggestion that anything had gone wrong at the government or police end. And the police surely are a government agency for protection of the people.

Why was the government standing automatically on the side of those who were hurt against those who had hurt? This was no trial, it was an exercise to determine the truth. Just the basic set-up of the Mishra Commission hearings looked all wrong.

The government–police team—and team they were—had set out to deny that I was present at Rakab Ganj gurdwara when I said I was, and where I had seen Congress MP Kamal Nath when the gurdwara was being attacked. Over a second affidavit, where I had testified that I had seen and heard Congress MP Dharam Dass Shastri putting pressure on the police to release arrested Congress workers, they did not seek to deny my physical presence, they simply took no note of anything, I had written in my affidavit. This affidavit was not challenged, it was ignored.

Over another affidavit, the police lawyer denied, which is to say he spoke words of denial, that I had seen bodies close to the Durgapura Chowk gurdwara I had visited along with Joydeep Gupta, a reporter from *The Statesman*. The lawyer simply said I had not seen them, just as DCP Sewa Dass from the Delhi Police had when I ran into him outside the gurdwara.

~

The history of queues in the line of failed justice is by now a long and undistinguished one. It has included many whose cause was just and who found no justice. Three days in 1984 produced about the longest such queue independent India has known.

I am not asking for a place in that queue. Perhaps, unknown to an ignorant and non-legal chap such as me, the Supreme Court judge was right in his immensely superior grasp of law to brush my affidavits aside. My prime quarrel is not that the judge—later to be appointed Congress party member of parliament—had discovered that all things considered, there was no substance in my affidavits.

My quarrel, and a silent one that quarrel has been all these years, is that all things were in fact not considered, that nothing I said was.

This does sound awkwardly and unfortunately like some personal grouse. It isn't. This is not a moan why *my* affidavits were not considered. The concern is over a process of justice that disregarded what to me would be just ways. Far more serious matters than any I had raised were disregarded, I speak here of the affidavits I had filed because those arose from what I saw.

Those eyewitness affidavits I'd filed had raised some questions. Mishra did not address those questions to dismiss them for particular reasons—he did not look at the questions, going by the report he submitted. I am no lawyer, and certainly no judge. But I have seen and reported scores of cases down the years. From what I have seen, it would be usual to dismiss submissions with some declared reason for doing so, unless these were obviously outlandish. My submissions were dismissed because I could not establish in line with the judge's expectations that I was there at all when I said I was.

I had in fact two witnesses to prove I was there at the Rakab Ganj gurdwara: Kamal Nath, MP, whom I had met there and spoken to, and Gautam Kaul, additional commissioner of police, whom I had also met and spoken to. My affidavits had said as much. Surely the government then had no ground to suggest I was not there when I said I was. If there were doubts over my presence itself, surely the honourable judge might have found it elementary to suggest that we put that to Kamal Nath and Gautam Kaul.

So, was it a question of just when I was there? The exact time on the watch? I remember those scenes vividly, but I made no minute-to minute noting of when exactly I saw what, and at precisely what time I spoke to whom. I don't think I looked at my watch even once through the time. But the judge could take for granted at least that I was there when Kamal Nath and Gautam Kaul were.

A reference to these two witnesses—and strong witnesses as these things go—would have made unnecessary the second demand for a logbook from my office to prove where I was and when. It would have been known to the lawyers, and to Justice Mishra, that the head office of a newspaper does not log reporters' movements in the field—this is no trade secret. But really, this whole argument was a distraction—some things, many things, the Mishra Commission simply did not want to know.

My affidavit from Rakab Ganj gurdwara had noted also that a platoon of armed men from the CRPF stood by as the crowd advanced again and again towards the gurdwara. They made no attempt to stop them, push them back, or to disperse them. Gautam Kaul, far from leading the police into dispersal of the crowd, ducked to a side at one point when the crowd advanced. It seems therefore an inevitable question to ask: why were the police force there taking no action?

Gautam Kaul produced his own affidavit too, claiming firm and effective action, and naturally, denying he ever ducked to a side. I was never asked to substantiate my account against his denial. That inquiry panel was not to know of itself who was right and who not; but clearly we could not both have been right. No questioning came to ascertain whether my account could have been accurate or not. My account had raised a serious question: if a top police officer had chosen to be inactive, and visibly so in the face of street violence, what was this saying about the police and of the message going out to the rest of the police from the top?

The presence both of Gautam Kaul and Kamal Nath under the circumstances raised awkward questions: was a Congress party MP in some sort of understanding with violent crowds? Maybe he wasn't, but the inquiry commission did not come to that conclusion following any sustained questioning or cross-examination.

Why were the police standing idly by in the face of a violent crowd? Did the police have good reasons to do nothing? I was not cross-examined over their disciplined paralysis that I had seen. I was then the only independent eyewitness on the scene—separate from those advancing crowds, from the Sikhs within the gurdwara, from the police, and from the Congress leader.

Again, at the Karol Bagh police station, here was an eyewitness account speaking of a Congress-I MP threatening the police, inside a police station, demanding release of his party men who had been arrested for loot. What more obvious (and more tactlessly revealed) evidence could have arisen of a connection between looters and Congress leaders? Here too I was the only independent eyewitness, away from the Congress-I and the police. At no stage was I asked to present evidence as witness.

The government lawyers asked about my affidavit over the Durgapura Chowk gurdwara. One of the government lawyers declared that I hadn't seen any bodies. It is a recorded fact that killings had taken place at and around Durgapura Chowk gurdwara. To me it was clear that a quick cleaning job had been done there in time for Rajiv Gandhi's scheduled visit but that it had not been clean enough.

Again, I was not cross-examined over this, my statement was simply denied. The problem with the inquiry commission was not what it found after due process, but that it did not go down the way of due process. It did not ascertain, it did not make even a show of ascertaining; it only dismissed. Or accepted.

My distress over being silenced was nothing before what the survivors who were eyewitnesses would have endured. So many of them, in thousands, had seen loved ones burnt alive before them, they saw who killed and later so many said who had killed. And they didn't get a hearing that counted for anything. The killers they saw went unpunished. What they had seen was traumatic; what I saw was, I thought, telling. Justice Mishra didn't think so.

~

When the Mishra Commission report came out, it spoke for itself—and not in the way intended. My little brush with that inquiry was meaningful to me but, in the larger scheme of things, inconsequential. Whatever my own experience, the inquiry would only be as good as the report it produced.

The Mishra Commission got going with the support of the Citizens Justice Committee (CJC), an umbrella organization of human rights groups that came together to secure the justice for the 1984 victims. It was led by former Bombay High Court judge V.M. Tarkunde, a widely revered campaigner for human rights. H.S. Phoolka took over as its legal counsel. That was to become for him the beginning of a long, long struggle.

The Mishra Commission was set up in May 1985. After that, nothing happened for a while. Almost nobody came before it, the commission waThe Kusum Lata Mittal inquiry ordered in 1987 vits and evidence from survivors and witnesses to present to the commission and that was when the procedures got going. But the CJC soon found itself drawn into a spat with Justice Mishra over questions of openness. The CJC opposed secrecy in the proceedings imposed by Mishra. Other differences arose over the death toll. Finally, the CJC insisted it wanted to cross-examine senior officials and Mishra wouldn't allow this. In March 1986 the CJC withdrew from the Mishra Commission.

Justice Mishra declared in his inquiry report to follow that the decision of the committee to walk away from the inquiry created 'some amount of embarrassment in the working of the Commission'.[1] This 'embarrassment' arose over some media reports—Mishra really did not want the media anywhere near his inquiry.

Once the CJC had quit, Mishra, who had barred the media from reporting the hearings at the commission, was unhappy that members of the commission spoke to the media about their decision to leave. 'Having withdrawn from the proceedings, the Committee should not have helped a debate to be raised in the Press,' Mishra said.[2] Members of the CJC were then no longer a part of the proceedings, the media itself hadn't been from the start. The judge wanted conversations between two entities that had nothing to do with his business any more to keep communications 'in camera'—legal language for shutting up publicly.

Among the disputes that arose through the spell where the CJC worked with Mishra was the question just how many Sikhs had been killed in Delhi after the assassination of Mrs Gandhi. R.K. Ahuja, then home secretary with the Delhi administration, who set about determining the death toll following directions from the Mishra Commission reported in 1987 that 2,733 people had been killed in Delhi.

Whether that official final count is the last word on the death toll is far from certain. The path towards coming to some sort of number had been as tortuous as it was painful. All sorts of numbers came and went before the Mishra Commission. The commission confronted an admittedly difficult question.

Mishra noted that in parliament the government had spoken of 2,146 killed. He then noted that Delhi Administration had listed 2,307 dead. The first information reports of the police placed the figure at 1,419—about half the total later admitted officially. So, even by official admission, Delhi Police did not record about half of all the murders later established. Other factors arose to suggest the death toll might be higher than the official numbers; Mishra admitted that many charred bodies had been found on which no post-mortem had been carried out, and that the dead would have included several from a 'floating population'[3] that moves in and out of Delhi.

In the face of such uncertainty over the death toll, the CJC began its own investigations and came to a different assessment that it then presented to Mishra. Mishra said in his report that the CJC had at first filed a 'grand total' of 3,949, which it later reduced by 149 on ground of duplication while adding seventy names. The CJC, Mishra noted, then presented a final figure of 3,870.

Mishra, clearly peeved that the CJC had withdrawn from his inquiry, pounced on what he saw as 'an arithmetical error in the totalling of the number'.[4] Given the CJC's additions and subtractions, the correct number, he said, by their account should be 3,874, and not the 3,870 as the committee had written in its statement.

Mishra triumphed over this difference of four he had spotted. If counting was to be his forte, Mishra sat on far shakier grounds—and far more seriously. Not 3,874 and 3,870, Mishra demonstrated he could not tell the difference between five and six when it mattered.

In describing the policing set-up in Delhi while surveying the scene in which the violence erupted, Mishra said: 'By 1984, the Union Territory had been divided into five police districts, each being called a Range in charge of a Deputy Inspector General of Police (later, Addl. Commissioner of Police).'[5] That's three serious errors in one sentence: One, Delhi comprised not five but six police districts (north, central, east, New Delhi, south and west). Second, each district was not called a range. There were two ranges only, called Delhi and New Delhi, each divided into three police districts. Third, the officers in charge of those districts were additional commissioners of police right then and not later. In 1984 there were no deputy inspector generals of police in Delhi.

The difference went far deeper than nomenclature. Under the commissioner system, the police had different kinds of powers. The Supreme Court judge inquiring into a law and order breakdown in Delhi demonstrated that he had no idea how the police in Delhi were set up—this he had exhibited himself in a considered report following a long inquiry.

Mishra had got his facts wrong, and few thought he had got his conclusions right. He declared in his report that the riots were not organized by the Congress party. A pleased Congress government later appointed him the Chief Justice of India, then chairman of the National Human Rights Commission, and finally nominated him a member of the Rajya Sabha from the Congress party.

Mishra set down several reasons for his conclusion clearing the Congress. On the evening of 31 October, he notes, thirteen gurdwaras were attacked. 'These incidents of October 31, 1984 appear to have been taken by way of involuntary reaction of a deep sense of grief, anguish and hatred for the assassins. There can be no scope to contend, and much less to accept, that at the initial stage on October 31, 1984, the violence that took place was organised.'[6]

What the judge did not note was that of these thirteen gurdwaras, ten stood in the area around the All India Institute of Medical Sciences (AIIMS), where a large number of people had gathered through the day and where the cry 'Khoon ka badla khoon' was first raised. It was from here that these people branched out to attack gurdwaras. There could after all be some scope to contend, if not accept from this alone, that the attacks branching out from here just might have been organized. A very large number of Congress party men had gathered outside AIIMS. The cry for bloody revenge was raised here, and the violence spread from here. This is not for a moment suggested as evidence or even indication that these were party-led attacks that evening. But nothing here establishes innocence either that Mishra was pronouncing on just this basis.

Mishra reasoned further that Congress party men could not have been involved because 'the gloom that had spread and affected the Congress men in particular would not have permitted any such organisation to be handled'.[7] By this reasoning, the men spreading the violence outward from AIIMS that evening, the men crying for blood, were necessarily not from the Congress because party men had been immobilized by a pall of gloom, they were feeling far too sad to attack anyone. It is on the basis of this reasoning that the judge was pronouncing 'not guilty'.

But he notes a change the following day. On 1 November, he says, 'the riotous mobs followed almost a uniform pattern everywhere'.[8] He sums up how they were killed: 'The riotous crowd followed the pattern of burning all the Sikhs who were either killed or were in the process of dying as a result of fatal assault and injuries.'[9] He found that 'there is clear evidence that a common pattern had been followed by big crowds'.[10] A common pattern surely would suggest some organization. As Mishra describes, something had changed overnight.

What changed? Mishra's answer: 'The change in the pattern from spontaneous reaction to organised riots was the outcome of the takeover of the command of the situation by anti-social elements.' Who were these 'anti-social elements' and just how did they come to take over command of the situation?

Mishra's answer: 'It is said that Satan too has a process and when taking to satanic activities the anti-social elements took to their organised process. This is how—and in this sense—violence in Delhi was indeed organised but such organisation was not by any political party or a definite group of persons but by the anti-social elements.'[11]

A sitting judge of the Supreme Court of India had seen the hand of Satan in the killings. Satan, such as he is, is known to plant immorality, he has no known record of also then organizing the lot that he inspired into immorality. It was violence by this Satanic lot that he found was organized. Justice Mishra offers no thoughts on where this Satan came from, but he does describe whom Satan entered.

It was the lower classes. Justice Mishra says in his report: 'The existence of jhuggis with their poverty stricken and underfed people in close proximity of multistoried modern fashionable buildings with the rich section of the society often gives rise to peculiar problems. Incompatibility in the living process between the two classes of people brings about in the poor section a sense of frustration and generates a sense of hatred as also a lust for the property of the well-to-do. In recent years respect for human life has been fast vanishing. Fear of, and regard for, law are also reduced. Moral convictions have perished. There is, therefore, anxiety to avail every opportunity by the jhuggi dwellers to cut the rich to size.'[12]

Mishra offers a class theory. But this theory, such as it is, appears to have little relation to the facts of those days. No doubt loot could be seen as class-inspired and it was Sikhs these gangs could loot because they could get away with it. But each of those gangs out to loot numbered no more than a hundred, if that. In a city of millions that would add up to less than a class revolt. Loot, in any case, is one thing, murder quite another. The really rich were neither murdered nor looted.

We didn't get a class revolt that then 'naturally' led to killing in some police districts in Delhi. Criminality is not the same thing as class anger. Such anger that spilled out was never aimed at all the rich; the attackers mostly hadn't got near enough the seriously rich to loot them. Because there the police had been vigilant. A crowd did advance into the plush Friends Colony in south Delhi on the morning of 1 November. Additional Commissioner of Police Gautam Kaul himself led a police force to drive them away.

The Sikhs killed in Sultanpuri and Trilokpuri were not rich by any means. Nor the Sikhs killed in Sagarpur area around Delhi Cantonment, or Jahangirpuri in the north or Mangolpuri in the west or Seemapuri and Nand Nagri in the east. These are the places where almost all the killings took place.

Attempts at loot and loot itself hit some of the more prosperous areas too. And there Mishra's class theory might carry a kernel of truth, though if a theory is that limited, it can't be a theory at all. But within these limits too Mishra's report betrays serious ignorance about Delhi, and about the particular violence he was examining over three days in Delhi—and pronouncing judgment upon. He seems to have got his facts wrong about the 'multistoried modern fashionable buildings'.[13] Almost nobody among those killed in Delhi then lived in a multistoreyed modern fashionable building. The Sikhs living in such buildings were then about the safest in Delhi.

Delhi saw petty theft and loot within the deprived areas where the killings came, not just heading outwards from these areas to wealthy targets, though that too came. Violence of that kind unleashed by small groups is more criminal action than class anger aimed at the bourgeoisie of Delhi. Or even the bourgeois Sikhs of Delhi if you were to allow that class anger was selected for free expression so long as it could be aimed at the Sikh haves. Class anger launched by groups of a couple of hundred or so, or even just a score, that did not touch the rich, that did not even lust substantially for the property of the well-todo, that arose in select areas to aim at the select—all these add up to any suggestion that Delhi had seen a Red Revolution of sorts, that people had arisen from jhuggis to 'cut the rich to size'.

The satanic view Mishra so philosophically expressed was perhaps a step, a short step, closer to the truth than his Marxist offering. Respect for human life has been vanishing; true, moral convictions have been declining; regard for law has been reduced. And that made carriers of all of the above traits 'anti-socials' that Mishra says organized the riots. The difficulty with this theory is that antisocials may share commonality, but that does not make them therefore organized. Mishra saw an organized pattern to the violence from 1 November. He said also that antisocial people organized the violence. So who then actually organized these 'anti-socials', and how? At that point the Mishra report drops over a precipice into silence.

Mishra's final defence of the Congress party is that if the Congress leadership had organized the killings, many more would have been killed. Undoubtedly a logical suggestion, that had the Congress really got into the act, they could have killed many more.

'If the party in power or a minister or well placed person had masterminded or organised the riots, the same would had taken even a more serious turn. It is the case of all parties before the Commission that in certain area there was no trouble of any noticeable degree and two reasons have been advanced for such a situation—(i) effectiveness of the local police; and (ii) raising of combined defence of the local residents. If the Congress party or a powerful force in the party played any role, neither of these two elements could have functioned in the manner each of them has been ascribed.'[14]

Had the Congress been involved, he further reasons, Sikh members of the Congress party would have been spared. He found 'there is no single instance placed before the Commission where the plea of Sikh that he belonged to the Congress had ever been acceded to by the rioters'.[15] Mishra suggested that submissions from the Delhi Sikh Gurdwara Prabandhak Committee had helped his inquiry 'fortify the conclusion that some people of the Congress party on their own had indulged and participated in the turmoil for considerations entirely their own'.[16]

In the end, he noted that the Congress party had passed resolutions on 1 November, calling for peace and harmony. Given these resolutions, 'it is indeed difficult to allege, much less discover, unseen hands of the party behind the violence perpetrated so dastardly over members of the Sikh community at Delhi.'[17] (Mishra might have reasoned better even in bad grammar.) The home ministry too, he noted, had issued a circular asking for vigil in maintaining peace and harmony. And therefore, Justice Mishra said, the government administration could not have been responsible. Rajiv Gandhi himself had made an appeal for peace and calm and therefore he could not be held responsible either. This, then, was the final reasoning: The Congress party had passed a resolution, the government issued an order, Rajiv Gandhi made an appeal for peace. And therefore none of these was involved. It can get elementary to the point of embarrassment to point out that Justice Mishra left no room for a gap between statement and action. Statements of intention are never enough to establish innocence, most judges would know.

But behind the image of the ground shaking under a falling tree (Rajiv Gandhi's way of describing the killings as an inevitable consequence of the assassination, and to which Justice Mishra made no reference) lay disturbing in-between questions that Justice Mishra's simple sweep did not include. Did the Congress government move swiftly, and effectively, enough to put down the growing violence? Was any attempt made to restrain party leaders who had been seen with the violent crowds? Did the Congress government launch prosecutions and disciplinary action against the police? Or were such moves that were being made in that direction restricted and then stopped? Whose was the hand that had stopped Ved Marwah from completing his inquiry if not that of the Congress government?

But, while saying the right things, it was clear to me, as it was to all I spoke to, that the government had not taken any firm steps to stop the killing where it did happen. True, it did not stop a few police officers doing the right thing, but it then made no effort to ensure that the rest would do the right thing. That some party leaders, if not all, may have done their bit to shake the earth seemed fine with the Congress leadership.

Justice Mishra drew a parallel. The Sikhs, he said, had been right to say that all of them must not be blamed for the actions of two assassins. And so, he argued, even if some few juniors from the Congress party had been involved, the whole party must not be blamed for it. Not a reasonable parallel. That all Sikhs should not have been blamed for two assassins is one thing; that all within an organization should not be blamed for what some within it do is another. Organizations do not parallel society. They are close-knit places where by definition a connected set of people work towards a single purpose. An organization cannot so easily disconnect itself from the doings of its members, and top members at that. It was not a particularly sensitive parallel either— the Citizens Justice Committee found the thinking and language of the Mishra report 'breathtakingly crude'.

~

I quit full-time crime reporting in 1986 to take up responsibilities as chief reporter with *The Indian Express* and then wound up all city reporting responsibilities when I joined the political reporting bureau briefly in 1988. That ended any active reporting in relation to those killings. In the years of city reporting after 1984, my engagement in any active follow-up of the 1984 events was limited and only partly because nothing really happened.

The one who never gave up the struggle to speak for survivors, and to seek justice for those killed, was H.S. Phoolka. He worked indefatigably from the start to bring the guilty to justice. His has been an up-and-down struggle—mostly down after what arose as moments of hope. But he has never given up.

By way of reporting, Manoj Mitta took over after the few of us who had reported those events in those days wound up. He followed up on the fate of the 1984 victims incisively. He dug out buried reports, reports that cornered the government and political leaders into taking note and to begin some move at least in the direction of justice. If the injustices of 1984 were not allowed to be forgotten, it was due primarily to the efforts of Phoolka and Mitta.

My thoughts shared over these pages are no substitute for an account of their efforts, that they themselves have put down exhaustively in their jointly written book *When A Tree Shook Delhi: The 1984 Carnage and Its Aftermath*. They have continued to follow up the consequences of that massacre also after the publication of that book in 2007.

When I presented myself before the Mishra Commission, I didn't have the full legal picture of the circumstances in which it was set up. That I discovered only later, through Phoolka personally and later his book. That's when I discovered the extent of the problems, to put it mildly, with this commission headed by a Supreme Court judge.

In his chapter 'A Farce of an Inquiry', Phoolka details how it came to be that over a period of a month after it set out to receive affidavits, the Mishra Commission received just one: no one seemed to have any faith in it. Mishra then sought help from the CJC of which Phoolka was a member. It was this group that set about securing affidavits to be filed before the commission.

Mishra decided early on to bar any media reporting of the hearings. That, Phoolka writes, 'should have made us see red' because he was violating a 'universally accepted requisite of fair trial'. Nevertheless, the CJC went along with the inquiry. Eventually, Phoolka says, 2,905 affidavits were received—of which two-thirds were against the victims and read mostly similar to one another: 'The same set of assertions was repeated in those affidavits in more or less the same language.' These did not narrate personal experiences, they only offered the opinion that the killing was not organized.

Of the rest, 550 were filed by Mr Phoolka. These were categorized by Mishra as 'pro-victim'. This is how the bulk of affidavits were divided. By Mishra's own categorization, there were very few affidavits that were classed as independent and outside of those categories. My affidavits would have been among those few.

This categorization itself was odd, it suggested that the 'pro-victim' affidavits had taken a dedicated and partial position, and so had others. I thought this kind of clubbing would reduce the individual validity of each account. And Mishra entertained the submission of a large number of affidavits that should have been declared inadmissible if all they were offering was an opinion that the killing was not organized. By an outward count, the 'anti-victim' lot was outnumbering the pro-victim start straightaway. But far more upfront indications of bias came to surface.

Phoolka's account in his book details how affidavits defending the Congress began to fall apart on the very first day of the hearings. Forgeries and fraud surfaced in several of these. Some reports on this did appear at first in the media that were later blocked.

Former chief justice of India S.M. Sikri, working with the CJC, declared that 'the unusual procedure adopted by the commission subserves the purpose of those who are interested in shielding the culprits and suppressing the truth'. The committee wanted to crossexamine senior officials and the police commissioner in

October– November 1984, Subhash Tandon. Mishra refused. At the end of March 1986, the committee withdrew from the Mishra proceedings. Mishra went ahead without the CJC; he pronounced that no Congress leaders were involved; he did find fault with the police but no officer was indicted in law as a result.

Phoolka's account that I read later was in line with my own experience before Justice Mishra. Standing before his perched lordship I had glimpsed briefly in the treatment of my affidavits what Mr Phoolka discovered at such painful length.

The Mishra Commission set up by the Congress government only brought reminders of how the government was now failing to deliver justice after refusing to protect Sikhs earlier. It showed how the government was continuing to shield criminals. At the first stage over those three days, government knowledge of the crimes that were being unleashed, coupled with its inability to stop them, could be argued to be a conspiracy where leaders and officials of the government had ended up wilfully supporting criminals and killings.

The cover-up that came later added up to condoning murders. At an individual level, that's culpable in law. If that act of condoning is processed through structures and institutions by the government, then the government becomes culpable. The reason that a straight application of law in that scenario seems fuzzy is that individuals merge into institutions. How do you prosecute an institution? Possible, of course, but that would take strong government will. Where were the signs of that? None that the Mishra Commission brought; that inquiry only established that the government was covering one kind of failure with another.

The Rajiv Gandhi government had resisted all calls for setting up an inquiry commission in the weeks and months after the killings. Rajiv Gandhi declared it would only 'open up old wounds'.

All murder trials do, but no one has suggested responsibly that they should not therefore be held.

The Mishra Commission was set up as a concession to a demand by Akali leader Harcharan Singh Longowal. Longowal could not select the judge for it; the government did.

Why would the government want to stifle truth? These questions were being asked at the time of both the ruling party leaders and government officials—the realities of Delhi do not separate them quite as sharply as the Constitution of India does. Accusations sprang up all around, and with reason, that government 'leadership', or the lack of it, had made the killings possible. To argue by inference for a moment, in the style of Justice Mishra, why would the government wish to shield the guilty if it had nothing to hide? Why would it want to set up a show of an inquiry that would prevent any real inquiry? Was that need to set up a show really, a show of complicity?

The show cast a long shadow. After the Mishra Commission was set up, police records were denied to the police themselves. Where are all those records now that were handed over to the commission? A new government set up a new commission of inquiry in 2000 headed by retired Supreme Court judge G.T. Nanavati to inquire into the riots. The Nanavati Commission asked for the records that were with the Mishra Commission. It didn't get them.

~

I travelled down from London in 2001 to depose before Justice Nanavati. I did believe, but only a little, that the Nanavati Commission may succeed at last, because it might want to. The law still held, facts could be at hand, records could be summoned, I thought, many of the killers and their protectors were still around. They could be prosecuted, if prosecution someone wanted.

The Nanavati Commission was set up by the BJP government. It took five years to submit its report. When it did, it was in early 2005, soon after the Congress had returned to power. I would not have guessed when I appeared before this second commission that it would take that long to hand in its report.

I went across to the office for the Nanavati Commission at the Vigyan Bhavan annexe in Delhi to give evidence, which meant I'd say what I could remember, and say what I'd said before. I planted myself before Justice Nanavati accordingly. He asked me about Rakab Ganj gurdwara where I had seen Kamal Nath and Gautam Kaul. I was crossexamined over when I went there and what I had seen. A government lawyer asked me exactly when I was there and I did remember it was around four in the afternoon. It was some relief to hear Justice Nanavati declare during my cross-examination that seventeen years later I could not be expected to recall at exactly what time.

Memory finds its own ways of selection and holding on to a selection. And now thirteen years after deposing before Justice Nanavati, one exchange through that deposition stands out sharply in memory. For the rest, I had nothing new to say, no one had anything new to ask.

That one exchange through otherwise routine repetitions stayed with me for the discomfort I caused by mentioning Rajiv Gandhi. I was describing my brief meeting with him in Amethi, where he had been campaigning for the election in December 1984. The clerk writing down what I was saying stopped writing the moment I mentioned Rajiv Gandhi. He looked to Nanavati for guidance.

The judge queried me a bit dismissively over what I was saying. He seemed distinctly discouraging of any mention of Rajiv Gandhi, without actually stopping me. But I was saying what I was, and some reference to Rajiv Gandhi was included finally.

What was written down, I can't remember. The mechanics of such deposition seemed rather basic to me. Through the deposition I had not spoken fully for myself the way I might have wanted to. That was just the way such statements are structured. Someone would write down their summary on a sheet based on what I said, the equivalent of a newspaper report of a speech. I was then asked to read and sign that sheet, which I did; I had after all said what had been summed up. The essence of what was on that sheet wasn't other than what I'd said, but it wasn't all of it. The reference to Rajiv Gandhi was minimal rather than full.

True, I could have insisted on the recording of a full account of what I was saying. But such ways of summarized representation seemed the convention. They weren't doing to me after all what I didn't do to others daily in the course of my work as a reporter. In any case, I believed that no note would be taken of this reference eventually. The content of that reference stood well short of anything dramatic. What struck me was the firmness with which Justice Nanavati didn't want to hear the name of Rajiv Gandhi. Where this reluctance came from I don't know, and don't wish to guess.

No doubt, such proceedings are carried out in a matter-of-fact way, and are no indication in themselves of findings ahead. But it seemed that this was all just procedure being completed, from which nothing would result. I saw no hunger to hear more from me, and faced no effort by lawyers to draw out any meaning from the facts I had narrated. Perhaps the disinterested listening was a response to my affidavits in which they had seen all they needed to.

~

The Nanavati Commission, ordered by the BJP government in May 2000, submitted its report in February 2005. It did take a few steps forward from where the Mishra Commission had left off. Given where Mishra took his inquiry, that is not necessarily saying very much.

I hardly have the credentials to challenge the august status of the judges behind those findings, but in truth I believe that the Nanavati report is still not the last word on the subject. For a start, the shadow of the Mishra report fell heavily upon this second inquiry. Justice Nanavati noted in his final report that 'the full record of Justice Mishra Commission did not become available to the Commission'. He had sought it through his officials but it had become clear, he said, from affidavits filed before the commission 'that in spite of their efforts the remaining record was not traceable'.[18] The Nanavati Commission began its inquiry with one hand tied.

Sensitive police records from 1984 had been taken over in the following year by Ved Marwah's team for the purpose of his inquiry.

These were then handed over to the Mishra Commission. That commission declared the Congress leadership innocent and disregarded all manner of evidence produced before it. And then, the records were diverted somewhere, and Nanavati could not get them. And no one else having the records did anything with these. Exactly what was in those records that was denied to Nanavati?

The bulk of the 185-page report we finally got from Nanavati is a recount of attacks and incidents date-wise and district-wise. Some of the background within the Mishra Commission is simply repeated by the Nanavati Commission—though Justice Nanavati did correct the total number of police districts in Delhi then from five to six.

Considering that the bulk of Nanavati's report is a repeat of the data presented before Mishra and the Kusum Lata Mittal report that followed, Nanavati took a remarkably long five years before he submitted his findings in 2005. He had his own take over the submissions I had made that were different from Mishra's. And as it later became clear, heavy political clouds of several colours hang over Nanavati's report (see the last chapter 'BJP Shadows').

The report notes Rajiv Gandhi broadcasting all the right things, but raises no difficult questions in relation to Rajiv Gandhi. Several difficult questions needed asking. Did Rajiv Gandhi as Prime Minister order the pursuit of cases against the suspects? Did the Prime Minister want 3,000 murders in his capital city investigated or not? Did Rajiv Gandhi order such investigation? In the face of massive and provably criminal failures of his government administration, did he order the prosecution of anyone within the government? Or order the prosecution of his own MP he himself had acknowledged to have been involved?

Who could have stopped the killing or at the least reduced it? What kind of chain of command lay behind the police inaction, or complicity? These shady areas, the commission did not explore. The truth lay in those shades, and the commission didn't go that way.

Who, finally, could have ordered the guillotine dropped on the Marwah inquiry? Who, if not the Prime Minister, had described those killings as an inevitable shaking of the earth upon the falling of a tree? What were the implications of presenting that image? Nanavati noted that the violence was organized, but did not probe and did not say who organized it. Questions crowded into those shaded areas. No inquiry asked these questions.

In my deposition before Nanavati, he had gone out of his way, and certainly out of the proper way for a commission of inquiry, to dissuade me from saying anything about Rajiv Gandhi at all. The reason was apparent then, the report he produced confirmed it. He had declared his alignment with Rajiv Gandhi's tree view before he was called to conduct the inquiry, he showed his support for Rajiv Gandhi through my deposition and his final report was in line with this view.

'The events leading to the assassination of Smt. Indira Gandhi show that it was not an unconnected event,' Nanavati concluded. 'There was progressive deterioration in the situation in Punjab since 1981. Violent activities of the extremists elements in Punjab had increased. Many Hindus were killed by Sikh extremists. Manoeuverings by the political parties during this period to gain political advantages and exploitation of the tension had led to a smouldering resentment against the Sikh community. Probably, there was a desire on the part of some persons to teach a lesson to the Sikhs. The assassination of Smt. Indira Gandhi by her two Sikh security guards appears to have triggered the massive onslaught on the lives and properties of Sikhs in Delhi. Smt. Indira Gandhi was a popular leader. She was the Prime Minister of India. It was, therefore, not unusual that on coming to know about her assassination by her Sikh security men, the people reacted angrily.'[19]

The conclusions simply bypass evidence of organized attacks—the rumours of poisoned water spreading systematically all around the city at the same time, the killing by the use of as unusual a murder weapon as burning tyres all around the city, the clearly commandeered mobs that were not formed of local people, the organized identification of Sikh homes. Nanavati concluded that the violence was not organized after himself noting facts that would suggest quite the opposite—quite his style.

Nanavati writes that mobs 'either came armed with weapons and inflammable materials like kerosene, petrol and some white powder or were supplied with such materials soon after they were taken to the localities where the Sikhs were to be attacked.'[20] From 1 November, 'attacks were made in a systematic manner and without much fear of the police; almost suggesting that they were assured that they would not be harmed while committing those acts and even thereafter. Male members of the Sikh community were taken out of their houses. They were beaten first and then burnt alive in a systematic manner.'[21] Does this sound like organized attacks or spontaneous outpouring of political grief?

'In some cases tyres were put around their necks and then they were set on fire by pouring kerosene or petrol over them. In some cases white inflammable powder was thrown on them which immediately caught fire thereafter. This was a common pattern which was followed by the big mobs which had played havoc in certain areas. The shops were identified, looted and then burnt. Thus what had initially started as an angry outburst became an organized carnage.'[22]

Nanavati notes also in fact that the organized violence was led by Congress-I leaders. 'Large number of affidavits indicate that local Congress(I) leaders and workers had either incited or helped the mobs in attacking the Sikhs. But for the backing and help of influential and resourceful persons, killing of Sikhs so swiftly and in large numbers could not have happened.'[23] Who then within the Congress-I leadership of Delhi could have been influential and resourceful? Surely, the party's battery of MPs sat at the top of the party leadership in Delhi.

Nanavati repeats Mishra in blaming junior Congress-I people acting in what he too saw as personal political capacity, but also acknowledges that these would have necessarily had to be 'influential and resourceful persons'. Was it junior party leaders and workers then who had proved that influential and resourceful? He insists it could not have been senior Congress-I leaders. 'There is absolutely no evidence suggesting that Shri Rajiv Gandhi or any other high-ranking Congress-I leader had suggested or organized attacks on Sikhs. Whatever acts were done, were done by the local Congress-I leaders and workers, and they appear to have done so for their personal political reasons.'[24]

At the same time, outsiders from the scenes of killing, Nanavati notes, coming 'in large numbers could not have been brought by ordinary persons from the public. Bringing them from outside required an organized effort. Supplying them with weapons and inflammable material also required an organized effort. There is evidence to show that outsiders were shown the houses of the Sikhs.'[25] And yet Nanavati stops short of conclusions arising from the facts he himself notes. It could not have been ordinary persons who organized all this. But as he sees it—in the face of overwhelming evidence of the involvement of at least some Congress-I MPs, evidence that he accepts—it could not have been senior party leaders. Could there be some discrepancy here?

After declaring a collective innocence of high-ranking Congress-I leaders, Nanavati names Congress-I MPs he believes were involved. His Commission is 'inclined to take the view' that there is credible evidence against Sajjan Kumar for recording a finding that he was 'probably involved as alleged by the witnesses'.[26] He notes that there is 'evidence suggesting that Shri Dharam Dass Shastri was actively involved in the riots,'[27] that there is credible evidence that Dharam Dass Shastri had instigated his men to organize attacks on Sikhs. On Kamal Nath, Nanavati records at the least that he found his explanations unconvincing. And yet he declares that there is 'absolutely no evidence' that high-ranking Congress-I leaders had suggested or organized attacks on Sikhs. The word 'discrepancy' again comes to mind.

Congress-appointed Supreme Court judge Mishra killed justice over 1984, BJP-appointed judge Nanavati buried it.

~

A useful by-product of Justice Mishra's inquiry was that he started off some others, among them a probe into police failures by Kusum Lata Mittal. This was to have been the Kapur Mittal Commission, where former Uttar Pradesh government official Kusum Lata Mittal was to team up with Justice Dalip Kapur. Following early disputes, Mittal went ahead on her own and in her report produced a reconstruction of events based on police records.

Three rather startling facts emerge from Mittal's report that studied police records and the discrepancies in them.[28] So it was able to note both what the police knew and what they did or didn't do.

First, it became evident that the bulk of the attacks on gurdwaras in Delhi came within the space of a few hours on 1 November. Within the span of violence over most of seventy-two hours, the attacks on gurdwaras came mostly on the morning and early afternoon of 1 November, the day after the assassination. This was the period just after busloads had been driven to Teen Murti Bhavan to pay their respects to Indira Gandhi. And from there this lot had driven back, or been driven back. The attacks came after mourners, as they were called, were shown live on Doordarshan raising the slogan 'Khoon ka badla khoon'.

Second, the pattern of attacks documented shows that many of the gurdwaras were attacked sequentially by the same group; and that it was invariably a relatively small group. These men attacked one gurdwara, then moved on to attack a second and a third. At gurdwaras where Sikhs within tried to defend themselves, the police were seen joining the crowds in attacking the gurdwaras. Of police protection for these gurdwaras there was none, barring Sis Ganj.

Third, it is clear from the documented pattern that most of the killing of Sikhs also came on 1 November. The evening of 31 October had seen scattered attacks, later came the lethal ones. This pattern has been noted by both the Mishra and the Nanavati Commissions.

The killing pattern was much the same—burning Sikhs alive.

Bands across the city had clearly been armed with fuel, tyres and other weapons overnight. Of about 3,000 Sikhs estimated to have been killed, almost all lay dead by the night of 1 November. Some scattered attacks continued on 2 November, and at a few places also on 3 November and in the couple of days following. After the evening of 2 November, records show that less than fifty Sikhs were killed; all the rest were killed earlier.

The evening of 2 November brought a political landmark. About 5.30 p.m. that evening Prime Minister Rajiv Gandhi summoned the lieutenant governor (LG) of Delhi, P.G. Gavai, according to official records. Rajiv Gandhi issued a firm order to Gavai; he said all killing must stop within fifteen minutes. The fact is that almost all the killing had been over for fifteen hours before this fifteen-minute ultimatum came.

At 10 p.m. that night, the LG testified that he was again called to the Prime Minister's house. Now, the general manager of the telephones department too had been invited because of complaints that people could not get through to the police emergency number, 100. After days and nights of failure to get through to the police on phone, it was being decided at 10 p.m. on 2 November that the telephones department should do something about this. By then the killers were done.

True, Rajiv Gandhi had made public appeals for peace earlier. But this most firm executive order he gave as Prime Minister came well after the earth had stopped shaking, more or less.

By way of information, these records that the Mittal report relies upon offer a fairly full picture of just what happened and where in Delhi at that time. Mishra and Nanavati had noted a pattern to the killings: the Mittal report reproduces the contours of that pattern. Its dry documentation is a gut-wrenching read.

~

It records the attacks that began on 31 October, which included several on gurdwaras in south Delhi at places such as R.K. Puram, a neighbourhood of government housing for junior officials spread between Ring Road around Chanakyapuri and Outer Ring Road along Munirka. This violence followed the assembly and later dispersal of crowds outside the All India Institute of Medical Sciences where Mrs Gandhi's body had been taken. The report also takes note of incidents in other areas of Delhi that evening. This violence stopped well short of any mass murders.

The following morning brought attacks on gurdwaras. These attacks, evidently, were not an immediate expression of any class-driven revolt of the kind Mishra suggested; groups descended on gurdwaras simultaneously, and not primarily for personal gain. In the poor areas where they stood, these small gurdwaras would house no gold, no piles of cash to enrich the raiders. The attack, say, on the Maujpur gurdwara in Seelampur, located just to the east of the Yamuna on the way to Shahdara, did not yield wealth to the attackers; they did not imagine they were looting a bank or its equivalent.

The Takshila Guru Harkrishan Public School was burnt around here, as the Guru Harkrishan Public School had been in Vasant Vihar—these schools were not attacked for money. The Preet Vihar gurdwara was burnt down, several bodies were discovered here later. People had entered to kill, not to loot. In this neighbourhood, other gurdwaras were burnt in and around Nand Nagri that morning, to the north-east of Shahdara, and approaching the Indian Air Force base at Hindon.

Across Delhi to the west, much the same pattern became evident. The Mittal report says that Congress party MP Sajjan Kumar addressed a meeting that morning in Sultanpuri, a 'resettlement' colony of tworoom tenements located between Pitampura and Rohini. One of the first targets after this meeting was over became the gurdwara in C Block of Sultanpuri, and then one in Budh Vihar, a little to the north.

The report documents that it was small groups on the move that killed where they went. It cites eyewitnesses reporting a convoy on the move near gurdwara Tikana Sahib in Punjabi Bagh that left attacks behind them: at one place they were seen numbering no more than only a few men in one white Ambassador car and a couple on a motorcycle.

About 11 a.m., after setting fire to the gurdwaras in this area in the west, the crowd set fire to Guru Nanak Public School. Twenty minutes later, Guru Singh Sabha in Bhagwan Dass Nagar, close to Punjabi Bagh, was burnt. All these attacks on gurdwaras came more or less simultaneously; the attackers were organized and equipped; it's hard to see groups who could be described simply as antisocial launching these simultaneous attacks in a similar way, and simultaneously. Delhi had no club then called Antisocial whose members communicated with one another towards a common purpose.

The attacks on the gurdwara did bring theft, attackers grabbed what they could. But that appeared to have been an incidental outcome of the attack, not its primary purpose; these were not instances of organized theft. Those men entered gurdwaras to burn and to kill.

Gurdwaras stood as just the best-known place to locate Sikhs to kill, they were the most identifiably Sikh place to destroy. But the Mittal report documents that the killing followed a pattern on the streets, and in their homes.

In the west district, just as in east Delhi, the police ordered Sikhs into their homes, and then the groups attacked and killed, as the report says, 'with the full connivance of the police'. The report says the police then dragged bodies away from the streets and burnt them. 'There is enough evidence to show that dead bodies were being burnt or systematically removed soon after the killings.'

Not a single arrest was made over these attacks in the west. 'This was quite natural because the evidence goes to show that police was completely in league with the mob,' the report notes. Many hundreds were killed in Sultanpuri alone in west Delhi.

The killings crossed the line of mere anger into a methodical, and remorseless, hunt. In nearby Nangloi in west Delhi, a very low-income area, the Mittal report noted that no attacks came on 31 October; what did take place was a meeting of local leaders. The attacks followed the next day. The report describes one such.

Gurdeep Kaur's family received warnings of an advancing crowd.

Nine men from the family hid themselves inside a tubewell, the report notes. But the men in the crowd came and spotted them. The Sikhs were dragged out and burnt alive. Two girls too were burnt alive. By the time the crowd was done, at least a hundred Sikhs lay dead in Nangloi. Only one case was registered. No one was arrested.

Word was spreading quickly among Sikhs about the emerging pattern to the killing. In Fateh Nagar and Shiv Nagar, close to Tilak Nagar in west Delhi, Hindus and Sikhs formed joint resistance groups. Together they saved everyone in the area on 1 and 2 November. Police officers then came and ordered Sikhs to go inside their homes, but here the Sikhs refused—they knew by then what that would mean.

The Mittal report documents such incidents of police connivance all over the city. A retired major in this area said his licensed gun was seized by the police and he was taken to the police station. When he asked for a receipt, he was beaten up. His call to help Sikhs under attack was ignored. A case was registered—against him. Three cases were registered in this area, one each on 1, 2 and 3 November, all of them against Sikhs. The police said no deaths occurred here; Delhi administration later counted sixty-three.

In Najafgarh in west Delhi the Mittal report tracked a single group of killers on the move.[29] The murders, the arson and the looting came at different places and at different times but sequentially—they were the work of one lot on the move from one place to another. The group advanced from Gaushala Road, burning and looting along the way through Chawla Stand, Roshanara, Dhansa Stand, Dharampura and Dichau village.

They then entered a local hospital to attack Sikhs who were already injured. The police recorded that eight of the injured Sikhs waiting for treatment were killed. Five survived. They were then sent in a private truck to Dr Ram Manohar Lohia Hospital. Was this spontaneous expression of sadness over the death of a beloved leader? Or even of just anger? These looked like killers who had been organized into a mission.

A local police unit later argued that they could not act because the police had insufficient arms—after declaring also that the police force in the area was equipped with three semi-automatic rifles, one Sten gun, thirty-six rifles and seventeen revolvers or pistols. 'Were these insufficient?' the Mittal report asks. In any case, none was used.

Was the bunch of men, and no more than a bunch, that stopped trains at Tughlakabad to pull Sikh passengers out driven by grief? Or even by greed? That was no way to mourn clearly. And these were no muggers focused on Sikh pockets. They were out to murder.

At 10.25 a.m. on 1 November, reports came into the police control room that the Frontier Mail had been stopped at Tughlakabad by a group hunting Sikh passengers.[30] This train runs from Mumbai to Amritsar, and was certain to have a number of Sikh passengers on it. The Mittal report says that the control room flashed out a collective signal at 10.54 a.m. to all police officers saying that Sikh passengers were being taken down from the Frontier Mail at Tughlakabad and assaulted. After this, other trains were stopped at Tughlakabad, and Sikh passengers dragged out and killed through the day.

The crowds damaged the starter signals around 4 p.m. That meant that mail trains that do not normally halt at Tughlakabad had to stop there. Among these were Punjab Mail and the Rajdhani Express.

After an admitted seventy-four Sikh passengers were killed at Tughlakabad, the railway authorities cancelled further trains. One passenger's tale tells the story of the trains, the passengers and the police. This was no ordinary passenger, he was the former railway minister Madhu Dandavate, who happened to be on a train passing through Tughlakabad that morning. At Tughlakabad, he said, 'I found two Sikhs killed and thrown on the platform and then their dead bodies were set on fire on the platform. The police standing on the platform made no efforts to prevent either the killings or the burning of Sikhs.'

It was a different story when his train stopped at Mathura, in the state of Uttar Pradesh. 'At Mathura when the train stopped, commandos and police party were already ready for action on the platform. Therefore, there was not much of influx into the train.'

In their reports of events at the Tughlakabad station, the Delhi Police omitted Madhu Dandavate. 'The presence of Prof. Madhu Dandavate, MP and former Railways Minister, was perhaps too inconvenient for the Delhi Police,' the Mittal report said.

Another former minister encountered the ways of the police. Dr Sushila Nayar, a former Union health minister, sent a letter on 6 November to P.V. Narasimha Rao, then union home minister. The Mittal report quotes an extract from her letter:

> I write this to you with a heavy heart. My cousin brother Shri D.P. Nayyar, who retired as Education Adviser in the Planning Commission some time ago lives in Sarvodaya Enclave (Delhi), C-145. He has a Sikh neighbour. A mob came to set fire to the Sardar's house on November 1, Shri Dev Prakash's son telephoned to the police. The police asked 'whose house is burning? Is it Sikh's or Hindu's? He replied 'It is a Sikh's house.' 'Let it burn,' was the reply. This poison in the police is dangerous for our country.

Across in New Delhi district, Ram Vilas Paswan, MP, gave shelter to a fleeing Sikh in his house—and still could not save him. A mob burnt down the garage in which the aged Sikh had taken shelter.

It was such bloody killings that added up to the estimated 3,000 or so. None of the attackers was arrested; when Sikhs put up some resistance and survived—most didn't—they were arrested. Sikhs did put up resistance at gurdwaras, but they mostly failed before the wellresourced and supported attacks. Many died trying to save their gurdwaras.

The army came in too late; to be effective it would have had necessarily to liaise with the police. Had the police wished to be effective, they had enough force of their own. The police did not fail because they lacked numbers, they failed because they lacked will.

Army commanders themselves, the Mittal report reveals, had been rapidly alert to the situation, and were keen on deployment. As early as the morning of 31 October, within an hour or two of the assassination, the military's general officer commanding (GOC) for Delhi area, A.S. Vaidya, called the police commissioner, but did not get through. He tried all day to reach the police chief, without success. He only got through finally at 11.30 p.m. on 31 October to offer army support.

General Vaidya had meanwhile ordered the movement of a brigade from Meerut to Delhi at 10.30 a.m. on 31 October. The brigade had reached Delhi by midnight on 31 October. This reinforced a Brigade Regiments Centre, with an engineering regiment and two regiments of artillery consisting of about 6,000 men.

The civilian bureaucracy itself had moved fairly fast. A number of companies of paramilitary forces had been airlifted from other places by the home ministry. That brought the total strength of the paramilitary forces to sixty-one available companies by the morning of 1 November. Military and paramilitary forces were available, and early enough. These were not called. No surprise, considering that the Delhi Police themselves got no firm orders.

The LG suggested to the police commissioner at 7 a.m. on 1 November that he should call in the army. The police chief said he would first like to take a round of the city. He finally agreed to call in the army around 10 a.m., a full twenty-four hours after the army had offered itself, the Mittal report says. Those turned out to be a lethal twenty-four hours. Dispatch of army units came much later on 1 and 2 November, and effective deployment still later—or not at all.

When the military finally was called in on 1 November, the Mittal report notes, 'there was quite a lot of confusion about co-ordination with the Army'. The army was expecting to deal with magistrates and not directly with the police.

By 2 November, the army had been called out into several of the troubled areas. They did not actually do very much, they didn't have to. Finally just the sight of the army was enough; it signalled an intention of the government to put down the violence. A signal from the government was all that really was needed.

~

Murder of Justice

Away from all the expectations from the Supreme Court commissions, and their betrayal of those expectations, justice was being handed out by a single junior judge sitting in East Delhi, even if it was just this one judge delivering it. That delivery of justice also delivered a byproduct whose reach spread far beyond the failure of law in individual cases; it showed how justice itself was murdered after the killing of those thousands.

Prevention had failed, protection had failed. That still left the government one last chance, to bring justice over the murders. We've had some poster justice by way of a life sentence for Sajjan Kumar, Congress party MP then. That stands well short of justice for over more than 3,000 murders. Almost everyone got away with murder.

It's argued usually that punishment could not be handed out because cases had not been registered properly to begin with where they had been registered at all, that reliable witnesses did not come forward, that evidence was destroyed by killers or erased by the police. But in the face of all that, a few were nevertheless convicted. And of those, most were convicted by a single judge, Shiv Narayan Dhingra. He handed out sentences in one case after another.

Questions came pouring over such exceptional sentencing of accused persons. If the law is the same and the cases similar, why did one judge hand out punishments, and others acquittals? Can guilt over murder be decided by the mood, or inclination of individual judges? How could a judicial system allow such extremes? Was Dhingra wrong to punish, or were others wrong to acquit? Were the other judges prejudiced or politically pressured? Or appointed on an understanding that they will not convict the 1984 accused?

Some answers to these questions came unfolding through the course of a chat with Justice Dhingra. We met at the quaint

Samay Yaan study room in R.K. Puram. The chat turned out to be as chilling as it was revealing. Given below is an excerpt of what Justice Dhingra had to say:

> When I was appointed some time in 1994-95, Mr S.S. Bal was the special court judge for trying the 1984 cases. He had been appointed additional district and sessions judge in 1988 and was made special judge in 1989, dealing with the 1984 cases. Mr Bal had never done criminal cases. Neither in the course of his practice nor as judge. He was a revenue advocate. The sole reason for his appointment was that he was close to Mr H.R. Bhardwaj, who was then the law minister. There were innumerable other judges then with experience in criminal law, but he was appointed. In 1994-95, I replaced Mr S.S. Bal; I was made special judge for the 1984 cases at the Karkardooma court. There were a lot of cases pending with Mr Bal, lying almost unattended, those included the Trilokpuri cases.
>
> There were basic reasons why he did not proceed. In Trilokpuri about 200 murders had taken place. And the police had registered one case, one FIR for those 200 murders. More than 100 persons had been named as accused. On every date, Mr Bal would mark attendance of the accused. Five or ten would be absent, he would issue bailable warrants for them, and give a new date. On that new date, they may appear but another five or ten would not. He would then cancel the warrants of those who had appeared, and issue fresh warrants for those who had not appeared. This had been going on since 1989 till the time I was appointed. For five years this game was going on. This was a strategy. In some cases, where there was a separate FIR, he conducted a trial, but he disbelieved every witness.
>
> But most of the cases were pending. In some of those cases, local elected leaders, such as municipal councillors and the MP Mr H.K.L. Bhagat, were the accused. He had not even

opened those cases. When I took over, I asked the special public prosecutor, Mr Tandon, who had been appointed by the government for conducting these cases, why just a single challan had been filed in the cases of the 200 or so murders in Trilokpuri. Under the law, no more than three cases arising from the same event can be tried together. So, he should have requested the court to give direction to the police to file separate challans. Mr Tandon told me that he had made this application for separation of challans about two to three years earlier. I found that application but saw that no order had been passed on it.

I immediately took up that application, and passed an order for the prosecution to file a separate challan with respect to each murder. So the challans were separated. Now in each case, instead of having a hundred and more accused, I had those who had been named which were two or three or so per case. Then I began the trials. I found that in the case where H.K.L. Bhagat was accused, he had not been summoned. He had been named in the affidavit of the victim, but he had not been named as an accused by the prosecution. So I summoned him, and also other political leaders in other cases who had been named, such as Dr Ashok Kumar. I started recording witness statements.

During examination of witnesses, most judges sit as dumb umpires, and blow their whistle if they see something going wrong. This has not been my way from the very start. I have always believed it would be my duty to find the truth and give justice. I would not allow advocates to overawe the witness, to threaten them, to shout them down. So witnesses became confident, and they began to appear and give evidence. I completed the trial in about 250 cases.

I remember one incident. There was one Rampal Singh, he was a local leader, he had been accused in three or four cases. At one hearing, when he found that people were being convicted and sentenced, he said that they are small people, the ones responsible were others, the ones who were leading them. I said he could give a statement to testify who the real killers were, I would make him a witness and record his statement. He said that he will think about it and let me know at the next hearing. I called up his case at the next hearing, I was told that his dead body had been found on the railway platform.

In all, I convicted perhaps 30 to 40 persons. In some cases, I gave a life sentence, because these were serious offences like murder, looting, burning of houses. Most of the cases in my court were cases of murder. In the Kishori Lal case, I awarded the death sentence because he had committed several murders one after another. Almost everyone went in appeal. All those convicted had a battery of lawyers provided by the Congress party. But none of my convictions was set aside.

H.K.L. Bhagat was summoned as an accused. He was the MP of the area and a stalwart of the Congress party, so he brought top-end advocates. Their strategy was to challenge each of my orders in the High Court. And they started making complaints against me, reporting all sorts of things I can't even remember. Every time a complaint was made, the High Court wrote to me seeking my comments. I had to do that two or three times a week. I was fed up, I went and met my inspecting judge. I told him that if you feel there is substance in these complaints, hold an inquiry. This sort of demand for comments is affecting my work in the court. I said that I'm not afraid of these threats. I will do whatever I feel is right, whatever is in the interest of justice. But this nonsense must stop.

Counsel for Mr Bhagat made sure that they dragged the case on and on. They kept going to the High Court. In one of the appeals, they made personal allegations against me. Fortunately, the High Court judge, Mr Jaspal Singh, was good enough to persuade them to withdraw the personal allegations.

When I left after three years, no case was pending in my court except that of H.K.L. Bhagat. The moment I completed three years, I was the single transfer made from that court, they wanted to get rid of me. They did not want me to complete the trial of Bhagat.

During those three years, my annual confidential report was not written. At the end, I was downgraded. I wrote to the High Court that you can give me whatever grading you want, but as long as I am a judge, I will keep up my work of searching for truth and standing for justice. That created a stir in the High Court, they were saying how can a judge write like this.

H.R. Bhardwaj said openly that he will not allow me to become a High Court judge. My name was superseded twice, three times, my seniority was lowered. I filed a writ petition against that in the Supreme Court. The hearing before a two-judge bench continued for three days. The bench appeared to be with us, but when a decision came a month later, I was declared junior, they did not accept my argument.

Only later was I made a High Court judge after Mr Markandey Katju from the Allahabad High Court became the Chief Justice of the High Court. When he was to send the names, he looked at my history. He called me, he made inquiries, and then told me that if my name is not sent, nobody's name will be sent.

Later, in 2018, I was asked by the Supreme Court to head a committee to review 196 cases that had been written off. I examined all those cases. I found that FIRs had not been registered at all, or not registered properly. Hundreds of cases were clubbed in one FIR, in one instance 500 cases were clubbed into one FIR. These cases were being sent to judges for trial. And judges were not taking any active role to see that justice was being done. A committee was set up after the Mishra Commission had given direction for the registration of FIRs only in 1989. And the judges were writing in their judgment that there is long delay in the recording of the FIR. What then is the fault of the victim, or the witness?

You may have a high view of our judicial system, but I have a very low view of the kind of judiciary we have.

A loaded account from a leading judge. To flag some thoughts on his account below, even if these would seem obvious:

- Justice Dhingra's orders were all challenged, and upheld in the face of these challenges. They would appear then to have been soundly reasoned and justly delivered.
- His predecessor looking at the same cases made no move to deliver similar orders over a period of five years. His ways seemed intended to block justice or to delay justice indefinitely, which would be much the same thing.
- The preceding judge enforced an illegal practice of clubbing too many cases together despite being alerted to that by the prosecutor.
- Dhingra was harassed continually over his three-year term trying the 1984 cases, his elevation to the High Court was blocked until Justice Katju came along as Chief Justice of the High Court.
- A High Court judge tells us he has a low view of the judiciary.

~

And H.S. Phoolka has become of course the name of the campaign for justice over 1984. When we met, we couldn't remotely think that 40 years on we would still be talking injustice and inaction. But tragically that is what we did at our meeting at Mr Phoolka's office in Defence Colony in New Delhi, now in May 2024. Some excerpts from our chat:

SS: We know the official count for those killed in Delhi, the figure is 2,733. Is that the last word? What about the deaths on the trains, the bodies dumped outside jurisdictions, so many people who were not accounted for?

HSP: No, that's not the last word. There were many who were killed who could not be counted. I will give you an example. Mohinder Kaur's husband was bringing her back to Mumbai. They boarded the train from Amritsar on 31 October, with their two-month-old daughter. The train reached Shahadra on the morning of 1 November. At the station a mob looking for Sikhs found her husband, beat him up badly and left him for dead. Some passengers brought him back into the train. But the mob returned to set the bodies on fire, to wipe out any trace they may have left. They could not find him, so they searched the train and found him under a seat where passengers had hidden him. They dragged him out on to the platform, and burnt him to death.

Mohinder Kaur's fellow passengers took her with them to Mumbai. After some time she returned to her village in Punjab with her brother. She got a job there in the dera of Baba Sewa Singh. She received no compensation. In 1996, the compensation amount was raised to Rs 3.5 lakh. I applied for her compensation, the financial commissioner was convinced the story is genuine but needed some document. We found a noting by the chowkidar in her village made in January 1985 about the circumstances of her husband's death. On that basis, she finally got the compensation.

SS: There would be many others who similarly had not been recorded.

HSP: There were many such cases. Many were also killed in trucks passing through Delhi at the time. There is no record of most of those deaths.

SS: To date how many have been convicted for murder?

HSP: Perhaps about 70 in different cases. That includes six in the Sajjan Kumar case, including Sajjan Kumar.

SS: We are talking about cases in Delhi.

HSP: Yes. At no other place has anyone been convicted. Not in Kanpur, not in Bokaro or any other place in India. In Kanpur chargesheets have been filed only now on the direction of the Supreme Court.

SS: Of the 70 convicted, a good number would have been convicted by Justice S.N. Dhingra.

HSP: Yes, most of them.

SS: How is it that one judge convicted so many, and the rest of the judges convicted nobody?

HSP: One judge, S.S. Bal, decided 123 cases, and acquitted in 120. In two cases, where he did convict the accused, he let them off on grounds of having undergone their sentence because they had been detained for a few days. This judge was especially brought in by the Congress-I.

SS: And in other cases, of rioting, looting?

HSP: Of the few who were convicted, many immediately filed appeals, and were released on bail. Some stayed in jail ten days, others 15 days or so, some did not go to jail at all.

SS: So, would you say that after the killings, justice itself was murdered?

HSP: Yes, justice itself was murdered. Just think how many were killed, and how few were convicted.

Look at how the process unfolded. When a murder case comes before a judge, he issues summons to witnesses. Summons are sent to the widow at the house where her husband was killed, and the house was burnt down. Obviously, there is no one there. Summons were sent only once, a report would come back that they have shifted. The judge passes an order that the witness is not traceable, and closes the evidence, and thereafter acquits the accused on the basis that no evidence has come forward. You would never have seen murder cases dealt with like this. It was just a sham. If the witness was not traceable there, the police should trace the person. These widows had received compensation, and therefore new addresses were available in official records. But unfortunately, neither the police nor the judge made any efforts.

In one case I dealt with, the police said the witness is not traceable, and acquitted the accused. That case then came up in the High Court. I was appointed amicus curiae. I traced the address of that lady and gave it to the High Court.

SS: What does all this say about the judiciary?

HSP: Judiciary was a near total failure. Some judges were clearly conniving with the guilty. Very few judges were up to the mark. Like Dhingra. Like Justice Sachar who gave an order against winding up relief camps in 1984. Like Justice Jaspal Singh. Like Justice S.B. Wad. And of course, finally Judges S. Muralidhar and Vinod Goel who convicted Sajjan Kumar.

The Sajjan Kumar case took so long. The Jain-Bannerjee committee had recommended registration of a case against him back in October 1987. But Justice Yogeshwar Dayal ruled then that no case at all should be registered on the recommendation of this committee. Yogeshwar Dayal was rewarded for this, he was made the Chief Justice.

The Sajjan Kumar matter then came up before the bench of Justice Wad and G.C. Mittal. Justice Wad told the government lawyer that whatever the recommendations of the Jain-Bannerjee committee, the court has the affidavit of a widow that Sajjan Kumar was in the mob that killed her husband and so an FIR must be registered. The government lawyer managed to take a two-week adjournment on 5 May 1988. The next date for hearing was set for 20 May 1988. On the evening of 19 May, a new Chief Justice was brought in. They wanted acting Chief Justice S.S. Chadha to change the roster, he did not agree. The new Chief Justice took oath on the morning of 20 May and had the case brought before him. He adjourned the case and continued the stay. There were good judges but they were bypassed.

When V.P. Singh came to power, we asked for the appointment of a new committee. The new Poti-Rosha committee again recommended registration of a case against Sajjan Kumar, and the Lt-Governor of Delhi accepted that. The CBI team went to Sajjan Kumar's house to arrest him, but Sajjan Kumar's people did not allow the CBI team to take Sajjan Kumar away after arresting him, and in fact took the CBI team as hostages, and set their jeeps on fire. Delhi Police didn't help them. An oral application was made before the High Court for anticipatory bail. I have never seen that before—a move for anticipatory bail after someone has already been arrested. Justice Chawla granted anticipatory bail and directed the registrar to call the CBI official at the house of Sajjan Kumar to release him.

SS: Ved Marwah had inquired into the killings and the police response. He had his report almost ready before his inquiry was called off by the government. What happened to his findings?

HSP: There were several parts to his report. The documents he had collected, police reports from officers like Gautam Kaul that were placed before him, and then the notes he made from meetings with police officers he had called. In those conversations, they told him the whole truth about who did what. The government told Marwah to stop the inquiry because the Mishra Commission had been appointed. Marwah submitted everything to the government, the government passed some of that to the Mishra Commission. And Mishra himself admitted to me that the statements that Marwah recorded on the basis of his meetings with the top police officers in 1984 were destroyed by the government. This had been done for obvious reasons.

SS: Those surely would have been crucial, more revealing than anything else.

HSP: Every police officer told him what had happened where, and where the instructions had come from. The government knew that this report will be very strongly against the government if it comes out. So, they stopped it on the ground that the Mishra Commission has been appointed. And then Mishra did not go into all this because he said it is not within the terms of his inquiry.

~

Rajiv Gandhi, do let's remind ourselves, was Prime Minister when Marwah's inquiry was smothered, when the evidence it gathered was destroyed. He necessarily had to have been in the know of such a decision and, as Prime Minister, to have led that decision to block truth and to destroy evidence. It turned out to be one of the most lethal blows that the government delivered to murder justice over 1984.

14

Now

Mohan Singh did survive the killings in Trilokpuri, miraculously. He did not just survive the killings then, he brought news of those killings to the offices of *The Indian Express*, and then on to the world. From the shock of that morning of 2 November 1984 when I saw him half-shaven and shattered in the office of the *Express*, I had always visited him on occasions when I visited Delhi. I had planned on this visit again in May 2024. His wife answered the phone to say he had died the day earlier.

So, this was a visit to join the mourning. I met his wife, his son, his grandchildren gathered on a dari spread out on the street where he had lived in Tilak Vihar, the allotted dwellings for the 1984 survivors and their descendants. Over the years the equivalent of a welcome arch had come up to announce to a visitor - there aren't many - that they will now enter the neighbourhood of the 1984 survivors; no one ever thought of offering housing to survivors individually and separately.

They were targeted as a bunch, so then the survivors had been bunched up. The two rooms of sorts that each family was given were much like the homes they left behind in those earlier resettlement colonies, mostly Sultanpuri and Trilokpuri. In that lay the only limited virtue of the resettlement, their second resettlement.

The triumph of residents is that they lived past 1984, that they even got a more or less like-for-like place to live, that each was given a few lakh rupees as compensation. What else could they ask for?

It was the afternoon of the bhog ceremony. We all sat on the dari with folded hands, his wife fought back hopelessly to halt her tears. Everyone in Tilak Vihar knew of the death, Mohan Singh had become a natural leader through taking on the challenges survivors faced, and of those there had been many. Mohan Singh had continued to lead Tilak Vihar survivors in rebuilding their lives as best as they fractionally could.

Too much had gone wrong with Mohan's health over the last couple of years. TB, liver issues, kidney issues, diabetes, the sort of illnesses that trigger an ending for just about everyone some time or other. As the count goes, a natural ending to a full life. It had been after all 40 years of living since the days of the Trilokpuri massacre that he survived when almost everyone around him did not.

Escaping those slaughter streets, Mohan Singh had set out for *The Indian Express* office to bring those killings to our attention. He had cut his hair, shaved off his beard as best as he could, but I could see when I met him at the *Express* office that this was too visibly less than the safety of a clean-shaven look. It would have been dangerously obvious to anyone who spotted him that here was a disguised Sikh on the run.

That was a look he had carried ten long kilometres from Trilokpuri to *The Indian Express* building. Hordes of killers were prowling everywhere looking out for such as him. He came carrying one of the grimmest truths India has ever known. It was Mohan's mission that took *Indian Express* reporters Rahul Bedi and Joseph Maliakan to Trilokpuri to report the worst of the killings those days. But for him that killing too could have been smothered under dust, denials and lies.

Tilak Vihar was never the picture of some beautiful survival. It only heaps together the leftovers from those massacres, how presentable would anyone want to make that? 'Tilak' translates as a holy mark; the mark its residents wear - inmates almost, you might say, given their imprisoning experiences - is distinctly unholy. Tilak Vihar could be named more accurately perhaps the Slaughter Survivors Colony. Or something worse, because it did not end with the slaughter and the survival. Killers had roamed free on the streets where its now residents lived before, untouched by the police all their lives. So call it maybe the Shared Injustice Colony. Those who now share never did go back to what was home.

The new home is typically a room dragged out into some space around. Bundled together into Tilak Vihar those tenements look as abandoned as they are. A tiled path to Mohan Singh's street runs through an intended park that is now garbage rotting amidst pools of stench. It's the only view through one of those tiny windows for families squeezed behind brickwork holding together without paint, straight lines or other such frills. It must take a spoilt outsider to find something wrong with a neighbourhood set in a garbage heap. To residents it seems to come with the inevitability of night and day. Only strange others think it might have been better.

From our silent moments on that dari, we returned through the garbage to the local gurdwara for the bhog ceremony. The kirtan within did what it could to soothe our disturbing togetherness. Ours was not a gathering that could find the luxury of just mourning, we never would know the innocence of people sharing faith and familiarity to mourn a death. Who didn't know the conditions in which Mohan Singh had fled Trilokpuri, or of the fate of the rest of their own?

Those memories sit etched into experience and have been structured into the gurdwara. The sangat at this gurdwara routinely pays homage first within a memorial room, built to the side just as you ascend the stairs to the sangat hall. The room is a gallery of photographs of the dead, with their names written at the bottom of the picture after 'Shaheed', and a mostly common date, 1.11.84. The photographs rise high from about knee level to the top of the wall. A partition screen set up in the middle displays photographs that ran out of wall.

Those pictures are not easy to face, these were people once, many just boys that you could see in their padkas. On each picture I found myself projecting a burning tyre until the face screamed into silence. Ghastly thought and had that just been thought. It's how most met their end, that kind of end is why those pictures are there together.

The gurdwara holds more of these pictures than it has room for. But there still could have been room in that gallery for one more. That one space is taken by a picture of Jarnail Singh Bhindranwale, whose battle with the government in the 1980s triggered the events that eventually created Tilak Vihar.

Bhindranwale's is not a picture the Indian government wants to see or wants anyone to see. As the government sees it the matter is done and dusted, these are people compensated and relocated. It counted the dead, counted the homes and closed the file. But there is no statistic for shattered living, no file-friendly measure for subdued anger.

Justice could have been the only balm. It never came. In its place has appeared that picture of Bhindranwale. Anger speaks through that picture, not mourning. The shadow of 1984 will not leave India for some time yet.

Slipping back to my recollection recorded in the earlier edition of this book, Mohan Singh had looked more unsettled than resettled when I visited him at his home in Tilak Vihar in the summer of 2014. Sitting on his bed, he still managed to look as tall as I remembered him thirty years ago the day he escaped the Trilokpuri massacre to tell us that tale at the office of *The Indian Express* of the murder of hundreds of Sikhs down a few streets.

I recognized him straightaway. He looked greyer and heavier, but still much the Mohan Singh I had met before. He couldn't tell me, we'd been out of touch too many years. To me that image of Mohan Singh in the *Express* office late that morning was unforgettable; to him I was a reporter he met that day, one among several others in the years following he met, who then disappeared. He remembered my name, but couldn't tell me by appearance; we'd grown old in different ways.

He'd been asleep in the front room with his wife by his side on a worn-out bed when I made my badly timed entry. In Tilak Vihar you don't think bedrooms. There was the front room, not that much bigger than the bed in it, with a similar room behind, and that's all. The front room had squeezed in a couple of chairs besides the bed, a youngish man sat in one of them, and a lady I later discovered to be a neighbour in the other. The man vacated his chair for me, I sat down and reintroduced myself.

Mohan Singh took my word for who I said I was, though he still couldn't place me. I asked after him. He didn't work much, he said, because he couldn't walk much. He had a problem with his legs, he'd been suffering for years. Over the years he had lapsed into idleness. His children had now grown up; theirs had become a joint family. The neighbour sat in on the chat on her chair, where else could she go without leaving.

Mohan Singh didn't have a lot to say about his unwell and unemployed state. Our connection went back to that point when the suddenly unleashed violence changed his life, almost ended it. He spoke now to me only about the justice he'd never got ever since. Not for himself, not for any of the neighbours now around him whose loved ones had been killed.

His story of a denied search for justice had begun within the hour of his escape from Trilokpuri on the morning of 1 November. He still remembered everything about that day of escape, when he had at first tried to get to the police headquarters across the Yamuna from Trilokpuri, because the local police had been backing the killers. 'They just did not let me in. Whom could I report to, whom could I complain to? They turned me away at the gate. I wanted to go in and tell them our people are being killed, our homes are being destroyed. There was this policeman with a gun at the steps to the building. He just didn't let me through.'

'I didn't know where to go from the police headquarters. I couldn't return, I knew they would kill me if I went back, or someone would kill me on the way back. So I came to *The Indian Express* and *Jansatta* office. I had faith in them for years. I used to drive an autorickshaw those days. I came and reported the situation to you all, and thank god you helped.'

Mohan Singh never went back to Trilokpuri, nobody who escaped the massacre ever did. 'We went to the refugee camp at Farash Bazar police station, near Jhilmil colony in Shahdara,' he said. 'We stayed in camps till we got this allotment in Tilak Vihar in 1985. And I have been here ever since.'

Like that morning when he was turned away at the police headquarters, Mohan Singh has by now been turned away from one door after another that he knocked to seek justice—by the police, by one inquiry commission after another, by the local administration, by political leaders. The injustice hasn't been easy to live with:

> MS: There were two Supreme Court inquiries, there were others. Why? Nothing was done. No killer was punished, nobody took legal action against the policemen who failed to save our people. I gave evidence before the (Mishra) inquiry

commission, I told them all I had seen, but then nothing happened. I saw people being killed, I saw who killed, I saw the killings take place in the presence of the SHO, and one police hawaldar. But no one was punished (the SHO was later only suspended for a while). I said this all over again before the Nanavati Commission, and still nothing happened.

SS: And who were the killers?

MS: It was local leaders, they were from the Congress party, we named them. (He did again, he still remembers the names.)

SS: And you had given evidence in writing?

MS: Yes. But nothing happened after the affidavits, nothing happened after the cases. That police inspector stood there and ordered the killings. And a hawaldar stood there and ordered killings. But in the end nobody was punished.

SS: What do you do now?

MS: I had to give up driving an autorickshaw. My knees don't carry me around any more, I am unemployed, I just stay here, that's all.

SS: What do you feel after all these failures?

MS: I am angry. How can I not be angry? If you have struggled for justice, if thirty years have passed, and you get no justice, how can you not be angry? Cases have been going on and on. Our people were killed, our homes were looted, we lost our homes. Everything was destroyed, we are like on the roadside now.

SS: How do you all manage in these two rooms?

MS: When I came here, it was with my wife and children. Now they've grown up, and I have grandchildren. Many of these houses have four families living in them. Yes, four families in two rooms. You see this space. Can you imagine what it's like? It's difficult, very difficult. None of us has any money to buy another place, to take another place on rent.

SS: Have Sikh leaders helped?

MS: They all speak around election time. Not before or after.

SS: And the Akalis?

MS: They are not paying our lawyers, they are not fighting our cases. And you, in the press, what can you say? How much can you say? And who is listening? Where were you all these years?

SS: I was away.

That's all I could say. Yes, I had abandoned their story, I'd walked away from it.

I was in the business of doing stories and moving on. But 1984 was never just another story, it sits locked into memories and feeling, it changed me and all of us who ran into it. Those moments of trauma then had built a silent bond between us, and I had walked away. My now useless guilt meant nothing.

But Mohan Singh has always stood out in my memory. Down the years it was in him that I saw everyone's story. It was through him now that I saw the injustice everyone faced and continues to. To me, it was his story that told everyone's story, then and now.

~

At the entrance to Tilak Vihar stands a shack with durries laid out on the floor. The afternoon I looked in to see Mohan Singh, I saw about twenty very elderly men sitting around, lying down, who looked like they'd had nothing else to do for a long time. They shared a table fan between them on that hot afternoon in May.

That shack has been built for the elderly to sit somewhere, the homes have no room for them. Such are the fruits of their survival.

Thousands had been killed; thousands of others now serve out a life sentence. It was at this shack that they directed me to Mohan Singh's house. In Tilak Vihar everyone knows who lives where, who lived where, who lost how many in 1984, and how.

Revisiting those memories takes no more than a walk through Tilak Vihar. The trouble with that walk is that you could stop by at just about any house, and hear what sounds like more or less the same story. And so, we don't look in at any house at all, if you ever go to Tilak Vihar that is, because we've heard it before, we know, and what can we do now?

So far as anyone knows or cares, those three days produces just two stories, not 3,000—the story of the one who died, and that of the one who survived. And we've heard both enough. Not many care to listen any more, beyond perhaps a moment or two around one anniversary or the other, while looking the other way.

This had now become another problem: to the outsider now Mohan Singh's agony, that of his neighbours, meant little. Everyone had decided that Mohan Singh and his like belong to a past best forgotten.

Does anyone want to hear about Sheila Kaur? She survived, unlike her husband. So I would know his kind of story and the Sheila Kaur kind of story well before I met her. The difference in detail, the difference that her family was killed in Sultanpuri and not Trilokpuri, brought little difference to the story of then, or to that of living with it since. She, like the other survivors, had lived to tell the same story, and had very soon run out of listeners.

Who wants to hear the same tragic story 3,000 times, and now thirty years later? But in turning away from those unfinished stories we turned away from the justice that could have brought the stories to some sort of close, brought the pain some kind of closure.

Mass killing has a way of killing interest in the individual dead, no matter that you can only die as an individual and that the loss with one is no less because others lost similarly. But when you kill enough, these stories become victim of their magnitude. We cover them with labels like 'massacre' or 'pogrom' or 'holocaust' or whatever, and leave them as a number.

In an eerily similar way—if also fundamentally different way—much the same happened with the 9/11 attacks that I reported from New York and Washington. People would speak blandly how so many of those 3,000 killed in those attacks 'just got vapourised'. You'd hear about a 'skyscraper chasing people running down a street'—that's how the rubble advanced from the collapsing towers. Expressions silenced expression.

Whoever wanted to hear all of those 3,000 stories, or could ever fit them all into their attention? For me that horror was frozen into a picture of a couple leaping from a skyscraper holding hands, just as Mohan Singh had become the enduring face of the Delhi killings. The nearest I could ever get to comprehending those tragedies was to approach that image, that face, with a sense of scale. I didn't get far. I could count the numbers, but I couldn't feel the magnitude.

Two tragedies, one in New Delhi, one in New York; 3,000 killed in one, 3,000 killed in the other. But what a difference for those the killings left behind. In New York the government went after the attackers, in Delhi the government and its police made sure first that the attacks were not stopped, and then that the government not go after the killers. It made a difference too that in New York they were attacked by obvious aliens, in Delhi the aliens had arisen from among the victims. America got Osama bin Laden in the end to get some justice. The Delhi killings never did lead to justice.

So Mohan Singh suffers today in ways no 9/11 survivor or a loved one of the dead ever had to.

I did not witness the killing in New York, I did in Delhi. I could never comprehend the full horror of those stories, I could not open my mind to feel the full shock of those deaths. Like everyone else, I too turned away from such deaths, except for fleeting moments, and in those to acknowledge them only distantly.

It wasn't just time that brought distancing, it came right then. I could not look at bodies of Sikhs to begin to understand the pain of their last moments. How does anyone ever get to feel the pain of a man necklaced to death with a burning tyre? In time that horror became a number, that number 3,000 itself froze into a cold total, a chilling statistic. Such limited comprehension that we could build around the lives that went out behind these numbers was soon crowded out by disrespecting disputes and obdurate denials.

Leaders and officials generated words to cloak facts, raised arguments to cover truth. I cannot believe that those who spoke words of denial really believed what they were saying. This language of a predetermined position only saved perpetrators and their protectors.

Mohan Singh and his neighbours now share stories that are heard no more. The stories stand clubbed, not the suffering. The stories of injustice haven't ended because the injustice has not. Justice must have a way of bringing closure to tragedies that the survivors of 1984 have never known. The other face of injustice was a negation of the truth they knew. The truth about those killings died about 3,000 times those three days.

~

I still wanted to listen to Sheila Kaur, if only to invite assault on my complacency. Up close, the cloning of tragedies vanishes, the suffering in a house in Tilak Vihar is no less because the circumstances of a neighbour's loss were similar. Or those of the many thousand who survived and fled to Punjab or found scattered shelter to make a new start somewhere else. Sheila Kaur's story is like that of Mohan Singh's family, her struggle is of course her own.

She was lying on her bed with many children of varying ages when I mistimed my visit to her house as I had to Mohan Singh's. A family picture on the wall presented a picture of what used to be family. The two men in the picture, her husband and his brother, were both killed, she said. She spoke in Hindi, not Punjabi—theirs was a family of Sikhs from Rajasthan who had settled in Sultanpuri. Hear her:

> I came to my husband's home in Sultanpuri after my marriage. We had an all right life. Then came that day. They came with lathis, with knives. They came with cans of kerosene. There were three men in the house when they attacked. They were all killed one by one. They beat them with lathis until they were bleeding and fell unconscious. Then they set fire to them. My husband, my husband's brother, and my father-in-law. They were all killed before us. They were killing everywhere. Three days they kept killing. They started on 1 November, and they were killing until 3 November.
>
> It wasn't the neighbours. They came from outside somewhere. The neighbours saved us, saved all of us they could. Then they threatened the neighbours, that if they saved a Sikh, they would kill them. Some people went and hid in the house of a Muslim neighbour. These killers came to know, they threatened the Muslim family. That family got scared, and asked the Sikhs hiding there to leave. Then those Sikhs were killed.
>
> I escaped the killing somehow. After the killing I couldn't stay any longer. For a year we were kept in some camp. Then we came here. Now I go and clean houses and wash dishes in Tilak Nagar. I do little assembly jobs at home.
>
> None of the killers was caught and punished. I just keep thinking of this, and every time I think I am angry. For thirty

years we have been waiting for someone to be punished. I don't know why we wait. In every house, it's the same. In some homes they killed three, in some five. We all know in which house they lost how many. It was terrible what they did. We were just poor people, I used to go out in the morning, cook in houses and come back. Are we the ones who killed Indira?

And you know, we have now lost our children also. They are on to drugs. And that is in every house here. We lost our men, and after that who was left to control our children? I couldn't. The mothers here couldn't. The children are now addicts, and we have no hope left for them. They could not get jobs, because they never went to school, they never had an education.

There are a few children who managed to find something, and stayed all right, but most have gone the wrong way. In some houses now the children have died of their addictions. In these thirty years I can't tell you how many of the children of those victims have died.

Now there are these little grandchildren. We have told them nothing. Who knows what they will think, what they will do? So we tell them nothing. Some of our children were just very small then, my daughter was just one year old. They didn't know what was happening. They came to know afterwards. And they are angry, that their father was killed like that. But what can they do? Some of our children used to say when we grow up we will kill them.

I gave evidence once. And after that there was nothing. We keep telling what happened when we get a chance. But it has led to nothing. We have gone to some courts to give evidence. I don't know why I have done all this. You don't know how it hurts in the heart. It's like a fire burning inside me. For thirty years I have been hoping. Now I am tired.

We struggle here. In these two rooms. I have my children, and my daughter-in-law. And the grandchildren. Outside we have converted a space into a third room. We are four families living here. In this room at night we fit two more beds. Three share one bed. Sometimes we have guests who come to stay. We manage in this space.

I have never been back to Sultanpuri. Those of us who survived, we all left. Some came here, others went back to Alwar, to Jaipur. Some people came and occupied our houses, we are told they just started living there.

~

Justice Still?

Just what is left now on the side of Mohan Singh and Sheila Kaur? The law, and nothing but. Justice never needed this commission and that, these only delayed and denied an application of law. Justice later needed only a government to put proven facts together with written law—and that is absolutely all.

In law, the number 119 for a start, possibly the least favourite number among the police within the IPC. Section 119 of the IPC provides that a policeman or police officer could be sent to jail if he omits to communicate or represents falsely a plan to commit an offence. 'Whoever, being a public servant, intending to facilitate or knowing it to be likely that he will thereby facilitate the commission of an offence which it is his duty as such public servant to prevent; voluntarily conceals, by any act or illegal omission, the existence of a design to commit such offence, or makes any representation which he knows to be false respecting such design,' can go to jail for up to half the term for the offence itself.

So that if a murder carries a twenty-year sentence, a police officer who knows it to be likely—and no more—that a murder may be committed, can go to jail for ten years if the murder is actually committed and he has concealed through an illegal omission the design to commit such an offence. And if it is a theft that may carry a two-year sentence, the police officer concerned could similarly be jailed for up to a year.

I saw such criminality of the police all through those three days in 1984 and everywhere I went—most people in Delhi did. The police knew there were crowds out there, and that those crowds were out to kill. The police did not stop them, made no move to stop them; they concealed from themselves—individually and institutionally—for the purpose of any action, the knowledge that these crowds were out to burn, loot and kill. They omitted to mention in communications with a view to action, they falsely represented the developing situation. All this stands well documented in the Mittal report. This is also what I saw myself.

Take the policemen in Vasant Vihar that morning of 1 November, the first lot I ran into. This was the area where the Guru Harkrishan Public School had been burnt down. These policemen were public servants who knew an offence had already been committed at that school—if I had seen thick columns of smoke rising from the school building from Malviya Nagar, surely they had from Vasant Vihar. They are certain to have known more, and earlier.

Yet, none of the available police force was ordered to prevent the arson; calls to the police by the residents were disregarded. The police do not exist to observe a crime, they are employed by the citizen of the state to prevent, and if it has happened, to investigate it, and to prosecute offenders. The Vasant Vihar police were effectively concealing the crime from themselves. That failure was criminal.

Section 119 sets down a legal illustration how the law would operate—the illustration is a part of the law. The illustration goes:

'*A*, an officer of police, being legally bound to give information of all designs to commit robbery which may come to his knowledge, and knowing that *B* designs to commit robbery, omits to give such information, with intent to facilitate the commission of that offence. Here *A* has by an illegal omission concealed the existence of *B's* design, and is liable to punishment according to the provision of this section.'

Sticking just with the offence of robbery (and that is only the given example in this illustration), who didn't know the mobs were out at the very least to rob? And that they then did so? The police, the As, knew that hordes of Bs were out to loot. How many As gave that information to their fellow policemen for the purpose of action? Specifically, how many police officers knew this and then failed to give orders for action based on that knowledge? Through omission of such information they facilitated the commission of the offence. These officers were and, to the extent they are around, still are liable to punishment under this section.

The police failure those three days was a failure of knowing negligence. Such negligence coming from the police is not just condemnable but punishable; it's not just offensive, it's an offence.

The law covers a known likelihood that an offence may be committed; given that the level of arson evident in the skies above Vasant Vihar, anyone might think it a known likelihood that more such crimes could be committed. The police in Vasant Vihar (on duty, in the sense that they were being paid for it but not in the sense that they were doing it) knew that on that main Outer Ring Road, a short walk from where they sat, hundreds stood blocking the road to stop cars and buses to look for Sikhs to attack.

Those men were intending to commit a crime, the police could not but have known that. The wireless records prove they did. They also prove what I had seen, that the police then did nothing about the crimes they knew were being committed, or that they did nothing that they were bound by law to do—to prevent crimes that were known to be intended to be committed.

The existence of that design to commit an offence was not a matter of interpretation. It was right there on the streets before the police. That police guilt stands provable today under a joint consideration of two levels of records—the wireless messages that confirm their knowledge of crimes and their own logbooks that show little or no action in response to that knowledge. Put the records together and they add up to clear cases for arrest—of policemen.

Records proving the knowledge of crimes and intention to commit crimes exist in the roznamchas of the police stations, the daily diaries. This record at a police station traps the point of divergence between information coming in, as established in wireless records, and action mostly not taken on the basis of such information, as evidenced in the roznamcha.

Where in the face of what we now know the police knew then such entries were not made, that omission is of itself an added offence. 'Every police officer making an investigation … shall day by day enter his proceedings in the investigation in a diary, setting forth the time at which the information reached him, the time at which he began and closed his investigation, the place or places visited by him, and a statement of the circumstances ascertained through his investigation,' Section 172 of the CrPC sets out.

Any failure to represent the scale of a developing situation as fully as it was possible to know stands as a related offence. In Vasant Vihar, at the least, offences of arson and assault had been committed in the knowledge of the police without a move by them to stop these attacks or to pursue the criminals responsible. Over the fire at the Guru Harkrishan Public School alone, every policeman in Vasant Vihar could have been jailed for years—and should have been under neutral application of law.

As the law sees it, the men on Outer Ring Road were intending to commit an offence—murder—by looking for Sikhs. It does not appear that at that spot on that morning any Sikhs were murdered. But under Section 119, even if that offence was not committed, the fact of a known and undeniable intention to commit such an offence should still have brought to each policeman on duty in Vasant Vihar, or at least to the officer in charge, a jail term of a quarter of whatever a magistrate might determine as the sentence for someone found guilty of setting out with an intention to kill.

More than 3,000 were murdered in Delhi; given the circumstances of such killing, thousands of policemen could under this law have faced up to ten years in jail. At least hundreds still can be prosecuted. This is expressly provided by the law. It has been in the hands of the government to apply the law all these years since 1984. Section 119 stands as a reminder of the extent of police criminality then and of the consequential criminality of failing to make legal moves to punish the police.

The evidence on what the police knew, and what they did not then do, given what they knew, can be brought against them now too if the government so chooses. Not by way of political negotiation but through a replacement of politics with law. All these years we've only had conversations about how 'the police stood idly by', conversations that the police have disregarded and the government dismissed. But under law it is possible to make arrests, and not make talk.

The police do not talk much about Section 119. Or other cousinly numbers that seek to police the police. They like that number 353 in the IPC. It mandates two years in jail for someone assaulting a public servant on duty.

Most of the police force did not actually kill, theirs was the guilt of inaction, but that inaction was criminal. Police passivity wasn't 'criminal' only in some morally declared way. That of course it would be when protectors fail to protect, and fail to stop perpetrators. But the police passivity was precisely criminal under the IPC and the CrPC. The police know this but have kept, well, a criminal silence over their crimes.

Police criminality stands established on not one but several counts. And it is criminality that stands established today—the facts stand on record, the law remains in place. Under no law does a murderer become automatically innocent after a lapse of time. Time stands in the way, but there is still time, for at least some prosecutions. Those could go some way in bringing closure to the Sikh experience of continued injustice over those murders.

The law does not lean on political moods, but the application of it has. The politics of 1984 erased the law itself. The absurd truth—but absurd only because we set it against common expectations of law and policing—is that thousands in the Delhi Police force of 1984 could have been arrested under a simple application of law. Yes, thousands, and yes, arrest.

~

Who in the police could face prosecution? The constable? The head constable? Or, up the chain, the assistant sub-inspector, sub-inspector, inspector, assistant commissioner of police, deputy commissioner of police, the additional commissioner of police, the commissioner of police? By strictly legal logic, all policemen who failed to act, which is almost all policemen, would be culpable. But it is true that the vast majority of policemen were only following orders, with limited possibilities of independent intervention.

Down that long chain of command, the critical points of failure lie on just a few levels. First, the station house officer, an officer of inspector rank who is always the most immediate trigger for action. They say in the police that whoever rules the country in name, it is the thanedar who really rules. The thanedar is the SHO, the one in charge of a police station area. It is he who knows his area most closely, the people in it, he would best know who's up to what on which street, and when people gather to make trouble, just who they are.

It almost never happens that a crowd can gather within the area of a police station, and the SHO won't know where the crowd came from and who leads it. Every SHO has at his command an informal force of informers, mukhbirs as they are called. This telling network is quite firmly established across all police stations—it is an extensive network that works in loose tandem with the Intelligence Bureau (IB).

This network of informers does often include men with a criminal past or people with known criminal associations of some sort. It has to, for the sake of effective policing. 'To catch a thief, set a thief'—goes the much repeated slogan of wisdom in the police. No officer commanding a district ever wants some spotlessly clean SHO with top marks from a police school. You couldn't rely on innocent babes to police effectively.

The effective SHO knows who can siphon information out from criminal networks. Who would know the underworld better than the underworld itself? And to know it, the police must tap some within it. The local police invariably find inroads into the underworld if they must police at all. Also, the local SHO is certain to know the politicized lot within his area. When looters and killers came out on to the streets in an area, the SHO's mukhbir network is very likely to have fed him substantial information on who had brought them there, who many of them were.

Through those days, many of the attacking groups came from outside the targeted neighbourhood, but not many of these bands had travelled so far out of their areas as to be absolute outsiders. And to the extent they were strictly speaking outside of the area of a police station, the mukhbir network would still give the police a fairly good idea where they came from—through other SHOs and their own mukhbir networks. Not every name immediately, but usually enough to lead on to at least some names.

The SHO would rely, of course, on more than his own intelligence service of scattered mukhbirs. Each police station includes several substations. They were headed usually then by a sub-inspector, and at more micro levels, kiosks staffed by constables. No one is closer to the people of an area than constables on street duty. This street-level police network is the frontline eyes and ears of the police and, naturally, the first face of police interaction with people. Enough records have surfaced to show that this street-level force was keeping its bosses informed all the way through.

It's nobody's expectation that following those days of killing half the police could realistically have arrested the other half—or that a few should have arrested all the rest. But the police logs make a compelling case for action against police officers heading pivotal points in the chain of communication and action.

Above the SHOs, the crucial pivot would be the DCPs, the deputy commissioners of police of a district. The DCP of a particular district would interact with all the SHOs directly, as he could with the officers immediately above, who would be either of the two additional commissioners of police for Delhi range and for New Delhi range, and above them the commissioner of police. The DCP could make all the difference to policing within his district. Where a district failed, it was the DCP primarily responsible—and who must face prosecution first.

The DCPs had to be in the know of what was happening, and where, through their SHOs and their buzzing district-level wireless network. Buzz it would, if only as a result of the overriding culture in the police force of transferring responsibility higher up and to create a record that would keep yourself in the clear should an inquiry follow. This sense of an 'afterwards' is much on the mind of every policeman— almost more, one might say, than the immediate situation he has to deal with that will generate the 'afterwards'.

This question of what to do in the here and now—or not—with a sharp sense of the afterwards is critical to determining what happened and did not happen along the police chain of command. Because in this lay the double-edged question: should a policeman fear the consequences more from failing to stop the crime before him, or from protecting Sikhs within the prevailing mood and political environment, that he might then live to regret as did the inspector from the armed police who fired and later said he hadn't? One path could be wrong policing, the other politically induced career suicide. Hadn't two Sikhs just assassinated the Prime Minister? And wouldn't people legitimately be angry? And if they were out on the streets, should you stop them, in the absence of a forthright command to do so?

The police almost everywhere took the second course, but while making some show of the first: in effect to do nothing under a show of having done something. Such halfway cleverness comes naturally to the police (and not only to the police). In Delhi those days this kind of cleverness had lethal consequences.

Down the chain of such communication, officers learn to read the tone. They've learnt through experience whether the officer above really wants action, or is creating a record for the asking for action. The difference between a command for action and a command for record is easy for a policeman to tell.

Such cleverness was intended, but that is not to say it always worked. The gaps and silences through this cover-up game are not difficult spot for an inquiry officer who had access to the records, as Marwah did for the period before his inquiry was abruptly halted.

Police officers are accountable for what they did or did not do and not just for what they said or did not say. Commissioner of Police Subhash Tandon has several things right to say. But that still does not cover inevitable questions: (a) what kind of information he actively solicited and finally was given? (b) what was his actual response to such specific information and the directions he gave or did not give? and (c) what were his own movements through the city at the time?

The record shows that Tandon was nowhere near the worst of what happened. But he was seen at places where some Sikhs had fired in self-defence—the records on this too are clear. The Kusum Lata Mittal report carries a detailed account of the records of Subhash Tandon, of the additional commissioner of police for Delhi range, Hukum Chand Jatav, and the additional commissioner of police for New Delhi range, Gautam Kaul. The records that speak for themselves would be accessible to the government, should the government wish to act upon them.

The debate over possibilities of prosecution has been dragged into all sorts of dead ends but not taken along the path of application of law. About the biggest of the ghosts raised was the debate about calling in the army. Justice Mishra suggests that a couple of thousand lives might have been saved had the government called the army in earlier. Perhaps so, because the sight of the army can be a deterrent, it comes as a strong signal from the government. That speculation does carry a degree of the logic of likelihood.

But what of the police themselves? Thousands and thousands of the policemen were around but not deployed. Whole units of the armed men from the Delhi Police were at hand, but were never called. And what was the army being called to deal with? Groups of no more than a few hundred at most. None of these groups was of a magnitude that even just a few policemen could not handle.

One woman police officer who was nine months' pregnant could confront attackers, and they vanished. Whenever the police showed some intention of force, these crowds disappeared. Delhi did not need an army, it needed will. Had the police been given firm leadership, they would never have needed the army.

And what if the police are in no position to summon the army and no order from the Central government comes? This is what Section 131 of the CrPC says: 'When the public security is manifestly endangered by any such assembly and no executive magistrate can be communicated with, any commissioned or gazetted officer of the armed forces may disperse such assembly with the help of the armed forces under his command, and may arrest and confine any persons forming part of it, in order to disperse such assembly or that they may be punished according to law.' So, army officers could have deployed units, strictly speaking, on their own.

Having done so, they could have corresponded with the police later. 'If while he (the army officer) is acting under this section, it becomes practicable for him to communicate with an executive magistrate (or the equivalent under the police commissioner system), he shall do so, and shall thenceforward obey the instructions of the magistrate, as to whether he shall or shall not continue such action.'

So, if such unrest were to appear before the eyes of the army, they did not have to remain witnesses. Officers could have stepped in on their own. That would be an exceptional act, but those were exceptional circumstances. And the law provides for such exceptional circumstances.

But who, realistically, would fault an army officer for what the police had failed to do—at critical levels in the chain of command: the SHO, the DCP and the commissioner of police? Hauling the police in for that failure even at this last stage could do the right thing for a little justice, at last, for the surviving Sikhs; but it also could do a lot of good to the police themselves. To think these thoughts is not to think wastefully of what might have been, but what can be, still.

~

Catching the police out should be relatively easy; rather, the police had caught themselves out, and prosecuting them even now is well short of impossible. But what of the political government of the day?

The police themselves no doubt are the street-level face of the government, the hand of the political government controls the police invisibly but surely. But the hand of the government did show itself directly too, it in fact showed in the most visible means then possible— through the government-owned and controlled Doordarshan.

Consider two facts, neither of which anyone can deny, not even the government:

First, that on the morning of 1 November, Doordarshan broadcast live a repeated call to kill made by supposed mourners at Teen Murti Bhavan where Indira Gandhi's body lay in state. These men raised the slogans, 'Khoon ka badla khoon' (Blood for blood). Millions saw this coverage on Doordarshan, and no one can deny, and certainly Doordarshan cannot and does not deny, that the government channel had broadcast calls for murder, live.

Justice Mishra, who evidently had a plentiful supply of clean chits to hand, gave the government a clean chit over this as well.

Over this broadcast, Justice Mishra says the following: 'The Union of India denied having undertaken any program in which Doordarshan had permitted shouting of a slogan——"blood for blood". It appears that after the dead body was taken to Teenmurti Bhavan on 1 November live telecast arrangement had been made covering the dead body lying in state and the people who would move around either in the room where the dead body was kept or the crowd that would fly (sic) past on the outer side at the lower level so that millions in the country who could not come to Delhi would be able to associate themselves with what was going on at Teenmurti Bhavan.

'In the morning of November 1, a group of people passing through the passage at the lower level did raise the shout "khoon ka badla khoon". Since the live telecast arrangements had then been working, the crowd along with the shout did come on the TV and their shout was heard. When directed by the commission, the director-general of Doordarshan appeared before it and explained the situation in which this part of the program had been covered and to substantiate the explanation, he exhibited that part of the cassette where the shouting crowd were seen and their shout was recorded.

'The Director-General explained that the officers of the Doordarshan never apprehended that a crowd paying respect to the departed leader would raise such a shout which on account of the live program would get televised. The moment this was realised the live telecast arrangement was switched off. When the cassette was played, the Commission found that the shout had been repeated for 18 times spread over 37 seconds.

'The impugned shouting came all of a sudden at high pitch which probabilizes (sic) the position that Doordarshan people could not have apprehended it. It melted away as the crowd was pushed ahead by the police. From the original cassette, the Commission has made a copy. Though it had been alleged that this telecast was arranged, the Commission is of the view that neither the Prime Minister nor any one in Government had any role to play in the matter and the Doordarshan authorities did not intentionally do anything.'

Finally, Mishra declares: 'The time lag between the objectionable matter being telecast and the switching off also is not unreasonably long to suggest, as alleged, that Doordarshan wanted it to continue. The Director-General of Doordarshan also told the Commission that care was taken thereafter to keep off any objectionable matter from being included in the live program.'

Again grammar is the least of the problems with the Mishra report ('probabilize', 'fly past' when he must have meant 'file past', 'apprehended' when he must have meant 'anticipated'). But are there errors of fact here? Was that slogan 'khoon ka badla khoon' repeated only eighteen times that morning, over a period of thirty-seven seconds? How did the judge count the thirty-seven seconds? A single thirtyseven-second period over which the slogan was repeated eighteen times? Or was the slogan repeated eighteen times, and the duration of each separate chant add up to thirty-seven seconds? Mishra's report does not say.

Doordarshan could hardly have claimed this broadcast to be eighteen continuous slogans raised over a single thirty-seven-second period. Was Mishra then right to aggregate that count to then minimize it as just thirty-seven seconds? Methodologically very strange.

Where did these figures of eighteen times and thirty-seven seconds come from? They came from Doordarshan. Doordarshan exhibited to the Mishra Commission 'that part of the cassette where the shouting crowd were seen and their shout was recorded'. Mishra does not say he saw, or asked to see the record of the entire broadcast that morning during the course of which he or his staff had heard that cry eighteen times over a period of thirty-seven seconds, however you count those thirty-seven seconds. Mishra issued his clean chit on the basis of a recording volunteered by Doordarshan that he appears not to have accepted as handed over to him. He pronounced on the basis of the cassette given him.

I saw this live broadcast that morning of 1 November before I began chasing smoke signals around the city. And I saw that broadcast for more than thirty-seven seconds. For very much more than that. Just about everyone I spoke to had seen that broadcast. Had we all watched it over those same thirty-seven seconds only? And remembered it from the same little stretch if that is what it was?

Granted that if thirty-seven seconds it was, we would all have remembered that bit more than the rest. But this was not just thirtyseven seconds by any means. I do not remember that broadcast as some slogans shouted for a total of a fraction of a minute; nobody I ever spoke with remembers those as some fleeting broadcast promptly removed.

The way to determine the truth would be to check the entire broadcast that morning, not through a cassette of doubtful length volunteered by Doordarshan purporting to claim that what was submitted was all that was broadcast that morning. While we await (indefinitely) copies of the full broadcast, the undeniable fact stands that in broadcasting even for just the length it admitted, Doordarshan had broken the law, it had committed a crime. By its own admission not once, twice, but eighteen times.

The IPC (Section 153A) provides for up to three years imprisonment for promoting disharmony or feelings of enmity for any reason, or for an act that could be prejudicial to the maintenance of harmony and cause feelings of insecurity among a religious group. Doordarshan officials were not themselves calling for murder, but they were responsible for amplifying that call. The law on abetment and conspiracy kicks in over any crime. The case for prosecuting Doordarshan is clear.

It doesn't take legal knowledge to understand that broadcasting a call by one group to kill members of another religion is, at the least, as the law says, a promotion of disharmony, that it is at the least likely to disturb public tranquility. That is enough to book Doordarshan under Section 153A of the IPC, read with, as lawyers like to say, the provisions within the law on abetment and conspiracy. Is multiplication of a call to kill before millions not at the least prejudicial to maintenance of harmony, and is it not likely to disturb public tranquility? In holding the megaphone to that call, Doordarshan had made itself an accomplice.

As required by law, it was for Doordarshan to provide copies of that entire footage from that morning to the police well before the Mishra Commission came along. The police should then have trawled through the footage, identified those men calling for murder, and checked them out against the crimes that followed that were consistent with their call. It might have solved the Rakab Ganj murders, and more. The police could have just arrested the men for making the call. It did not occur to the justice of the Supreme Court conducting that inquiry that this would be the course of action for the police to pursue under the law. That Doordarshan made no such offer, that the government did not lean on it to hand that evidence to the police, that the police never asked for it, pile up into layer after layer of government complicity in criminality.

Lawyers could certainly negotiate a long course around the wording of law and interpretation of the broadcast endlessly and profitably. But the police, the government, have clear grounds to launch a case, make arrests, and prosecute—and to let a judge decide the rest.

Sure, the bureaucracy within Doordarshan was only obeying orders. But guilt does not evaporate for want of an obvious suspect within reach for immediate arrest. The institutional guilt was clear, and it would be for Doordarshan and the government to decide how it must answer for it. For the purpose of the police, a crime had been committed by individuals within an institution and they were, they are, bound to register a case. It's not odd that they now should; what is odd, and criminally odd, is that they haven't as yet.

It may never be possible to fish some surviving Doordarshan official out of retirement to now prosecute. But for the police to register a case, even now, would bring some acknowledgement at last that they recognize an action to be a crime that they haven's so far. The case would be an official record of a recognition by the police of criminality on the part of the government in 1984, a criminality that the party then in government has consistently denied. Deny such criminality the Congress party bosses still would—but the content of the case would be in public for all to see and to judge. The public would see that law had been applied. In the Doordarshan broadcast lay an oblique point on which the criminality of the government could be nailed—it was not that oblique either.

The law on abetment (Section 107 IPC) covers any of three kinds of actions that can be considered abetment: first, instigation; second, to engage in a conspiracy, 'if an act or illegal omission takes place in pursuance of that conspiracy'; and third, 'intentionally aids, by any act or illegal omission, the doing of that thing'. Did Doordarshan instigate attacks on Sikhs by broadcasting a call to kill them? Did it conspire in the killing by putting the megaphone to that call? Was there an illegal omission in failing to stop the broadcast of such a call? Let a court decide. But at least, there is a case here for a court to decide.

It is usual practice for the police, for Delhi Police certainly, to slap on all the sections and charges they can when they do register an FIR. The prosecutor then sifts and sorts what he would pursue in court, for the magistrate to judge the extent of guilt if any. Several sections of the Indian Penal Code require the police to register a case to begin with against Doordarshan.

The guilt of the government has been known but not caught; this is where it can be caught.

This little, this later, might still be a little, if only a little, better than continuing to abandon justice. Even 40 years on now. The greater problem is still the will, not collapsing time frame.

It might still come as some late balm on the wounds of the families of the killed. Those wounds still hurt. This little too might mean a step towards some closure for the families of Mohan Singh and Sheila Kaur, and their many neighbours near and far, now and from then. They are Indian citizens and this law is their law too.

But we are now on the very edge of saying, should have been their law too.

The guilty are now mostly dead, after lasting out the time span nature granted them without legal interruption. Perfecty respectable dads and uncles, Mr So-and-So, and So-and-So Ji. If the killing they did ever bothered them, they didn't let it show in their lifestyle. The jaimala to their bride one day, the burning tyre to the Sikh another, all in a life's work. If conscience had to work, it wouldn't have brought guilt later, it would have prevented the killing then.

One thing remains, that matter of truth. That can still be acknowledged. How much such acknowledgment could heal those devastated by that very truth, who knows? But acknowledged or not, and denied endlessly, the truth is now more or less known to anyone who wants to know it. That no government or its commissions has managed to kill.

15

BJP Shadows

This murder of justice we've been talking about past all those killings was without doubt carried out by the Congress-I government and its commands running through legal institutions. In a better world, the Congress-I leadership could have acknowledged the truth to then prosecute its own; no one is surprised that it did not. But as some of us can see now and couldn't then, justice was not killed, nor truth smothered, without some devastating blows from the BJP and its like.

Those blows began to fall as early as April 1985 with the appointment of the Mishra Commission. We forget now that the name Ranganath Mishra had come to mean hope when he was appointed to lead an inquiry into the killings. We forget perhaps because that window of hope had opened only a crack, and so very briefly. We'd been naïve to think that a judge appointed by the Congress-I government would go after the truth, we should have known it was concealment he was after. But we could hardly have guessed Mishra would make so much room also for a Jan Sangh leader's moves to silence Sikh victims.

That leader was Ram Gopal Shawlwale, formerly member of parliament from the Bharatiya Jan Sangh, the party from which the Bharatiya Janata Party emerged following a brief tryst with the Janata Party. Shawlwale, who was Jan Sangh MP from the Chandni Chowk constituency in the fourth Lok Sabha from 1967 to 1971, resurfaced politically over the 1984 killings at the head of a group that announced itself as the Nagrik Suraksha Samiti, Arya Samaj. It was through this group that Shawlwale led his moves against Sikh victims.

Shawlwale appeared before the Mishra Commission as the opposite number so to speak against H.S. Phoolka who led the case for the Sikh victims. 'Shawlwale was the main functionary of the Nagrik Suraksha Samiti, pursuing the cases on their behalf,' Phoolka tells me. Shawlwale more than pursued cases. In his account of those proceedings, Phoolka records that lawyers from the Nagrik Suraksha Samiti 'drove some of the victims to tears by subjecting them to insulting and insensitive questions'. Why was a former Jan Sangh MP leading these moves?

These were no isolated moves. Shawlwale led a well-organized and clearly well-resourced campaign against the Sikh victims. He and the lawyers he brought to bear against the Sikhs became a leading, certainly the loudest, voice in proceedings before the commission. With more than a little encouragement from Mishra himself.

Justice Mishra notes at the start of his report submitted in 1986, that at the start of proceedings 'parties appearing before the Commission for the Delhi inquiry were called upon to disclose their stand in writing' in regards to what he described as 'the allegations in regard to the incidents of organised violence'.

Sikh victims were represented before the Mishra committee primarily by the Citizens Justice Committee (CJC). The CJC made the following initial submission to the Mishra commission: 'From the materials available to the Committee, prima facie, it appears that the violence in Delhi was premeditated, organised and was perpetrated methodically in a systematic manner so as to lead to the irresistible conclusion of central direction, guidance and control. This task was without doubt performed with the complicity, connivance and active involvement of the administration as well as the members of the ruling party.'

A second submission came from the Delhi Sikh Gurdwara Management Committee, which adopted a position similar to the CJC. It submitted: 'The stand of the DSGMC is that the mass violence and carnage which took place in Delhi and other parts of the country from 31st October to 7th November, 1984, on the assassination of the Hon'ble the then Prime Minister, Shrimati Indira Gandhi, was an organised violence. It was committed in the same pattern not only in Delhi but also in other parts of the country including Kanpur and Bokaro against the Sikh community.'

The third view, the counter view against Sikhs and in support of the police and the government came from this Nagrik Suraksha Samiti, Arya Samaj, headed by the former Jan Sangh MP. This group made the following submission: 'The stand of the Samiti is that the riots, arson and looting which took place in the wake of assassination of Smt. Indira Gandhi were not the handiwork of any organised group of people. To say that the riots were organised is wholly incorrect. The fact and the truth of the matter is that the riots, arson and looting which took place immediately on the assassination of Smt. Indira Gandhi were all sporadic and spontaneous and got erupted on grave provocation and anger on account of the tragic assassination of the late Prime Minister, Shrimati Indira Gandhi who was greatly loved and respected by the people at large.'

This argument that the killings were a spontaneous eruption driven by grief and anger over the assassination was in line with Rajiv Gandhi's tree argument—that when a big tree falls, the earth shakes 'a little'. That was the line taken inevitably by the Congress government and by the police. It's a line that saw the killings as natural consequence of the assassination, not as criminal acts that must bring justice later if not prevention before. Under this line, any masterminds and leaders who may have organized the killings would get away with murder because there would be no masterminds and leaders at all. Only a tree had fallen, and they were not the ones who felled it.

This view was presented in overwhelming numbers before the Mishra commission. The commission received in all 3,752 affidavits as counted in the Nanavati Commission report later. More than two-thirds of those were classified by Mishra as 'affidavits against the victims'. These affidavits broadly said that the violence against Sikhs was natural, that Sikhs had in effect asked for the violence that hit them and asserted that Congress-I MPs from Delhi and other party leaders were not responsible for what happened.

An odd classification to begin with—'affidavits against the victims'. Who were these couple of thousand people filing affidavits against shaken Sikh survivors now seeking justice? Thousands of Sikhs had been killed. And now a Jan Sangh leader was mobilizing affidavits in thousands to make sure that many of the accused would not be punished.

The Nagrik Suraksha Samiti had taken a lead in filing such anti-victim affidavits and followed up those submissions with cross-examination by aggressive lawyers intended to crush depositions from victims and their families. In this Shawlwale was supported by a couple of other groups that were also created to submit affidavits against Sikh victims such as the Citizens Forum for Truth and the Citizens Committee for Peace and Harmony. These groups appeared from nowhere apparent then or later, it never was very clear who ultimately was behind those others.

Phoolka soon discovered that most of these groups' 'affidavits against the victims' were 'stereotyped'. He notes in his book co-authored with Manoj Mitta, *When a Tree Shook Delhi*, that 'the same set of assertions were repeated in those affidavits in more or less the same language'. Transparently fake, that is. Rather than describing personal experiences, 'the affidavits were full of general opinion that the violence was not organised, and the Congress leaders were innocent'. The commission, he said, was 'flooded with scores of copies of each template in the guise of affidavits filed by different persons'.

It all began to fall apart on the very first day of the hearings. On day one, only one of the 13 witnesses summoned, who had filed 'anti-victim' affidavits, turned up. The affidavit of that one person, Faqir Chand, said: 'There was no organised violence and none of the Congress-I workers, or councillors incited or instigated people to indulge in violence.' A long sentence written in English by a witness who admitted he cannot speak English. He identified the affidavit as his from his signature in Hindi. As Phoolka recounts, he admitted in the hearings that he did not know the contents of that affidavit, that they had not been read over and explained to him.

The next day another 'anti-victim' witness, Ajit Singh, testified that he had not signed the affidavit said to be his. It had similarly asserted that 'the propaganda that riots were organised or organised by Congress-I or its leaders is false'.

A third witness completed the unravelling. This witness, Basant Singh, said he had been forced by the police to sign an affidavit that had said: 'The member of parliament from our area (H.K.L. Bhagat) rendered utmost help and assistance in helping Sikhs in that locality. I want to say further that the local police also helped us and gave us full protection.' Basant Singh discovered the content of 'his' affidavit only when he saw it later. In presenting his evidence before the Commission, Basant rose to say the very opposite. This hit the media. Mishra announced he was now throwing out all 'anti-victim' affidavits. Better three unravelling publicly than 2,200.

But Mishra wasn't done yet, nor the authors and leaders of those affidavits aimed at Sikhs and defending the accused. Most of those summoned at the start did not appear, it's not clear whether there was anyone behind these affidavits to appear at all. But some of those affidavits finally did find their day. Towards the very end of the hearings, Mishra re-opened proceedings to summon many claiming to be witnesses behind a number of these affidavits. Mishra cited some of their content to exonerate H.K.L. Bhagat.

~

It would be as misplaced as it would be hasty to read into the submissions of the Nagrik Suraksha Samiti some sort of Hindu plot against Sikhs, even if this was a move against Sikhs from an avowedly Hindu group led by the member of a politically Hindu party. For a start who doesn't know, and Sikhs certainly do, that Sikh lives were then saved in tens of thousands, who knows even hundreds of thousands, by Hindus—we really should say, people who happened to be Hindu. They were really the lawful against the lawless, the human against the inhuman. They were people to whom it was unthinkable that a Sikh neighbour be harmed. Their move to defend Sikhs was spontaneous, their moves to defend them became organized. Protection rings were set up everywhere around Sikhs. It was these friends and neighbours that we categorize as Hindus who saved most Sikhs, it wasn't the police.

Those who killed were Hindu too, but again only outwardly people we would categorize as Hindus. The binding force that organized and drove them was a oneness with the Congress party; they turned to kill as hordes loyal to the Congress party whose members happened to be Hindu. Some Hindu dacoit kills as a dacoit, not as a Hindu; not every killer who happens to be Christian kills as a Christian. Banal truisms, but where religious leanings can blur and burn so easily, the distinction is worth underlining.

Undoubtedly the mobs of killers had an awareness of themselves as Hindu to the extent that distinctly non-Hindu Sikhs were now their targets. Sikhs became politically approved targets triggered by the assassination, not from some long-running religious hatred. Mobs were led to attack a certain kind of identified others as induced duty, not from any call that killing Sikhs would uphold uniquely Hindu beliefs. The law stood suspended if those you killed and looted were Sikhs. The mobs targeted the unprotected other, not a religious other even if it was an outwardly religious sign that marked out this other.

When it came to the Mishra Commission hearings, the ground had stopped shaking, even if a lot of shaken people still stood on it. But past the stage of anger and reaction here was intervention from a Hindu group led by a former Jan Sangh MP on a legal stage against Sikh victims, and in support of those accused as killers. Here was an association that could stretch anywhere from a declaredly Hindu sympathy for killers to culpability in joining the government and the police to smother justice.

Politics of a Hindu kind defined Shawlwale and his career. He had been elected at the peak of the Gau Andolan in the sixties, a movement in which he had played a leading role. Shawlwale kept up his politically Hindu campaigns through his years as MP and later principally through association with a number of Arya Samaj organizations.

With a name like his, shawls had to come into it. Shawlwale ran a shawl business, and was for a spell president of the Shawl Merchants Association. That family business is now run by his grandson Ajay Kumar who I met at his tiny shop down the narrow Moti Bazaar in Chandni Chowk, the sort of a shop you wonder does any business at all till someone tells you it may well earn more in a day than many people do in a year.

Ajay sees Shawlwale as a Hindu hero, and he believes all Hindus in Chandni Chowk do as well. 'There was a mandir in the middle of a road in Chandni Chowk in British times, until they removed it in 1936. Shawlwale ji ran a campaign and got a new mandir built, you can see it opposite the Old Delhi railway station, the Vankhandi Mandir. That made him famous.'

Ajay counts other famous Hindu victories that Shawlwale led. The removal of meat shops from Lala Lajpat Rai market, the long opposition to the Nizam of Hyderabad. Politically, in Chandni Chowk, the famous election victory in 1967 against the then union railway minister from the Congress party, Lala Shyam Nath.

Shawlwale pursued Hindu causes well past his years as Jan Sangh MP. 'The Arya Samaj mandir in Green Park was destroyed by Jagmohan,' Ajay Kumar recalled sitting in the dim wealth of his shop. 'Shawlwale ji went to meet Indira Gandhi. She never had time for anyone, but she would always meet our grandfather.' The intervention, he said, led to the rebuilding of a new Arya Samaj mandir in Delhi's Green Park. Strong personal ties between top leaders of the Congress party and of the Jan Sangh were clearly not unusual then, as they apparently are not amongst some leaders of the present-day Congress party and the BJP.

Shawlwale's political resurgence, if you can call it that, over the mobilization he launched against Sikh victims in 1984 was entirely in line with the Hindu wave he rode through the Punjabi Suba agitation. That political wave in the sixties called for Punjab as a Punjabi speaking state; it was opposed by the champions of Hindi. The split broadly, though not entirely, aligned Sikhs with Punjabi and Hindus with Hindi. It led to the split of Punjab and the creation of primarily Hindi-speaking Haryana from within Punjab.

Shawlwale had pursued the fallout of that split strenuously while in Parliament. 'What is the government doing to protect minority languages in Punjab?' he asked (2 August 1968). 'Is it true that Hindi has been removed from signboards at government offices and on road milestones? That use of Hindi has been stopped by the Punjab government?' The government accepted in response that this was substantially true.

It was an issue Shawlwale raised repeatedly. 'Is it true,' he asked (20 December 1968), 'that the 40 percent Hindi speaking people in Punjab are being denied their linguistic rights? If the Gurmukhi script is given prominence, what are the rights for minority languages?' On 16 May 1969, he asked again if the use of Hindi has been replaced by Punjabi on milestones in Punjab. Shawlwale's other interventions in Parliament ran along familiar Jan Sangh lines—cows, Christian missionaries, Muslim groups and Pakistani spies. He was concerned over everything he saw as not entirely respectful of Hindus, to the extent that he raised a question in Parliament over what he saw as disrespectful portrayal of Hindus in the film *Padosan*.

Shawlwale kept up his passions over what he saw as the marginalization of Hindi and Hindus in Punjab through his political career at the Mishra Commission hearings that spilled over into a position against the Sikh victims of 1984.

Could this have been an expression of grief over the assassination of Indira Gandhi? His grandson tells us he had after all met her on some occasions. Would the production of a couple of thousand affidavits, by early signs some of them false, before a commission of inquiry set up six months later be an expression of grief? Would employment of a group of lawyers with a reputation for being rough in their ways—a reputation they proved before the commission again and again against Sikh survivors looking for justice—be an expression of grief? Shawlwale's intervention appears more in line with his long Hindu-fed political opposition to Sikhs than an outpouring of personal grief.

The BJP of today is no doubt not answerable for the position taken by a former MP of the Bharatiya Jan Sangh. And the Nagrik

Suraksha Samiti is no wing of the BJP. But undeniably one of the strongest attempts after the Delhi killings to defend Congress-I leaders and to silence Sikh victims was launched by a former Jan Sangh MP. The BJP of today can only answer for its own actions and decisions. There does arise questions for the BJP of today too.

~

The election of a BJP-led government in 1998 and again in 1999 brought new hope over 1984. The Congress had an interest in perpetuating injustice, it was thought, surely the BJP did not. It could on the contrary perhaps have a political interest in getting after Congress killers beyond what it rightfully should do now in government.

In line with that hope, campaigners turned to the Atal Behari Vajpayee-led BJP government to seek another inquiry by another judge of the Supreme Court. The BJP government—or the BJP-led government within the National Democratic Alliance (NDA)—accepted these demands and picked Supreme Court judge G.T. Nanavati in May 2000 to conduct a new inquiry.

Mishra had ruled entirely in line with that Rajiv Gandhi image of the earth shaking a little upon the felling of a mighty tree—the tree view call it, legally more than metaphorically because the cause and consequence reasoning of that view would leave no one to blame for murder, no one guilty. This from Nanavati was to be a proper Supreme Court inquiry—or so the campaigners thought.

Why did the BJP government pick Nanavati? By then Nanavati had already declared his views on the 1984 killings, he had delivered a judgment in a particularly serious case on 1 December 1998. The BJP government with L.K. Advani as home minister had that order before it. In that order, Nanavati set out very much the tree view of the killings, the view that would want to crush the case that the killings had been organized by party and government leaders.

A judge who held this tree view and had demonstrated it by delivering a ruling in a 1984 case based on declared reasoning along those lines could hardly have been expected to offer a conclusion at variance with his own stated view and in opposition to what Mishra had found and what the Congress-I government had wanted to be found. Nanavati had absolved the government already in a ruling over 1984 killings. And of all judges it could have picked on, the BJP government picked this one.

That 1 December 1998 order from Nanavati delivered together with Justice S. Rajendra Babu commuted the death sentence passed on Kishori Lal to life imprisonment. Judge S.N. Dhingra had convicted Kishori Lal, a butcher from Trilokpuri, of serial murders. Such conviction itself was rare, Dhingra is about the only judge who passed conviction orders at all over the 1984 killings—and the government of the day punished him for punishing anyone (see the interview with him in the chapter 'Commissions and Omissions').

Reducing a death sentence into life imprisonment is not the issue here, or of itself a reflection on Nanavati—much of the world rejects the death sentence. Nanavati was not offering any principled view against capital punishment. What is telling is his 'tree-like' reasoning against a death sentence for Kishori Lal.

Dhingra had convicted Kishori Lal along with Mohammed Abbas and Dull Chand; the latter two were given life sentences. The court found that these three were among a mob that attacked the houses of Sajjan Singh and others in Trilokpuri. The judgment records that Sajjan tried to hide but was dragged out and knifed in the stomach. Both his hands were cut. A quilt was thrown over him and he was burnt to death. According to a witness statement by his wife presented in court, Sajjan's last words were, 'Kishori, you were my friend, why you are killing me?'Two other Sikhs, Hoshiar Singh and Inder Singh, were killed there.

Mohammed Abbas and Dull Chand were acquitted on an appeal to the High Court against Dhingra's order. But the High Court confirmed the death sentence on Kishori Lal. A further special appeal was then filed against the death sentence passed against Kishori Lal, which then came up before Nanavati and Babu.

Nanavati and Babu summed up the defence for Kishori Lal. 'He has contended that the offence was committed under the influence of extreme emotional disturbance and in a state of frenzy following the unfortunate gruesome and tragic assassination of Smt. Indira Gandhi. When the entire country was engulfed in sudden and tremendous shock and distress, which also ignited anger and violence amongst a section of people showing their anger which led to the acts of riots, arson and killing of the members belonging to Sikh community.'

Nanavati then accepts the defence arguments that the circumstances lessened the crime: 'It is common experience that when people congregate in crowds normal defences are lowered so that the crowd instinct assaults on the sense of individuality or transcending one's individual boundaries by offering a release from inhibitions from personal doubts and anxiety. In such a situation, one can well imagine that a member of such a group loses one's self and the normal standard or sense of judgment and reality.'

He adds further psychological underlining of a kind: 'The primary motivational factor in the assembly of a violent mob may result in murder of several persons. Experts in criminology often express that when there is a collective action, as in the case of a mob, there is a diminished individual responsibility unless there are special circumstances to indicate that a particular individual had acted with any pre-determination such as by use of a weapon not normally found. If, however, a member of such a crowd picks up an article or a weapon which is close by and joins the mob, either on his own volition or at the instigation of the mob responding to the exhortation of the mob playing no role of leadership, we may very well say that such a person did not intend to commit all the acts which a mob would commit left to himself, but did so under the influence of collective fury.'

Consider what Nanavati is accepting, together with Babu, and over what. Kishori Lal was considered to be extremely disturbed over the assassination. Nanavati then notes that Kishori Lal was not alone in this. The 'entire country' he notes was engulfed in shock and distress. But it would be known to Nanavati as it is to all of us that the entire country was not in the dock before him, the entire country had not set out to murder the nearest Sikh. The case before him, the case of Kishori Lal, was the case of one in a billion who had been sentenced to death. Nanavati points to the distress of a billion who did not kill, in order to lessen the guilt of the one before him who had. The facts he points to are an argument for the very opposite of what he concludes.

Nanavati was accepting through his reasoning that in this one case the distress Kishori experienced should excuse to a great extent his decision to stick a knife into a friend's stomach, cut off his hands and then burn him alive. That this was to an extent an understandable outcome of distress over the assassination of Indira Gandhi. Kishori Lal had been convicted of several murders, that is the reason he had been given the death sentence. As Nanavati's reasoning goes, he would have been more distressed than others who had killed in such supposed distress.

Nanavati argues that the pressure of a congregated crowd can overcome individual decisions so as to make the individual less responsible then for his actions. But in any case, the facts before Nanavati establish that Kishori Lal did not act as a part of a congregated crowd. He went into the house of someone he knew to kill him; no crowd could ever gather in a Trilokpuri house and in this instance no crowd did. Only three had been accused in this case of killing at one particular place, and three is well short of a crowd. That they were aware that others around had been killing yet others was seen by Nanavati as a mitigating factor. A sense of a crowd elsewhere if no crowd there.

Nanavati sees such a broader oneness with members of a crowd killing elsewhere because they had together shed their 'inhibitions' over killing, and through such solidarity cast aside 'personal doubts and anxiety'. Killing certainly would be an uninhibited sort of thing to do if you gathered that others too were similarly uninhibited at the time. Nanavati also cites those 'experts in criminology' to excuse Kishori over the murder weapon. So, if Kishori Lal had picked up a knife he saw rather than carry one of the many he would have owned as a butcher, he then only acted in collective fury more than he might have by himself. Nanavati's reasoning demands pause at every step.

It's fundamentally an argument that suggests that if many kill many, the responsibility of every killer among them stands lessened. Nanavati consequently appears to justify the police move to bundle hundreds of killings into a single collective case in Trilokpuri. Nanavati's judgment argues that 'all these killings had taken place in a chain of events occurring on one night and day and, therefore, pertained to one incident. Looked from that angle, it could not be stated that the appellant (Kishori) was indulging in criminal activities one after another.'

He further excuses Kishori Lal for not leading a mob. 'None of the witnesses has stated that Kishori, the appellant, was the leader of the mob or he exhorted the members thereof to do any particular act. His role appears was only as a member of the mob.'

The killer that is, should be punished less because he was just a killer and not a leader of killers.

Nanavati points to the defence offered by Kishori's lawyer: 'He submitted that the appellant is not habitual criminal; that he was probably instigated to indulge in riots by leaders belonging to political parties.' Remarkably, that observation is made only in passing. Under law, such an allegation would point to conspiracy involving political leaders. Under conspiracy laws, a conspirator who instigated a killing, or even knew of it and did not report the one planning the killing, could be held just as guilty as the one who killed. Nanavati made no move to pursue the case to its legally logical next step to rope in conspirators that Kishori's lawyers were pointing to.

Finally, Nanavati excuses Kishori Lal for not assaulting women. His judgment suggests that some threat appears to have been made to molest Sajjan's wife. 'She is clear that several blows were inflicted on her husband. She is not able to state as to what happened to her husband when she was asked to leave her husband on the threat of dishonouring her but she is definite that her husband was killed. Her version appears to be natural and probable when she stated a mob attacked her house and there was threat to the lives and honour of women, it is quite natural that she had to go out of the house.' For the reason that Kishori let them, he deserved a lesser sentence.

The ruling says: 'We may notice that the acts attributed to the mob of which the appellant was a member at the relevant time cannot be stated to be a result of any organized systematic activity leading to genocide. Perhaps, we can visualize that to the extent there was unlawful assembly and to the extent that the mob wanted to teach stern lesson to the Sikhs there was some organization; but in that design they did not consider that women and children should be annihilated which is a redeeming feature.' This before the appellant was no mob, but mobs did not spare women and children everywhere.

Nanavati goes far beyond the call of an appeal ruling in this one particular case to declare that the killing was not organized—after suggesting that it would to an extent be understandable, and to an extent excusable. To this he adds the 'redeeming feature' that Kishori and others had not killed the women while killing the men. We have here a Supreme Court judge ruling that the redeeming feature of a murder case was that only three were killed and not others who could have been killed, who happened to be women. And for that reason, a killer deserves a lesser sentence.

Nanavati reversed the earlier High Court order that had confirmed Dhingra's death sentence for Kishori Lal. Nanavati notes that 'the High Court took note of the fact that, though there has been long lapse of time between the date of commission of the offence and conviction of the appellant, the acts attributed to the appoint affect the basic feature of our Constitution, viz., secularism; that the appellant indulged in riots resulting in killing of innocent persons, looting and burning their properties would send shivers to any person; that mob caused havoc of which the appellant was a member; that no leniency, mercy or sympathy should be shown.'

Summarizing the order further, Nanavati says 'the High Court opined that the court has also to keep in view the society's reasonable expectation for appropriate deterrent punishment commensurate with the gravity of the offence, the public abhorrence for the heinous crime committed by the appellant and thus the High Court concluded that this was one of the rarest of the rare cases where such (death) sentence should be imposed.'

In dismissing that High Court order, Nanavati concluded: 'It is no doubt true that the high ideals of the Constitution have to be borne in mind, but when normal life breaks down and groups of people go berserk losing balance of mind, the rationale that the ideals of the Constitution should be upheld or followed, may not appeal to them. In such circumstances, nor can we expect such loose heterogeneous group of persons like a mob to be alive to such high ideals. Therefore, to import the ideas or idealism to a mob in such a situation may not be realistic.' Nanavati appears to have reasoned that the Constitution that protects the rights and safety of citizens can understandably not quite apply when it may be needed most.

Could anyone fail to spot here the falling tree as seen by Rajiv Gandhi? The argument that so much killing was excusable to an extent at least, that to kill many is to have killed every one of them less. These views of Nanavati were all before the BJP government when it appointed him to lead another inquiry, to do better than Mishra had.

Nanavati had Babu by his side in reducing Kishori Lal's sentence from death to life imprisonment. But he appeared to think he had much of Indian society on the side of a reduced sentence, that society was at the least divided enough to stop many from wanting a heavy sentence. 'It is no doubt true that courts must be in tune with the notions prevalent in the society and punishment imposed upon an accused must be commensurate with the heinousness of the crime. We have elaborated earlier in the course of our judgment as to how mob psychology works and it is very difficult to gauge or assess what the notions of the society are in a given situation. There may be one section of the society which may cry for a very deterrent sentence while another section of the society may exhort upon the court to be lenient in the matter. To gauge such notions is to rely upon highly slippery imponderables and, in this case, we cannot be definite about the views of the society.' Justice Nanavati appears to think that some in society condoned these killings, and that the court must take some cognizance of that.

Through this ruling, the BJP government had before it Nanavati's fundamental views that would see murders as less a crime if politically provoked. Such political provocation could itself be evidence of a lack of political organization. 'When an amorphous group of persons come together it cannot be said that they indulge in any systematic or organised activity. Such group may indulge in activities and may remain cohesive only for a temporary period and thereafter would disintegrate. The acts of the mob of which the appellant was a member cannot be stated to be the result of any organisation or any group indulging in violent activities formed with any purpose or scheme so as to call an organised activity. In that sense we may say that the acts of the mob of which the appellant was a member was only the result of a temporary frenzy which we have discussed earlier. He did not play the role of a leader of the mob as noticed earlier. On the totality of the circumstances, we are of the opinion that this is not a case where courts below should have imposed a capital punishment.'

Why was anyone surprised then, that at the end of his inquiry Nanavati echoed Mishra's conclusions. He always was going to, he had made that known, the BJP government knew that when they picked him. He had talked tree loud and clear. And why would anyone be surprised that this same judge was picked to conduct the inquiry into the Gujarat killings of 2002. Or that his findings then should come in line with what the BJP government would have liked to see.

What may appear surprising is the politics on the face of it. This was a judge appointed by the BJP government to look at the failings of the Congress government and he still found as he did. True, he did so at the end of five years of inquiry only after the Congress was back in government. The conclusion was nevertheless in line with his views declared before he was picked for the inquiry ordered by a BJP government into failings under a Congress government.

The BJP government took a decision it knew was set to work against Sikh victims and work better for those who led the killings, even if this defies the logic of a party-political façade. What then of that expectation of opposition between Congress and the BJP? Was there some commonality of interest between the BJP and the Congress over 1984? Through these murky currents and undercurrents not easy to fathom, other signs have arisen pointing that way. One of those signs reads 'Kamal Nath'.

~

I could hardly have guessed which way Nanavati would go when I travelled to Delhi to depose before him. The Mishra Commission had brought hope, here was new hope. I had something to say, to repeat that is now before Nanavati, as eyewitness about Kamal Nath at Rakab Ganj gurdwara, about Dharam Dass Shastri at the Karol Bagh police station, about other violence I had witnessed. In the end I couldn't recognize my testimony in the report Nanavati produced.

He shouldn't have either, not as recorded. Because what had I said?

According to Nanavati's report, I 'reiterated before the Commission that Shri Kamal Nath did not make any attempt to control the situation near the Gurdwara'. According to Nanavati too, I had reported that a mob had attacked and killed at Rakab Ganj but that 'the Congress Member of Parliament and other leaders of the Congress Party were able to keep them under control'.[1]

So, what did Nanavati think I had said? He quotes me as saying opposite things.

If that indeed was what I had done, would this justice of the Supreme Court not have noticed that a witness before him was making opposing and not just contradictory statements, and those cannot both be correct? And then challenge me on this while I was testifying? Or later, spotted such an apparent 'discrepancy' while writing a report in which he attributes opposite statements to me within the space of a single paragraph? Nanavati does not flag this at all.

I do not now need to route my own testimony backwards through Nanavati. I know what I had said in line with what I had reported. I had testified that Kamal Nath clearly seemed to have control of the mob—not that he was able to keep them under control. This was in line with my report in *The Indian Express* the following day in 1984, and that is the position I have repeated consistently since then. Did Nanavati not hear what I had said and written, or did he not want to?

I have no idea where he got that other bit from, about seeing 'other leaders of the Congress Party' also keeping the mob under control. According to Nanavati's report, I 'stated that Shri Kamal Nath tried to control the crowd and the crowd was looking at him for directions'.[2] The latter part certainly is true, and only the latter part, that I did see the crowd looking to Kamal Nath for directions.

Nanavati's twists and turns follow more the style of a defence lawyer who has not done his homework than of an impartial judge conducting a fair inquiry. He again suggests that I was only certifying Kamal Nath's innocence. 'Shri Suri has said that Shri Kamal Nath had tried to persuade the mob to disperse and the mob had retreated for some time.'[3] What I had precisely said was that at one point after I had walked up towards him, Kamal Nath had held his hand up before a few persons in the mob and at that point they obeyed him. That was one split second within those hours, the one that really demonstrated publicly that he was in charge. How likely is it that some individual stranger would raise a controlling hand before a violent mob, and that anyone would take a single step back for even a moment. Those few right before Kamal Nath at that moment responded because that momentary gesture came from someone they saw as their leader.

Kamal Nath has long sought to use the inclusion of that single moment in my report as evidence from me that he was restraining the crowd. I had no reason to not include that moment, I had not arrived at that scene in any opposition to Kamal Nath, I didn't know he would be there. That moment did nothing to alter the overwhelming fact that this mob had obviously not been restrained before and since that moment, with Kamal Nath in their midst and clearly in charge. That one gesture at that one moment had obviously not kept the mob in check all day, and who said or saw that it had? Could a Supreme Court judge not see that? Or see that the description of that one moment only showed that Kamal Nath was in charge? All day this had been an unchecked mob that had killed. Kamal Nath had clearly not restrained the mob.

Nanavati does make note of one discrepancy as he saw it in my submission. 'The discrepancy that can be noticed between his affidavit and the evidence before this Commission is that whereas he had stated earlier that he had reached the Gurdwara at 4pm, now he has stated before the Commission that he reached there between 2 and 4pm.'[4]

Seventeen years had passed between my affidavit and the evidence I gave before Nanavati that brought up this discrepancy as he saw it. But Nanavati does allow for the passage of time to pardon a blurring of a timing-precise recall for Kamal Nath. 'It is also required to be considered that he (Kamal Nath) was called upon to give an explanation after about 20 years and probably for that reason he was not able to give more details as regards when and how he went there and what he did.'[5]

Nanavati's report on Kamal Nath is, to put this politely, a little mixed. Nanavati describes Kamal Nath as saying that he went to Rakab Ganj as 'a responsible leader of the Congress Party' on hearing of the violence. There he saw 'lots of people', and 'para military personnel were also present'.[6] It then gets all muddled over what Kamal Nath was up to or wasn't.

Kamal Nath is described as saying that he 'tried to find out from various persons in the mob as to why they had gathered there and why they were agitated. He was told that some Hindu men and women were kept inside the Gurudwara forcibly and that was the main reason why they were agitated. By that time the Commissioner of Police came there. He felt satisfied that police would be able to control the situation, so he left that place. He has further stated that while he was near the Gurudwara he had tried to persuade the crowd to disperse and not to take law into their hands. He had also told the crowd that since the police had arrived, it was their job to ensure safety of the Hindus, if any, inside the Gurudwara and that the police would be able to control the situation. He has denied that he gave instructions to any one to resort to firing. He has also denied that he had either led that mob or had any control over the mob.'[7]

Something missing here? It was two Sikhs who had been burnt alive here, no Hindu had been killed inside or outside the gurdwara. And yet throughout that summary, Kamal Nath is not described as expressing any concern for those Sikhs burnt alive, or about the attacks on the gurdwara. There was no record I found of Kamal Nath later following up on the murder of two Sikhs. As a responsible member of Parliament that he had claimed to be, why would he not care about those two murders enough to follow up with the police on who killed them?

It was the people with him on that street who had. Had he been as distant from that mob as he claimed to be, or at cross-purposes with them, surely it would have been consistent with that position to then seek justice over the killings, ask for the killers to be caught and prosecuted. None of that ever came, Kamal Nath only stated concern over rumours of Hindus detained within the gurdwara. The reassurance he said he offered to the crowd was that the police would look after the imagined Hindus within the gurdwara; not a word here about those two murders by that mob. Nanavati never raised such questions. He had never set out to.

Nanavati points to several oddities in Kamal Nath's testimony. He notes that the 'reply filed by Shri Kamal Nath is vague' and that 'he has not clearly stated at what time he went there and how long he remained there'. Nanavati sums up: 'The situation at the Gurudwara had become very grave at about 11.30 a.m. and continued to remain grave till about 3.30 p.m. The evidence discloses that Shri Kamal Nath was seen in the mob at about 2 p.m. The Police Commissioner had reached that place at about 3.30 p.m. So he (Kamal Nath) was there for quite a long time. He has not stated whether he went to the Gurudwara alone or with some other persons and how he went there. He has not stated that he looked for the police or tried to contact the policemen who were posted there for ensuring that the situation remained under control. He left that place after the Commissioner of Police arrived. He has not stated that he met him. He was a senior political leader and feeling concerned about the law and order situation went to the Gurudwara and therefore it appears little strange that he left that place abruptly without even contacting the police officers who had come there.'[8]

After finding Kamal Nath's position 'strange', Nanavati's final word on Kamal Nath is a blanket clean chit. 'In absence of better evidence it is not possible for the Commission to say that he had in any manner instigated the mob or that he was involved in the attack on the Gurdwara.'[9] No follow-up, no instructions to the police or anyone to follow up. Because there was that matter of law that this justice of the Supreme Court appears to have overlooked. And that the BJP government too has long chosen to overlook.

Nanavati's reasoning for dismissing all reports and affidavits critical of Congress-I leaders are recorded in his judgment. We can make our own individual judgments whether we find that reasoning convincing. But the BJP government knew before appointing him that this was the way his reasoning would be headed and that this would be the way he could therefore be expected to judge.

So, Kamal Nath was cleared by the Nanavati Commission after having been cleared by the Mishra Commission earlier. Kamal Nath has said, and said often, that no police case was ever registered against him. And in that he is quite right. In my understanding of the law in relation to the facts before me that day, this is the difficulty, that a case was not registered.

~

By 1984, I'd been a journalist for six years. Taking on the crime beat, I had as then required read the Indian Penal Code, the Criminal Procedure Code and the Police Act. So, I was aware of the law in relation to what I saw at Rakab Ganj, particularly Section 149 of the Indian Penal Code then (transferred straight over as Section 188 to the new Bharatiya Nyaya Sanhita). Another reminder of 149/188 could be helpful here: 'If an offence is committed by any member of an unlawful assembly in prosecution of the common object of that assembly, or such as the members of that assembly known to be likely to be committed in prosecution of that object, every person who, at the time of the committing of that offence, is a member of the same assembly, is guilty of that offence.'

It had been clear to me right then that there is a case here the police must pursue against Kamal Nath. I put that question now to greatly experienced and widely respected legal minds who could understand the position far better than I could. To Justice S.N. Dhingra, the judge who delivered more convictions over the 1984 killings than did any other, and who was later a justice of the Delhi High Court.

'Kamal Nath should obviously have been named as an accused,' said Justice Dhingra. 'Because he was present in the crowd, because he was in charge of the crowd, the crowd had committed a crime, and obviously he would have been leading the crowd. This has happened in almost all places, it's not only Kamal Nath. Mr Bhagat, Dharam Dass Shastri, others, were all leading the crowds. These were orchestrated murders. It was not spontaneous.'

And I asked H.S. Phoolka, who has devoted his life to legal pursuit of the 1984 cases, whether he thought Kamal Nath should have been prosecuted.

'One hundred percent,' he replied. 'It is very clear. He was a part of the unlawful assembly. According to your affidavit they were under his control. Then there is an affidavit of Mukhtiar Singh saying Kamal Nath was there and the mob was acting on his directions. Police records show that Kamal Nath was present. His claim that he was pacifying and protecting would have to be a part of investigation later. But an FIR would have to be registered first. During investigation he could give evidence, whatever he has. And then he could give evidence to try to satisfy a court.

'Before the Nanavati commission he admitted he was there. He said he was there to control. But he knew that offences are being committed. He knew that people had been burnt alive. He knew that the gurdwara has been attacked. Everything was in view, and still he remained a part of the mob. And if he says he was trying to control, what did he control? Did he control the attack on the gurdwara? Did he control the killing of the two Sikhs? In the Nanavati report, you can see that right till the end of the section on Kamal Nath he is leading up to recommend investigation against him. But right at the end he gave him the benefit of doubt. But benefit of doubt is for a court to give, not for a commission of inquiry. That was absolutely wrong on Nanavati's part.'

Was it not possible for the BJP government to proceed against Kamal Nath?

'It was very much possible,' Phoolka replied. 'This government could have moved against him very easily. Clearly, they did not want to proceed. Just as the Congress government did not.'

The simplistic outside view would be that a BJP government would not only not hesitate to prosecute a Congress-I MP once they had something on him, but might want to. Why they haven't is not clear. But very clearly the BJP government has long stalled any move against Kamal Nath.

~

I ran directly into signs of that unwillingness on two occasions, each telling in its own way.

In September 2019, I responded to a public notice inviting witnesses to come forward with evidence in the Rakab Ganj case. I wrote to the given email address (sho.sit84riots@mha.gov.in) to say I was an eyewitness and to express my willingness to appear before the Special Investigation Team (SIT) to record my statement. I never heard back.

If the SIT was opening a re-investigation over the Rakab Ganj violence and killings, it would have had something to go on, some prima facie evidence, or at least some sort of direction. A government investigation team had after all published a public notice inviting witnesses. If it then fell silent and made no further move, it's hard to see who but the political government of the day could have stalled the process that had been initiated.

I have since seen reports that Sikh leader Manjinder Singh Sirsa has filed a writ petition in the High Court seeking legal directions for reopening of the Rakab Ganj investigation. That as recently as February 2024 the court gave further time to the SIT to file a status report. As it happens, I am one of two principal eyewitnesses in this case. In the last five years, no one in the SIT has sought to record my statement in the case, it has not taken the first obvious step.

Additionally, and anecdotally, I had run into another tell-tale sign earlier. The first edition of this book came out in 2015. Shortly after, my college days friend Dhanbir Singh Bains, who became home secretary in the Punjab government, introduced me to the former sports minister and Akali Dal member Sukhdev Singh Dhindsa; we met over breakfast at Dhindsa's house in Chandigarh. Dhindsa very insistently set up a meeting for me with Arun Jaitley, then finance minister, for me to draw his attention to the events at Rakab Ganj and my position as witness as recorded in this book.

I had known Arun Jaitley over many years, but this was a meeting set up by a senior leader of the Akali Dal, then in coalition with the BJP in government. The meeting at Arun Jaitley's office in Parliament House proved quite extraordinary. I was shown into Jaitley's office and seated facing him. A TV news channel was playing on the wall behind me. Arun Jaitley had been looking at the TV screen as I entered, he peripherally pointed me to a chair. For a while after I sat down, Jaitley continued looking past me at the screen. I placed a copy of the book on the table and said something about the content, and about the view of Mr Dhindsa and others that the government had not moved against Kamal Nath but still could. Mr Jaitley perhaps did not hear. In any case, he said nothing.

After some time, Arun Jaitley broke the silence to say a few pleasant things about London, still looking at the screen mostly. Then again silence. It was a message. I had in any case nothing more to say. I thanked him for his time and left. He barely nodded back, still watching the TV screen. That was it, that was the meeting.

We could look at this meeting differently. Perhaps Arun Jaitley genuinely believed there is no case against Kamal Nath and his apparent unwillingness to take up this conversation arose from that belief. Taking this view Arun Jaitley exercised political judgment in line with his perception, and not because he was unprepared personally or politically to move against Kamal Nath.

Alternatively, the non-response, through almost a non-meeting, meant that the BJP government is not willing to touch Kamal Nath. As I see it, the silence that followed the brief SIT move to reopen investigation points to the way of this latter view. Of course, nobody needs to accept this view; many people have always thought very highly of Arun Jaitley—myself not least among them. I do think he could rightfully have taken up this Kamal Nath matter rather than dismissing it, but this is just my thought, even if the thought is shared by some senior legal figures. The legal world does of course produce more disagreement than agreement. What really mattered was that for whatever reason Arun Jaitley thought otherwise.

In the end, the move to reopen investigation had been the surprise, the aborting of that move was not. Now time is shutting the window on hope.

NOTES

1: Upside Down in Karol Bagh

1. Chapter 4: ACP H. C. Jatav (Range - Delhi).' *Kusum Lata Mittal Report*, submitted on 28 February 1990. https://www.carnage84.com/official/kusum/kusum.htm.
2. Justice Nanavati Commission of Inquiry, 2005, p. 7. https://www.mha.gov.in/sites/default/files/2022-08/Nanavati-I_eng_3%5B1%5D.pdf.
3. Sh. H.C. Jatav vs The Union of India on 11 May 2011. https://indiankanoon.org/doc/101496616/

5: Kamal Nath

1. 'Chapter 5: New Delhi District.' *Kusum Lata Mittal Report*, submitted on 28 February 1990. https://www.carnage84.com/official/kusum/kusum.htm.

6: Close Encounter

1. 'Chapter 6: West District.' *Kusum Lata Mittal Report*, submitted on 28 February 1990. https://www.carnage84.com/official/kusum/kusum.htm.
2. Ibid.

13: Commissions and Omissions

1. Report of Justice Ranganath Misra Commission of Inquiry, 1985, p. 7. https://www.mha.gov.in/sites/default/files/RanganathMishraVol_I_22102019_0.PDF.

2. Ibid.
3. Ibid, p. 23.
4. Ibid, p. 22.
5. Ibid, p. 8.
6. Ibid, p. 11.
7. Ibid, p. 13.
8. Ibid.
9. Ibid.
10. Ibid, p. 14.
11. Ibid, p. 31.
12. Ibid, p. 9.
13. Ibid.
14. Ibid, p. 28.
15. Ibid.
16. Ibid, p. 29.
17. Ibid, p. 28.
18. Justice Nanavati Commission of Inquiry, 2005, p. 13. https://www.mha.gov.in/sites/default/files/2022-08/Nanavati-I_eng_3%5B1%5D.pdf.
19. Ibid, p. 179.
20. Ibid.
21. Ibid, p. 180.
22. Ibid.
23. Ibid.
24. Ibid, p. 182.
25. Ibid, p. 180.
26. Ibid, p. 162.
27. Ibid, p. 145.
28. *Kusum Lata Mittal Report*, submitted on 28 February 1990. https://www.carnage84.com/official/kusum/kusum.htm.
29. 'Chapter 6: West District.' *Kusum Lata Mittal Report*.
30. Chapter 9: Delhi Railway Police.' *Kusum Lata Mittal Report*.

15: BJP Shadows

1. Justice Nanavati Commission of Inquiry, 2005, p. 22. https://www.mha.gov.in/sites/default/files/2022-08/Nanavati-I_eng_3%5B1%5D.pdf.
2. Ibid.
3. Ibid, p. 141.
4. Ibid, p. 22.
5. Ibid p. 141.
6. Ibid, p. 140.
7. Ibid.
8. Ibid, p. 141.
9. Ibid.

Index

About the Author

Sanjay Suri is a London-based journalist, and is currently, political editor, Europe, for CNN-IBN television. He studied at Delhi University and the London School of Economics. He is the author of *Brideless in Wembley*, *Naked Rain and Other Poems* and *A Gandhian Affair*.

P 5M

HarperCollins *Publishers* India

At HarperCollins India, we believe in telling the best stories and finding the widest readership for our books in every format possible. We started publishing in 1992; a great deal has changed since then, but what has remained constant is the passion with which our authors write their books, the love with which readers receive them, and the sheer joy and excitement that we as publishers feel in being a part of the publishing process.

Over the years, we've had the pleasure of publishing some of the finest writing from the subcontinent and around the world, including several award-winning titles and some of the biggest bestsellers in India's publishing history. But nothing has meant more to us than the fact that millions of people have read the books we published, and that somewhere, a book of ours might have made a difference.

As we look to the future, we go back to that one word—a word which has been a driving force for us all these years.

Read.

Harper Collins 4th HARPER FICTION HARPER NON-FICTION HARPER BUSINESS HCCB HARPERCOLLINS CHILDREN'S BOOKS

HARPER DESIGN Harper Sport HARPER PERENNIAL HARPER VANTAGE हार्पर हिन्दी